AMERICAN CHAIRS

Queen Anne and Chippendale

John T. Kirk

AMERICAN CHAIRS

Queen Anne and Chippendale

1 9 7 2  ALFRED A. KNOPF

NEW YORK

THIS IS A BORZOI BOOK

PUBLISHED BY ALFRED A. KNOPF, INC.

Library of Congress Cataloging in Publication Data

Kirk, John T   American chairs.
Includes bibliographical references.
1. Chairs—United States. 2. Decoration and ornament—Queen Anne style.
3. Decoration and ornament—Chippendale style. I. Title.
NK2715.K5   749.3   72-2239
ISBN 0-394-47328-0

Manufactured in the United States of America

FIRST EDITION

The way scientists get at the truth is not so much by avoiding mistakes or personal bias

as by displaying them in public, where they can be corrected.   BARRY COMMONER

ACKNOWLEDGMENTS

THE DEDICATION of this book expresses my gratitude to the teachers who directed my search to understand the visual: Leah M. Perkins of George School, Rigmor Andersen of The Royal Danish Academy of Fine Arts, and Meyric R. Rogers of Yale University.

I am further indebted to Meyric Rogers, my chief "American furniture mentor," who encouraged this book's inception, and to Jules D. Prown, who directed its early development. A Fulbright Fellowship made it possible to study English sources, and Delves Molesworth and Derek Shrub of the Victoria and Albert Museum kindly revealed English furniture to a provincial American. I am grateful also to Charles Montgomery and Benjamin Ginsburg for making helpful suggestions on the manuscript, and to Albert Sack who has for many years shared his vast acquaintance with high-style furniture, discussed the photographs, and suggested some important changes.

The sections on Southern chairs are almost completely the result of help from E. Milby Burton, Berry Greenlaw, Conover Hunt, Mrs. G. Dallas Coons, and especially Frank Horton, who read the Southern sections of the manuscript and made them more accurate.

Donald A. Shelley made the objects at the Henry Ford Museum available and Graham Hood opened up the collections and related information at Colonial Williamsburg. Israel Sack, Inc., has for years provided access to its photographic files. The American Philosophical Society made it possible to photograph some previously unphotographed chairs.

A book such as this is the product of much help, and Dick Benjamin, Wendy Cooper, Pat Kane, Jonathan Fairbanks, Gordon Saltar, Calvin Hathaway, George Bird, Charles Hummel, Berry Tracy, Carol Sanderson, Nan Ross, Mary Glaze, Ian Quinby, Morrie Heckscher, Margaret Stearns, and Philip Greven have contributed in a variety of ways. Genie Robbins has worked on the text. Freida Place typed and retyped messy manuscripts. Jane Garrett took a difficult manuscript and worked to make it more available to its audience. Various "interim Starksboro conferences" have, among other things, made possible a greater understanding of the extended family and the role of women in aesthetic development.

Above all, I am indebted to Elizabeth D. Kirk, who has seen this study more clearly than I as a means of understanding forms rather than as a goal in itself, and she compiled the material on which the appendix is based. And then there is Natasha.

JOHN T. KIRK

Daniel Bliss House
1972

Chronology of American Furniture Forms

FORMS	GENERAL DATE BLOCKS
Early 17th Century Furniture	1630–1680
Late 17th Century Furniture	1670–1710
William and Mary Furniture	1700–1735
Early Ladder-Back Chairs	1690–1720
Early Bannister-Back Chairs	1700–1735
Late Ladder-Back Chairs	1710–1800
Very Late Ladder-Back Chairs	1780–1880
Late Bannister-Back Chairs	1720–1800
Queen Anne Furniture	1730–1760
Early Queen Anne	1730–1750
Late Queen Anne	1740–1760
Country Queen Anne	1730–1800
Primitive Queen Anne	1730–1805
Composite Queen Anne and Chippendale Furniture	1745–1795
Chippendale Furniture	1755–1795
Straight-Leg Chippendale	1760–1795
Country Chippendale	1755–1810
Early Classical Revival Furniture	1790–1815
Late Classical Revival	1810–1840
Greco-Roman Revival Furniture	1810–1845
Early Greco-Roman Revival	1810–1820
Late Greco-Roman Revival	1815–1845
Fancy Furniture	1800–1840
French Restoration Style Furniture	1830–1850
Rococo Revival Furniture	1845–1870
Early Windsors	1750–1810
Bamboo-Turned Windsors	1805–1875

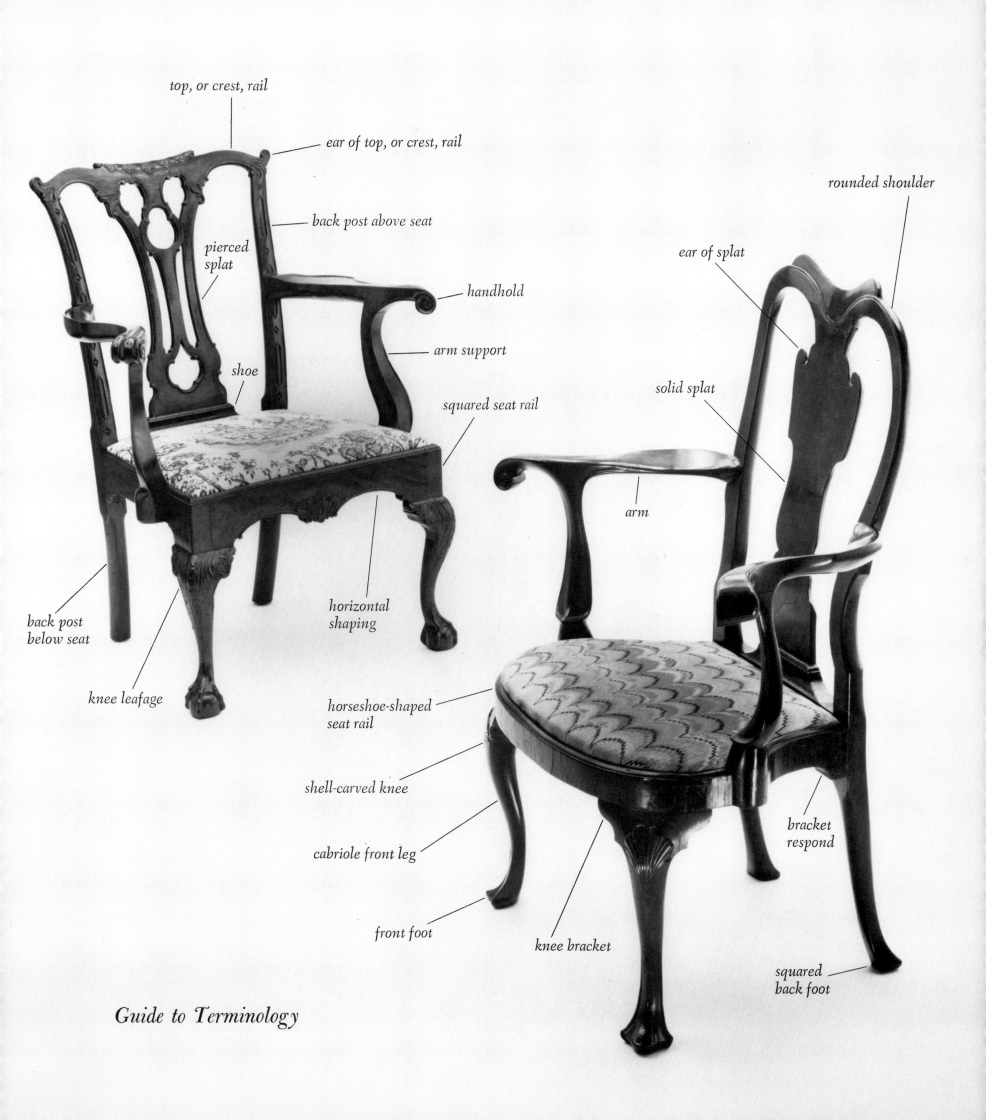

top, or crest, rail

ear of top, or crest, rail

rounded shoulder

back post above seat

ear of splat

pierced splat

handhold

solid splat

arm support

arm

shoe

squared seat rail

back post below seat

knee leafage

horizontal shaping

horseshoe-shaped seat rail

shell-carved knee

cabriole front leg

bracket respond

front foot

knee bracket

squared back foot

Guide to Terminology

AMERICAN CHAIRS

Queen Anne and Chippendale

INTRODUCTION

EVER SINCE people began to collect American furniture toward the end of the nineteenth century, there has never been any question that different areas or style centers in America used European ideas in different ways and that this produced regional differences in the furniture. Similarly, it was accepted that most furniture styles were based on European designs, to which American workers added many new variations of form and decoration. Neither of these ideas was then investigated in detail, for the place of origin of the furniture was not the primary concern. Rather, the more basic problems of whether a particular piece was American or European and at what date it was made became the crucial questions and the pioneer work was done in those areas. Not until Albert Sack published his *Fine Points of Furniture* in 1950 did any major work other than a catalogue attempt to come to grips with American regional differences in either construction or design, and studies on the European origin of designs are still limited to brief references and articles. It is perhaps revealing of the direction of new interest in American furniture that Sack's book was also the first to deal with the aesthetic qualities of pieces so casually lumped together and so reverently termed "antique."[1]

Is furniture art? Anything that invites a judgment as to its aesthetic merits is a work of art, whatever else it may be. Even a tool made simply for a practical purpose becomes a work of art to the extent that it confronts us not simply with the problem of judging its adequacy for that purpose but with the necessity of responding to its aesthetic goodness or badness. Furniture differs from tools in that aesthetic factors play a role far beyond anything demanded by its utilitarian function; like architecture, furniture

differs from what we usually mean by a "work of art" in that its aesthetic role must always be understood in terms of its practical function. Furthermore, this practical function is not merely to provide storage or a writing surface, but deliberately to embody the style, the atmosphere, and the associations in terms of which its owner is attempting to define himself. Furniture design has a special sociological dimension. A piece of furniture surviving from an earlier period confronts us not only with its own function and aesthetic qualities but with a forceful definition of its milieu and with the demand to be understood in terms of that milieu; it has become important for reasons besides those of which its creator and purchaser were conscious.

The critic of furniture must attempt to reveal how the object makes its impact in all these ways, and to do so in such a way that others' perception of it may be enriched by, but not limited to, the terms in which he himself views it. Insofar as the object is a product of and a player in a given historical milieu, the critic must judge and interpret the piece in terms of its original environment. For example, a Connecticut chair should be assessed in relation to its peers and not against the chairs of, say, Philadelphia, for the desires of both makers and buyers in each region were markedly different. When, however, he attempts to deal with the piece's aesthetic dimensions as such—to decide whether it is good aesthetically in the present—he views it in a broader perspective, of which the breadth or degree of inclusiveness is a matter of personal choice. In this study, I will be assessing chairs first in the context of their local contemporaries and then within the American eighteenth-century experience and to some degree in relationship to their English counterparts.

Various methods have been used in speculating upon what furniture was made where, but all have proved only partially helpful, and none has exhibited complete accuracy, something that can perhaps never be achieved. Since the problem is so complex, it is necessary to use all the available methods, modifying them as

---

[1] In 1950 Edwin J. Hipkiss published *Eighteenth-Century American Arts* (Cambridge, Mass.: Harvard University Press, 1950), a catalogue of the M. and M. Karolik Collection; it was the first major catalogue to regionalize its furniture, although a few earlier small catalogues such as *A Century of American Chairs* (New York: Ginsburg and Levy, Inc., 1942) had made a beginning.

required; and if possible, new ways of approaching the regional grouping of furniture must be developed. In order to look at methods of regionalizing, and to get at what constituted the achievement of each of the major early style centers, I have taken an isolated group of American furniture, applying a detailed analysis of structure and design to each piece without initially considering either its history or source.

Chairs of the Queen Anne and Chippendale period (1730–1795), really one continuous development without a break, have been chosen since this form shows the many facets of a gradual development, is easily handled, and is available in quantity. In order not to prejudge where the chairs were made, they were first grouped solely according to similar means of construction and design. Only after groups of like objects were formed was attention paid to their histories, labels, and similar documentation. Happily, when analyzed, enough of this secondary information was found associated with each group to provide the knowledge as to where they originated.

In studying the chairs made in Philadelphia, Massachusetts, New York, Rhode Island, Connecticut, and the South between 1730 and 1795, this book states some basic observations and indicates research that should lead to a much richer understanding of American furniture. If it does its job properly, it will stimulate further publication of already known or newly discovered material that may prove statements made here to be wrong, or only partially true.

This particular part of the eighteenth century was focused upon because the two styles of furniture form an easily discernible unit, and because these chairs are one of the high points of aesthetic achievement in America. Their makers were highly trained in craftsmanship and design and, since the time of a more slavish adherence to pattern books had not yet arrived, they attest clearly to the taste of their time and area of origin. In general, my discussion treats objects of a high artistic level of development; in reality, however, it must be admitted that all our regional areas exhibit a broad range of quality. Albert Sack classifies items as "Good, Bet-

1

Pad foot, Philadelphia-type, with distinctive ring (detail from fig. 45).

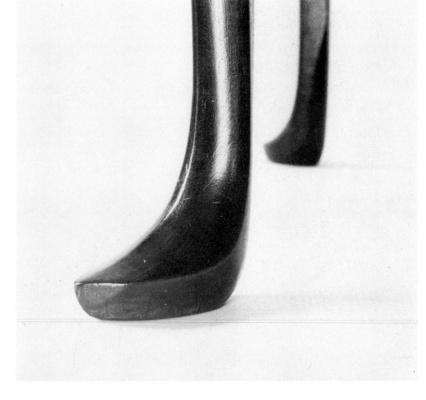

2

Slipper foot (from a Rhode Island tea table, The Museum of Art, Rhode Island School of Design).

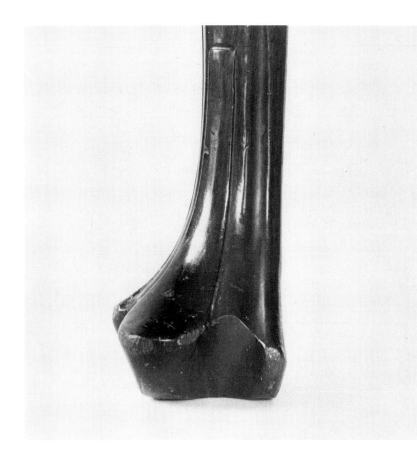

3

Trifid foot, Philadelphia-type, here with center tongue (detail from fig. 54).

The dating of American furniture is still in flux. This is not the place to argue the point in detail, but some reassignment of dates is necessary before we can proceed with a discussion of regional design. Early in the twentieth century critics tended to assign the earliest possible dates, since this seemed to give the pieces greater aesthetic and monetary value. Also, there has been an unwarranted tendency to attempt exact dates (as, for example: ladder-back chairs, 1700 to 1720; Queen Anne chairs, 1720 to 1750, etc.), with no room for chronological overlap or differences in the development of taste changes between regions. All regions were treated as one area when it came to dating details or motifs, with the result that claw and ball feet, say, came to be regarded as certain signs of 1750 to 1770, with no possibility that one area used them earlier or later. Most of the necessary redating will be dealt with more fully in its appropriate place, but the following summary might help to outline the general idea.

The standard designations used to cover the two types represented here are inaccurate. Queen Anne died in 1714, many

ter, and Best"; but the book has yet to be written which classifies our lesser products as "Poor, Worse, and Horrid." It is indeed a handicap that we have come to prize highly anything that is old, often with little real aesthetic discrimination.

Two more strictly historical problems proved inseparable from the basic question. That of European background is necessarily involved because our regional styles were in large part created by the influx of groups of European-trained cabinetmakers to particular areas of this country, where their former techniques and taste were relocated. English material supplies the clue to many developments, for almost every one of the designs and techniques formerly considered American inventions proved to have had European precedents. Therefore, at the risk of complicating the analysis I have introduced photographs and discussion of English material when it appeared crucial to an understanding of the American.

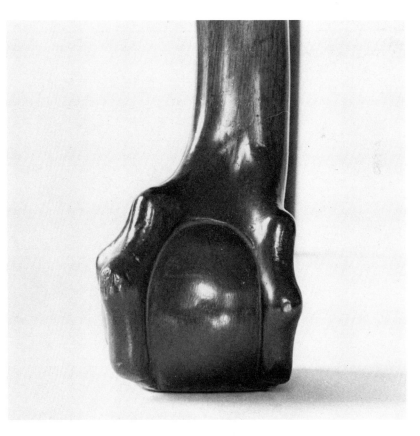

4

Claw and ball foot, Philadelphia-type (detail from fig. 70).

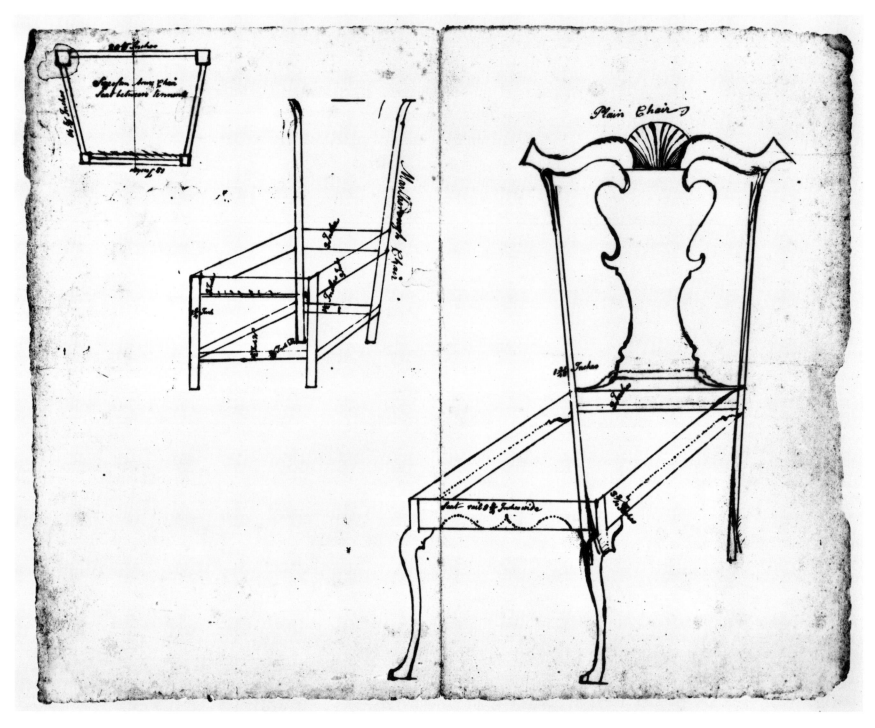

5

Drawing of "Plain Chair," probably 1766, by Samuel Mickle, Philadelphia (collection of the Philadelphia Museum of Art).

years before these shores received the style popular during her reign in England. Furthermore, much that is called Queen Anne in this country is, by English standards, early Georgian in style, particularly George I. Chippendale certainly never had any hand in creating American "Chippendale" chairs, and they would not have won his favor. Although he popularized and crystallized this taste and made it the first style period to carry a cabinetmaker's name, he was only one of the many who created it, and some of what we call Chippendale, particularly that of New York, is really English George II in inspiration. For simplicity's sake, in order to use familiar terms in the application of new analytical techniques, these two designations are begrudgingly continued here.

The dating of specific details, such as feet, seems to vary between areas. The dates in the table on page x have been used, but we must remember that although any form or detail can appear later than its time of popularity because of personal choice it cannot appear earlier, since it was not then in existence. Thus, a piece is *always* dated at least as late as its latest feature. The dating of Philadelphia furniture is perhaps the easiest at present since its high quality has already attracted many scholars. Philadelphia seems to have had an economic slump for ten years after 1720; from 1730, a new growth of business caused new building and thus a new demand for furniture. The Queen Anne style, long popular in England, was then adopted, providing a change from the stiffer William and Mary to new, luxuriously curved forms. This style developed in richness and lasted until about 1760, having overlapped the beginnings of the Chippendale (really a rococo development on the earlier style) by about five years. The pad foot (fig. 1) is given the date 1730–40 in Philadelphia, where it quickly gave way to the more graceful slipper foot (fig. 2), 1735–60, being paralleled about 1745 on late Queen Anne chairs by the trifid foot (fig. 3), which stayed in fashion until at least 1795. The last is usually considered to be a transitional foot between the Queen Anne forms and the claw and ball foot, 1745–95 (fig. 4) of the Chippendale era; but new information has changed our understanding of the situation. In 1786, Benjamin Lehman of Philadelphia compiled a descriptive list of furniture, designed to guide the cabinetmakers.[2] A guide in pricing the basic "chair with plain feet & Banister" was given first, with further elaborations listed, each with a suggested rise in price. What exactly this plain chair was has long been in question, but an eighteenth-century drawing suggests the answer. In a group of drawings, one dated 1766, by Samuel Mickle, apprenticed to Thomas Shoemaker of Philadelphia, there is one, figure 5, of what has been called a transitional chair and dated about 1750. This drawing shows a chair with a central shell and simple eared crest rail, a solid fretted splat, and cabriole front legs with the profile of trifid feet. Over the sketch of the chair is written "Plain Chair" and this seems to be the type of chair Lehman was referring to in 1786. It was simply a cheaper version of the more elaborate Chippendale chair. Thus, the trifid foot, far easier to carve than the claw and ball foot, which in Phila-

delphia has about the same dates, was cheaper; but it still provided the same necessary visual mass and three-part frontal play of projection and recess. Chairs such as that in figure 60 were therefore made at the same time as the more elaborate Chippendale version.

In Massachusetts the club foot (fig. 6), differing in form from the Philadelphia pad foot, appeared about 1730 and lasted throughout both styles until 1795, although it changed its form during the latter part of the period. The claw and ball foot was used there in quantity with Chippendale backs from about 1755, and at the same date the variation of the club foot with a thick sole or "shoe" appeared (fig. 7), giving the visual weight mass of a claw and ball foot; being lathe turned instead of carved, it was far easier to produce and therefore far cheaper, like the trifid foot of Philadelphia.

Rhode Island, Connecticut, and the South seem to have fol-

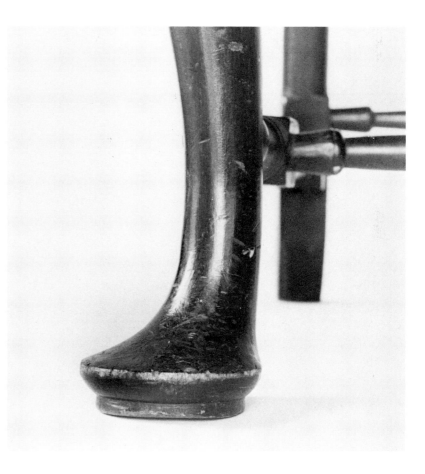

6

Club foot, New England–type, with a light shoe as found during the Queen Anne period (detail from The Museum of Art, Rhode Island School of Design).

[2] For Lehman's list, see William M. Hornor, Jr., *Blue Book, Philadelphia Furniture* (Philadelphia: privately printed, 1935), p. 210.

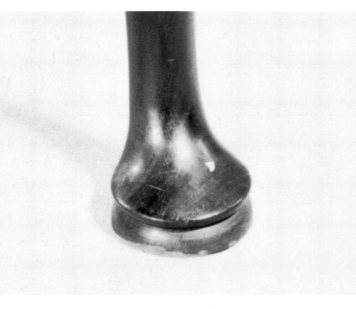

7

*Heavily shoed club foot, Massachusetts-type, as found on chair
with a Chippendale back (detail from fig. 111).*

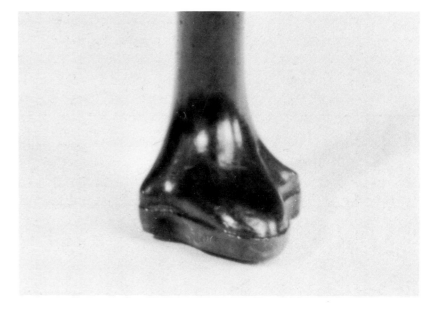

8

*George II foot, New York-type, found elsewhere in America only
on a few Philadelphia and Southern chairs (detail from fig. 151).*

lowed much the same pattern as Massachusetts. In New York, the pad or club foot rarely appeared on side or arm chairs, although more chairs with this foot may turn up at any time. Instead, we sometimes find a basic George II foot (fig. 8), which is known outside New York on only a few Philadelphia and Southern pieces, as well as the more common claw and ball foot. The claw and ball foot appeared in New York about 1740 and lasted until 1795. As will be seen, New York furniture is extremely difficult to categorize and date.

The regional variations that exist in dating forms of feet are also found to exist for other chair parts. For example, the use of shells as forms of decoration, the introduction of acanthus carving, and the piercing of chair splats each begin at a different time in different regional groupings. Such variation demonstrates the need to study the development of forms by regions rather than by simply stringing out pieces in a date sequence without regard to

their regional source. We must begin with an understanding of each region's own development.

Because of the wide-ranging nature of the comparisons, it has often been necessary to cite many examples in a single paragraph. Those figures essential to the argument are enclosed in commas, while those only elaborating the discussion are in parentheses and can be ignored by readers who do not wish to prove each point for themselves. Equally, readers with no desire to understand the more technical constructional discussions may wish to skip Part II, at least until they are compelled to it by having read the more general discussion in Part III.

Finally, I have not sought to employ the eighteenth-century terms for chair parts unless they are related to modern usage, since I am writing for modern readers. Rather, current terms are used unless they are truly misleading and then terms that are descriptive of forms, shapes, placement, or usage are introduced.

I

THE REGIONAL
APPROACH TO
AMERICAN FURNITURE

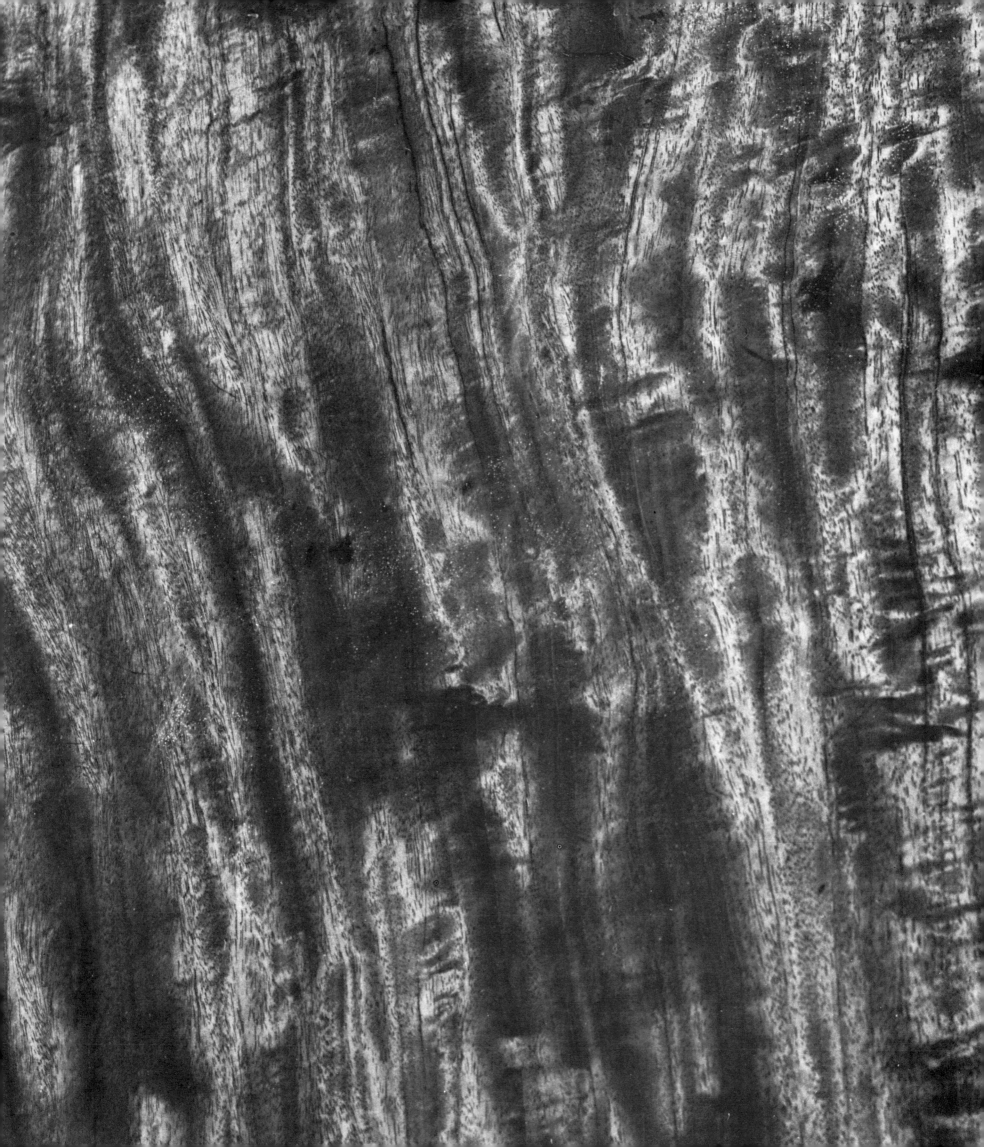

THE FUNDAMENTAL PURPOSE of studying good furniture, or indeed any work of art, is to understand each individual piece more fully, and, if it is a fine one, to perceive its nature to the greatest degree possible. To do this we need to know whether a chair's original context was Connecticut or Philadelphia, for no work of art can be appreciated or studied in a vacuum. It is an individual product and expresses and is expressed by its origin. The more information we have, the more accessible the piece becomes. As with any art, we need a context in which to understand it, although all background must finally become secondary as we focus on the one example. The great piece will ultimately stand on its own merits apart from its former context, yet it is always a part of that context and known through it.

The chairs we are considering, or in fact any piece of fine furniture, did not have a haphazard beginning. Each was a conscious creation of the maker, who drew upon European sources, was limited and focused by the nature of the material used, and conditioned by the milieu in which he worked, and all this was refocused by his particular sense of what was truly fine. Just as a sculptor develops a concept before he begins to carve, so a chairmaker designed the first piece of a new form. And as a sculptor refines and makes changes as he works, so a chairmaker refined and rethought again and again his creation as it came from the wood. A leg of a new shape must have been filed down slowly until it reached the right weight to visually as well as physically support the mass of the upper part.

We must remember that the material was wood, with its own positive and negative values. A great designer understands his material; perceiving its nature and accepting it, he utilizes its natural limitations. This interplay between the weaknesses and virtues of the material is continually at battle with the desires of the prevailing taste, creating a counterpoint throughout the history of furniture. The purpose of the object provides a third factor, and all three elements are continually balanced by a skillful designer-craftsman. In some respects, a furniture designer has to take into consideration more than does the sculptor; he stands next to the architect, who must also unify these three factors of prevailing taste, material, and use.

Furniture makers in different areas approached the possibilities and limitations differently, and to understand those differences is part of understanding where the objects were made. The taste of each area was conditioned by the previous experience of the people who first settled it, and this in turn conditioned those who came to the area. Taste changed somewhat as new groups arrived, bringing their particular approach to design; but basically the previous attitude prevailed unless the influx greatly outnumbered the previous settlers, which was rarely the case. The desire for a unified regional taste often ignored or overrode structural differences, since they are mostly concealed and do not affect the all-over impression of a piece. Each dominating style area developed an individual approach, with the result that though a man trained in one area moving to another might take the previous area's technical know-how with him, he adopted the exterior or aesthetic taste of his new home. For example, John Elliott (see fig. 62) came to America from England in 1753; in a chair made three years later, he shows a nearly complete adaptation to Philadelphia taste.[1] Again, Thomas Affleck came to Philadelphia in 1763 and for John Penn's Governor's Mansion made the now famous Penn-Affleck furniture in what was then the lastest London style. Within a few years he was making a claw and ball foot, solid splat, scroll crest rail chair related to figure 64,[2] a chair which would at that time have been considered twenty-five years out of date in London.

[1] Hornor, fig. 68. The validity of Hornor's information has often been called into question, since many of the documents he describes have now disappeared, and he frequently fails to cite sources. Although this causes serious problems, the book makes a major contribution to the study of American furniture.

[2] Horner, fig. 132.

Why did he, in a sense, revert to an old-fashioned design? Was it that Philadelphia preferred the earlier form? Was it Philadelphia's sense of having its own style, differing from that of London? Or was it that Affleck felt the Philadelphia forms were more aesthetic? We do not know. The point is that Affleck did, in fact, alter at least some of his work to make what was not the latest fashion out of London; he conformed to the taste of his new environment. Yet another case in point is Eliphalet Chapin who, having been trained in Connecticut, spent about three years in Philadelphia, after which he returned to his native area of East Windsor, Connecticut. Although one can easily discern Philadelphia's influences in his work (for example, the open fretted pediment, with floral terminal scrolls, best known on Philadelphia chest-on-chests), these pieces would today never be assigned to anywhere but the Connecticut Valley. They carry the flavor, the aura of the environment in which they were made; they are pieces created for use in a specific locale. We shall see how his key chair (fig. 193), seeming at first to have Philadelphia features, is in reality a composite of design attitudes from many areas crystallized into a distinctly Connecticut object, while Philadelphia's construction methods and details, not easily visible, continue to be used.

Having stated the value of a regional understanding, it seems best to begin our study by reviewing the approaches that have already been used in the regionalizing of American furniture, and to appraise their values and limitations. The problem is such a vast one that we must draw upon all the information previously culled and all the methods known.

Documents

The documents that can be summoned as evidence are early bills of sale, account books, wills, and letters mentioning the object in question and giving pertinent information about it, such as who made and bought it. But it cannot be lightly assumed that mention of a piece remains valid information. Most records are unspecific, stating, for instance, six "compass chairs." We believe this means six Queen Anne chairs, with horseshoe-shaped seats (although some Chippendale chairs had this form of seat), but which six? It is possible that the original owner had only six chairs made with this shape seat and that the connection between document and chairs is accurate; but what if the second owners inherited two sets

with the same shape seat and the bill became identified with the wrong set? This could cause confusion, and indeed often has. William Hornor, who develops this approach more than other writers in his *Blue Book, Philadelphia Furniture*, says that everything he shows was made in Philadelphia and that he has archival information for all his statements. But authorities now agree that plate 11 in his book is a Massachusetts chair; plate 189 a New York chest-on-chest, with typical New York gadrooning and feet (even Hornor considered it a strange piece for Philadelphia); and plate 47 a Rhode Island table. There are in fact many documents that assign a piece now known to have been made in one area to a different location. A Philadelphia lowboy in the Van Cortlandt manor house in New York is said to have been used in that house by Cornelia Van Cortlandt Beekman.[3] We know that New England sent large quantities of furniture as venture cargo along the coast and that New England chairs were sold in great quantity in Philadelphia.

Let us suppose a table made in Rhode Island was sent down the coast and purchased by a Philadelphia cabinetmaker, and that it was sold by him to a customer. The bill of sale or the purchaser's account book, the owner's will, or any other documents pertaining to this piece could place it as bought in Philadelphia, from a Philadelphia cabinetmaker. Recently, a table of the type made in Salem, Massachusetts, possibly by Samuel Field McIntire, turned up with an original New York Duncan Phyfe label attached, and was sold into a fine private collection with this interesting combination noted. A sideboard now considered by many to be a Salem piece, though it has a good Phyfe label, was mistakenly included in a show of furniture by New York cabinetmakers.[4] Probably both pieces were acquired by Phyfe, possibly from a venture cargo, with the intention of reselling them. Whether he passed them off as his own work we do not know, but at least today the untutored, observing the labels, would regard them as New York pieces. Of course, the strength of the documentary approach is that many valid records do exist. Hornor's book attests to this, for the majority of his statements appear accurate when evaluated in the light of other research.

[3] Joseph T. Butler, "The Family Furniture at Van Cortlandt Manor," *Antiques*, 82 (December 1962), pp. 645–6, fig. 6.

[4] V. Isabelle Miller, *Furniture by New York Cabinetmakers 1650 to 1860* (New York: Museum of the City of New York, 1956), no. 120.

Family histories

Allied to the documentary approach is that of the verbal or written family history. Here we have no early documents to keep memory, faulty at best, from building fanciful stories. For example, one historical house, built in the middle of the seventeenth century in Massachusetts, has always been occupied by a descendant of the original owner. The lady who lived there during the last generation wrote down all the traditions about the furniture now in the house, and verbal tradition became written tradition. The stories about one desk demonstrate the problem inherent in this method. This desk is said to have been carried by the original owner in the Revolutionary War, and upon it, traditionally, he wrote some of the letters still preserved by the family. The piece is made in the classical revival style. The front, with part of the top, opens forward to produce a slanting surface. Its heavy, round legs, which are not detachable, have broad, heavy reeding typical of furniture made in Massachusetts between 1800 and 1820. The case part is veneered and has no carrying handles. Surely, the damp encountered in travel under war conditions would have loosened the veneers, which were attached in that period by water-soluble glue, and the animal needed to carry such an object, legs and all, would undoubtedly have been put to better use. Considering these easily observable facts the desk could not have been the one used for letter writing during the Revolution, and an undoubtably true story has become attached to the wrong, though perhaps more attractive, piece.

Whereas specific tradition often proves untrue, strangely enough such general statements as "It was bought in Philadelphia" are more often accurate; again and again family histories do prove extremely helpful, for many times they add convincing weight when there are already other reasons for assigning a piece to a certain area.

Labeled and signed pieces

An approach that is heavily relied upon is the use of labeled, stamped, or signed furniture, which shows the original maker and thus the area of origin. Many cabinetmakers in the eighteenth century attached to their work their name and address, engraved upon small pieces of paper. Others stamped their products with their names, much as the silversmiths stamped their work; others again burned in their names with hot stamps; and still others signed their work in ink, pencil, or chalk. Many of the remaining identifying marks are the paper labels, though frequently only parts of the label or signs of former labels remain. Only a small percentage of the existing early cabinetwork was signed or shows signs of makers' marks. Undoubtedly there were originally more labels, for in many cases time and industrious housewives have removed forever this clue to an object's origin. With chairs the problem increases. Perhaps many of the labels were attached to the webbing under the seat,[5] and when the seats were re-upholstered the labels were lost. This lack of identification by the maker, or his customer, was intensified by the fact that up to sixty or seventy years ago no one set value on a label in the way we do now.

The problems with using labels to establish the origin of a piece are manifold. Let us take the natural ones first. Sometimes a chair was not upholstered by its maker, but the upholsterer attached his own label. Suppose it was later re-upholstered by an upholsterer or by a chairmaker who perhaps attached *his* own label. And again, suppose the man who sold the chair did not make it. We have noted the problem of pieces imported from other areas and sold with a Phyfe label. Another well-known case is John Elliott, cabinetmaker and retailer, who sold hundreds of European mirrors to which he attached his own label. Further, it is also known that some early owners signed, stamped, or branded their furniture. Where it is a well-known name there is little confusion, but an unknown name on a piece leaves us in doubt as to whether it is that of the owner or the maker.

These are some of the natural problems. The unnatural ones are far more difficult, since they are not meant to be recognized as problems. There are many pieces now bearing a label that have no right to that honor. It is easy enough to remove a label from a small box or from an unimportant or damaged piece. It is much more difficult to attach it to a different piece while reproducing all the circumstances that accompany a genuine label, such as proper wood color, wear, and so on, and we will discuss this later in detail. However, no matter how difficult, it is frequently done, largely because a piece carrying a label at least doubles its value and some-

---

[5] Meyric R. Rogers, "George Shipley: his furniture and his label. A set of side chairs," *Antiques*, 79 (April 1961), p. 374.

times raises it to ten times the price of the same piece unlabeled. Recently, a dealer was offered a sideboard, and although it was of fine quality he already had several good examples and let it pass. Two weeks later, the piece appeared in an important shop bearing a label it had not had when examined by the first dealer. The sideboard had passed through a small shop whose proprietor considers himself an expert at attaching old labels so that they appear original to the piece. It is possible to find old labels on new pieces as well—in Part III we will deal in detail with the problem of questionable chairs that carry authentic labels. Also, though it is harder to achieve a convincing result, people have attempted to attach new labels to pieces both old and new. To make a new label appear old by baking, acid fumes, or staining is as difficult as to make interior surfaces of unfinished wood appear old; luckily an expert has less trouble detecting this. It is far easier today simply to sign an object in pencil, chalk, or ink; a single chalk mark reading "Townsend" does astonishing things to the price of an ordinary Rhode Island piece.

The value of an honestly labeled piece is obvious. Of the many pieces illustrated in Hornor's book, all were in private hands and many of them had been in the same family since they were made. The pieces shown there, with the many forms of documentation, are of infinite value, and hundreds of other valid examples exist. A piece that carries a genuine label probably can be taken as typical of that maker's work, and it serves as a clue to what was made in his area. However, we cannot say that similar pieces are necessarily made by the same cabinetmaker, for related pieces were often made by different men. A poignant example of this is a well-known pair of case pieces, a highboy and a lowboy that match except for one carved ornament in the skirt; these were labeled by two Philadelphia cabinetmakers, William Savery and Thomas Tufft, respectively.[6] We know also that one carver often served

numerous shops, with the result that similar carving could appear on pieces made by different men.

Furthermore, carved parts of furniture could be purchased by anyone. In 1798, for instance, Francis Trumble advertised carved work, finished parts which could be incorporated by less experienced cabinetmakers into their own work. In 1747, Joseph Armitt had for sale "72 Banisters" (back splats); in 1775, Benjamin Randolph furnished Mr. Joseph Swift with materials for two arm chairs for £2.12s.3d. This included "'4 Back feet sawd. out, 2 Banesters, 2 Top Rales, 11 feet Boards for the Rales,' all 'Sawd. out,' '18 feet of 2½ Plank for Legs & arms &c' and '1 ½ Curld Hair for stuffing the seat.'"[7] The splat of the famous Gillingham chair in the Taradash Collection[8] is very close to the splat in the chair made by Duncan, shown in plate 344 of Hornor's book,[9] and could have been assigned to Gillingham on grounds of similarity if contrary proof did not exist. Apprentices tended to continue to make what they had learned under their master, and a lesser maker would surely attempt to copy the work of a more successful craftsman, just as he does today.

Structural details

Another method often used to determine the origin of a piece is to examine the similarity of structural details. We now know that Philadelphia cabinetmakers used in their chairs a quarter-round corner block, usually composed of two pieces, and that Massachusetts cabinetmakers used single pieces of triangular shape. The reason for such differences in technique between regions has to do in part with the European background of the makers or their teachers. Many of the early settlers in America came in groups: one such founded Massachusetts, another New York, another Philadelphia. Many of the successive migrations were also in groups: the French Huguenots, the Swedes, the Mennonites, and the Irish, to list only a few. And coming in groups, often they settled in groups.[10] Generally speaking, they came from

[6] Samuel W. Woodhouse, Jr., in "Thomas Tufft," *Antiques,* 12 (October 1927), pp. 292–3, discusses in detail a dressing table labeled by Thomas Tufft. Also, Clarence W. Brazer in "Early Pennsylvania Craftsmen," *Antiques,* 13 (March 1928), pp. 200–5, discusses the Tufft dressing table in relation to the Wharton highboy, the base of which matches the dressing table except for the introduction of a husk motif in the center of the skirt. Brazer says that the construction of the highboy reflects the work of William Savery, but that this highboy is "more correct than Savery's in its following of Chippendale's precedent. . . ." Husk carving like that of the highboy is found on other pieces attributed to Tufft by Carl M. Williams, "Thomas Tufft," *Antiques,* 54 (October 1948), p. 246. The only problem in attributing the highboy to Tufft on the basis of the almost identical Tufft-labeled dressing table is that Hornor found the Wharton highboy to be *thrice* labeled by William Savery; of course it could have been made by Tufft and labeled by Savery.

[7] Hornor, p. 207.

[8] *Antiques,* 49 (June 1946), p. 359 [illustrated].

[9] For further discussion, dealing with Gillingham's apprentices and partner who may have used the same back, see Hornor, p. 205.

[10] See migration of groups in the Appendix, p. 196.

one area of Europe and brought their own peculiar construction methods, just as they brought their peculiar accents.[11] Another reason for consistency within a region is that a master cabinetmaker would teach methods of construction to his apprentices and they, in turn, would teach the same skills and help to develop the use of a standard method. Just as details of style used by the most popular makers were copied, so did the less important makers copy methods in construction so that they could claim that their chairs were as fine and strong as the most fashionable ones.

Depending on direct examination, this way of determining the origin of a piece is one of the best as it does not rely on separate material that might mistakenly be associated with the wrong piece. However, it too carries dangers. Individuals and groups, and thus cabinetmakers, readily moved within America. These individuals took to new areas their former customs and many chairs show evidence of two or three regions. This could be because they were made on the border between style centers, receiving several influences; but it was also possible for a man trained in Philadelphia and later working in Massachusetts to combine details that he liked from both centers. We find, however, that in those known cases of a man having moved from one area to another, he often continued to use his previous techniques where they were not visible, but he adopted where it was visible the taste of his new locality. A good example of this is the adjustments made by Chapin upon his return to Connecticut.

Not only did men move, but pieces moved as well. We have already noted a Massachusetts chair, a New York chest-on-chest, and a Newport table all recorded in Philadelphia. Cabinetmakers were quick to take up new ideas if they seemed profitable, and pieces from other regions must often have served as models or sources of inspiration. When this borrowing occurs within a region, it confuses the issue of who made the particular object but not where it was made. But what if a piece was used as a pattern in another region? On September 16, 1788, General Washington wrote to Colonel Clement Biddle, who was in Philadelphia, " 'I will thank you to pay Samuel Powel, Esq. for a chair which he was so good as to procure for me as a pattern.' "[12] This chair was probably copied by workers on Washington's plantation. If it was accurately copied in every way, the resulting chairs would now appear to be from Philadelphia. This is, however, unlikely, for if the plantation cabinetmaker was highly skilled enough to repro-

duce it accurately, he probably would have introduced personal ideas; if, on the other hand, he was poor enough, the result might have been an indifferent "rural" chair with enough Philadelphia characteristics to have it appear as a rural Pennsylvania piece. The copies may look like Philadelphia, rural Pennsylvania, or Virginia chairs.

Woods

Related to the study of construction is the study of woods. The primary, or most visible wood, when not an imported wood such as mahogany, may suggest an area of origin. Walnut tends to be the wood of Pennsylvania and southward, whereas maple suggests New England, but walnut chairs existed in Massachusetts and maple chairs in Pennsylvania. Secondary woods, those not meant to be seen, were usually local woods; thus white pine is thought of as New England and hard pine as Southern. But we find, alas, that Charleston, South Carolina, after the Revolution, imported great quantities of New England pine, as it was far easier to work than hard or yellow pine[13] and American woods are known to have been used in English work. Recently there has been a drive to use microanalysis to determine the woods. When an accurate analysis is made, this can be helpful but, to date, there has not been sufficient surety of results. The notorious beech rear seat rail of one New York chair was reported as cherry, and two laboratories often give differing answers. Although woods may prove helpful they must therefore be considered cautiously.

Related pieces

Closely allied to the methods of detecting region by construction and by material is that of assessing similar pieces found in one area. Since most people moving in early times moved in wagons or boats, much furniture was left behind and pieces were repurchased or remade in the new locale. It is, then, usual that a large group of chairs, alike in both construction and design, dominates an area. The problem is the same one which haunts us in other methods,

---

[11] For an example of Irish influence, see pp. 166–7.

[12] Hornor, p. 206.

[13] E. Milby Burton, *Charleston Furniture 1700–1825* (Charleston, S.C.: The Charleston Museum, 1955), p. 34.

that of movement. Some families did take chairs or even large pieces to their new homes. Often, several families from one area moved together to a new area and it is possible that they took along similar objects, creating a style link with their former locality. In addition, there are problems raised by objects shipped as venture cargo. For example, a type of leather panel-back chair has been found in great quantities in both Massachusetts and Philadelphia, supporting the belief that it was made in both places. Now we know that over a thousand such chairs were shipped out of Boston in one year, and there is further evidence that quantities were purchased in Philadelphia. In 1742, Plunket Fleeson claimed to have " 'black and red leather chairs . . . cheaper than any made here, or imported from Boston.' "[14] Despite this movement of objects, however, a type predominant in one area may provide corroborating evidence of the typical work of that region.

With all the difficulties inherent in the problem of establishing regional types, it is unfortunate that the people who could have helped the most have often purposefully complicated the issue. Those who bought furniture out of homes where it had been for generations were predominantly dealers. True, the majority of such collecting was done before people paid attention to the question of what was made where, but even now most dealers are understandably wary of revealing the exact source of a piece for fear that the buyer or other dealers will go there and purchase the treasures that remain.

As the importance of regional origins became clear, many of the less informed people localized a piece on scant information, producing confusing and inaccurate traditions. Small details were called certain proof of origin, with no thought given to other factors or to the piece as a whole. Thus, any chair with a square back foot automatically became a "New York" chair, even if it was a Massachusetts or Philadelphia piece. Also furniture from some areas commands higher prices than pieces of basically the same form from other places, so that any feature that might suggest a higher priced region is all too often cited as the primary characteristic. A Philadelphia Chippendale chair, for example, is considered more valuable than a similar Chippendale chair from other areas. To some degree this is reasonable, for a first-rate Philadelphia example is one of the great forms produced in wood. Indeed, pieces are reconstructed or recarved to appear more like Philadelphia, just as lesser English pieces are often altered to appear American.

14 Hornor, p. 191.

Clearly, it is not easy to find the origin of an unmarked object that is small enough to be portable in a land where movement of individuals and groups was, and is, inherent in the foundation of the social structure. Any method that is really workable cannot depend on a stable society and, as we have seen, cannot depend exclusively on secondary information. It must therefore be based on information provided by the object itself.

It is possible to start by dividing the chairs into groups on the basis of their structure and details, but since we have overlaps among regions, such a grouping, though extremely helpful, is not enough; another factor still dependent on the piece itself needs to be brought into play. It must be a factor not easily transferable between areas, and it must be something that cannot have been totally controlled by one individual. Since it must have a continuing presence not altered by a few persons leaving or arriving, it should be at least partially in the control of the local purchasing group. The key must, in fact, lie at the junction between the buyer and the maker, where they both have some control. The maker cannot sell something sharply contrary to what is expected and a buyer cannot buy something that is not made. This junction, this interplay between maker and buyer, which is always present but generally unperceived, and which encompasses a complete region, makes that region's basic approach to an object's general design, the visual "feel" and emotional impact of a piece.

We will, then, concentrate on the object itself, seeking to group by construction and all-over design. In most cases the chairs themselves provide our data, with secondary sources avoided because of the past confusion they have caused. It is, of course, necessary to have some evidence with which to locate geographically the groups formed by direct analysis; fortunately, sound outside evidence was available for a sufficient number from each group to make sure of their original location. For this reason, chairs with good family histories, or labels, or other regionalizing information from a secondary source are ultimately necessary.

In Part II we shall see that the cabinetmaker's approach to construction and details, technical things learned as an apprentice, was fairly consistent within an area. It is important to understand how chairs in various regions were put together and, in conjunction with this, to realize variations in the handling of parts such as feet, seat rail, and back. However, some readers may wish to skip the more detailed discussion. Part III shows the cabinetmaker's approach to design, to the overall visual impact of an object, to differ with different areas. Six important areas with strong differences in design have been included: Philadelphia, Massachusetts, New York, Rhode Island, Connecticut, and the South. The first four look directly to Europe for their inspiration and stand separately from one another in their interpretation. In contrast, Connecticut depends on American style centers for inspiration and, using them as a source of basic forms, reinterprets these into local terms; and the South uses both American centers and Europe. One of the most interesting by-products of our research has been the increasing awareness of the American cabinetmakers' dependence upon actual European examples, rather than upon pattern book sources. This study deals with a specifically limited category, side and arm chairs, and mostly those with cabriole legs, in order to present most clearly both the subject and the technique of analysis. To apply this technique to all types of American furniture would require volumes of material. But the analytical method has been applied in passing to a few case pieces and tables, and it would be equally useful in examining simpler country pieces in which freedom, within a united attitude, becomes even more intensified as each area develops its own artistic expression in wood.

II

CONSTRUCTION
AND DESIGN
DETAILS

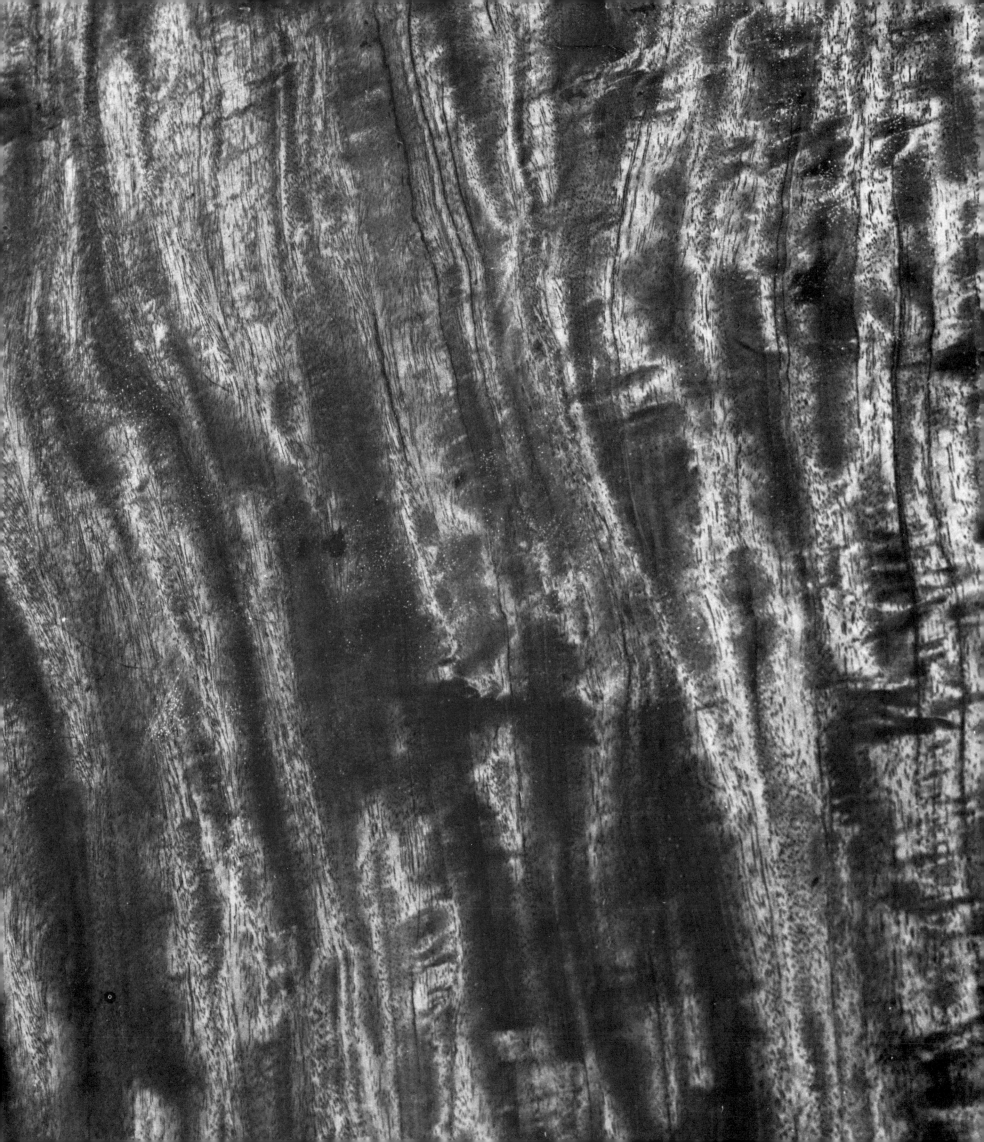

1. Philadelphia

In considering the cabinetmaker's approach to construction, it is most useful to examine the basic units of the chair separately, beginning with the crest rail and moving downwards (for photographs explaining chair parts, see p. *xi*). The physical needs of each structural part conditioned what was to become the popular taste, and in turn aesthetic changes influenced the shape of each visible part, for these two elements, taste and structure, are continually in both harmony and conflict. To give one example, the desire for a horseshoe-shaped seat (fig. 48) required the development of a new and stronger type of joint construction (fig. 16) because that particular form looked most satisfactory with members visibly thinner; in a slightly different way, horizontal shaping, an aesthetic rather than a structural need, developed as a visual treatment of the straight seat rail when it had the wide, strong joints required structurally by chairs with squared seat frames (fig. 45).

It is misleading to present a simple logical structural or stylistic development for any form, not only because styles overlapped but also because several were popular simultaneously, sometimes for long periods, while the interchange of motifs between coexistent styles was, of course, continual. Nevertheless, in order to clarify general shifts, chronological complexities must be simplified, and confusing but not basic facts (such as the production of fully developed Queen Anne chairs at least as late as 1800) must be temporarily ignored.

In the colonies the style previous to Queen Anne, that of William and Mary, was primarily composed of straight members relieved only by heavy turning and carving. The basic English William and Mary chairs, with caned or leather backs and seats, had developed through three structural stages, moving gradually toward a central emphasis: the first had a bilateral feeling, accented by finials, with the crest between the back posts; in the next, the crest was superimposed on the back posts to give more unity of line, eliminating the finials; finally, the back posts and crest rail became one continuous line up and across the top, which was greatly simplified so that the central splat under it dominated the design.[1] The coexistent and, in America, more popular bannister-back chair maintained the side finials and high elaborate crest of the first type of English chair. Examples of American caned chairs are rare, but the leather panel-back chairs were common in two forms and show the first and third stages of development. First, the finials accented the bilateral, then the splat was surrounded by one continuous line formed by the back posts and crest rail. The early Queen Anne style shows a straightness carried over from the William and Mary, but this gradually changes to the full-blown curves so typical of developed Queen Anne. Then, during the Chippendale period, there is a return to a new straightness so important to that style.

Clearly, the crest rail plays an important part in this shift of styles. In fact, along with the splat and feet, it is considered the determining factor as to which style the chair is to be assigned, and it is usually the most updated feature. The crest rail was lower in a Queen Anne chair than a late William and Mary chair, and was scooped in the center, providing a feeling of unity with the splat. In early Queen Anne, the meeting of the back posts and the crest rail retains the break in the curve at the outer corners of the crest rail, the re-entrant corners found on Chinese chairs that were ultimately the source of the English Queen Anne style (fig. 45). This break in the curved line soon disappears (fig. 47) and the back posts and top rail become visually one curve, while the rail continues to be decorated by an edge molding that continues down the back posts (fig. 47, etc.). It was the common practice to unite all major members of framed chairs by mortice and tenon joints and, except for one distinctive joint used only in

---

[1] For a detailed discussion of English William and Mary, see Luke Vincent Lockwood, *Colonial Furniture in America* (1901; 3rd edition, New York: Castle Books, 1957), vol. 2, pp. 33–55.

fully developed Philadelphia and a few Connecticut Queen Anne chairs, no other joint was used. (Dovetailing was, of course, the other major joint used in case pieces.)

About 1740, when the round pad foot shifted to the long pointed-pad or slipper foot, the scoop of the top rail became elaborated with a raised member that repeated the scoop below (fig. 49). This member gradually rose, becoming more and more elaborately decorated, until, as a central crown, its decoration became the main focal point (fig. 53). With the shift to bowed top rails, the center continued to be important and was lifted high. The shell as the central ornament then tended to replace the wave or S-scroll form, and the rail was carved at the center to give a resting place or cradle to the shell (fig. 68). In all the regions we shall study, crest rail decoration is cut from the solid and is not applied.[2] At times the shell, instead of being cradled in the top rail, projects from it. And it usually reaches higher than the ears or the rail itself, thus maintaining and reinforcing the central emphasis (fig. 69). Many of the simpler chairs, for economic reasons, are merely curved, without shell ornament.

The ears, appearing in the Chippendale period, were at first plain and straight-ended (fig. 60). Later they became knuckled or divided into three parts, with the center ridge much larger, bolder, and longer, and the thin side ridges usually ending in scrolls (fig. 69). As the Chippendale chair reached its developed form, which is perhaps the fullest rococo expression in American chairs prior to the mid-nineteenth century, the top rail sometimes carried carved forms of flowing leafage, and the ears repeated the form of the central shell accent (fig. 70). This form of top rail is sometimes, though rarely, decorated with a carved rope design (fig. 67). About 1755, parallel with the bowed crest rail, there developed a "double" serpentine top rail, with the side turning down instead of up (fig. 80) and the ears generally in the form of modified scrolls. These usually crown a vase-baluster or Gothic splat, which will be discussed later. A few top rails were pierced to long openings, perhaps to serve as handholds since they generally appear on low or "slipper" chairs, which were perhaps frequently moved about (fig. 63).

Because back posts were always treated differently above and below the seat, they will be discussed as two units even though they were always one piece of wood on side and arm chairs (on wing chairs this was not always the case). From the beginning of

[2] In all regions all carving on the crest rail, splat, back posts, knees, and seat rail, except for an applied central shell (as on fig. 69), is cut from the solid.

9

Reverse-curve back posts, echoing curve of front legs (side view of fig. 52).

the Queen Anne style, the back posts above the seat were S-curved on the side plane (that is, when viewed from the side) (fig. 9). About 1740, they began to move in an S-curve on the front plane as well (that is, viewed from the front), ending the downward curve some inches above the seat (compare figs. 47 and 48). This created a continuous interplay of reverse curves from the inside of the back posts upwards across the bottom edge of the crest rail, and down to the outline of the splat with its additional composite of reverse curves. On the outside, the basic line went up the back post across the top rail and down the other side. To complete the feeling of curves, a few cabinetmakers made the back post above the seat completely round in section instead of flat on the front and round behind (compare figs. 52 and 53). The innermost and outermost curves of the back posts above the seat were sometimes applied pieces so that the lighter stock could be used (fig. 48), but this practice was more common in New York.

With the beginning of the Chippendale style, movement and interest was largely concentrated in an elegant splat, and the back posts were straightened, becoming in effect a visual frame. To provide visual lift, the back posts diverged upward carrying the eye to the ears and thus to the crest rail crowning the all-important splat. The outer edge of the back posts was edge-molded when the top rail had the same decoration (fig. 61), although the fluting decoration (fig. 69) that is known in Philadelphia and elsewhere in America, having been a standard practice in England, was sometimes used. A variation of this, only rarely seen on Philadelphia chairs, is stop fluting (fig. 72).For a related but less visually emphatic decoration, molded front faces, termed in the eighteenth century "ogee" molded,[3] were used. This decoration usually appeared only on chairs with a Gothic or vase-baluster splat (figs. 82 and 87) and not with the simple baluster form of splat. Carving rarely appeared on the posts; simple carving (fig. 85) is sometimes found, but the Lambert family chairs (fig. 71) and the Jones family chairs (fig. 95) are nearly unique, not only in Philadelphia, but in America.[4] Sometimes the ears of the crest rail were carved to frontal scroll forms that appeared to be part of the post rather than part of the rail to which they actually belong (fig. 71). This feature is also found on many English (fig. 59), and perhaps Irish, chairs, which are in other ways very close to Philadelphia products.

Comfort was not originally a part of chair design. Seventeenth-century chairs had rigid straight backs, often with no backward rake, and many bannister-back chairs of the William and Mary period showed a simple strong backward rake. It was only when the reverse curve made it possible that chair backs developed

a comfortable shape. We have seen that the back post of Queen Anne chairs S-curved backward, and the splat followed the same curve, producing a harmonious movement and making physical comfort possible. When we take into consideration the height of eighteenth-century man, we see that the curve in the splat supported his lumbar curve, which is now understood by doctors, and typists, to be most in need of support.[5] This "spooning" of the splat continued in Philadelphia as long as the posts remained reverse-curved on the side plane; then, along with the posts, it was modified during the Chippendale period to a simple backward curve, reducing the amount of comfort but providing a surface more appropriate for elaborate piercing and scrolling. Except in rare cases, like the rather crude chairs by John Elliott (fig. 62), Philadelphia splats were made with some curve.

Some of the unpierced splats were of veneered pine or tulip poplar, as veneers could more easily provide the elaborate grain patterns that were so popular (fig. 50). However, such a veneered splat was not nearly as common as a splat of solid wood chosen for its handsome grain. The general ignorance of early practices was typified recently by the case of a customer who returned a Philadelphia Queen Anne chair after years of ownership because she had just realized that the splat was veneered; the dealer cheerfully met his guarantee, repaying the original purchase price. He sold the chair within a week for about five times that price, for it was completely genuine!

Except for the Gothic form, the outline of the splats seems to be based on the baluster shape (for example, figs. 45, 49, and 66); as we have seen in noting the sale of eighteenth-century chair parts, splats were called "Banesters" and in Lehman's 1786 list of prices "Banisters." The simple baluster form so common in New England (fig. 97) is not found on high-style Philadelphia chairs, although it appears there on simpler rush-seat chairs (fig. 44). On the earliest Queen Anne chair included here (fig. 45), the splat is a typical English form of cupped baluster which is extremely satisfying in design. A typical early baluster splat with pointed ears (fig. 47) looks like the left half of the splat of the chair Chippendale used in his *Director* when discussing perspective drawing.[6] Very quickly the splat copied the early English

---

[3] Lehman's list, Hornor, p. 210.

[4] Because elaborate carving is highly prized by collectors of Americana, many chairs of doubtful origin have been eagerly accepted as American.

[5] Modern research by Swedish doctors and Danish architects reveals 21 cm. or 8¼ in. as providing maximum comfort. The chairs we are considering provide the support at 6¾ to 7 in. The difference is accounted for by the fact that people are taller today.

[6] Thomas Chippendale, *The Gentleman and Cabinet-Maker's Director* (London, 1754 and 1755), no. IX.

Georgian forms of complex interrelated reverse curves and fretting, often with scroll ears (fig. 52).

In the Philadelphia Chippendale chair there are three basic forms of splat. The first (fig. 10) is a baluster form pierced to scrolled strapwork. This splat generally is composed of upper flanking scrolls, dropping in curves from the top rail to extend about one-third the length of the splat. From the bottom, or shoe, spring three bars, the center one dividing about one-third of the way up to join the outer straps which continue to curve, support the upper scrolls, and terminate at a central overlapping form of two curving straps. The ends of the scrolls are often carved to volutes. The central curved straps, starting at the top rail and ending where the center bar splits to join the sides from below, act as the uniting member. Without the structural and visual unity they produce, the top and bottom scrolls would create the effect of a splat divided into two parts.

The second basic form is the vase-baluster splat (fig. 11), in which the splat swells at the base, with the upper sides incurvated as in the classical Chinese vase form. The straps flow from the shoe to the top rail unbroken, connected by light lateral members that do not interrupt their movement. This form is rare and, as we shall see, it usually comes directly from English sources without the same degree of American reinterpretation found in the other two (fig. 79). The third basic form of splat is pierced to cusped Gothic tracery (fig. 12). In the basic form, the raised edges of the serpentine top rail flow into, and become, the tracery of the splat, which moves down in unbroken straps to the shoe. Near the top, the side members divide and the inner straps rake to meet at the center under some form of decorative terminal. Toward the bottom, the central member rests on a pointed "quatrefoil," below which are two vertical piercings, sometimes with their points up, sometimes down. The Gothic splat has two basic outlines (figs. 89 and 90). In the first, the outer straps come to a terminus and begin again about one-third of the way down the side; in the second, they join below a cusped bulge. A subgroup of the Gothic splat, with larger piercings in the upper part but similar below, is related in outline to the vase-baluster form (fig. 85).

These three basic forms encompass infinite variations and rarely appear in exactly the same manner, except in chairs made as a set. Other forms appear, but their outlines are usually related to one of the three basic splats. An example of a variation of type one (compare figs. 75 and 69) is a splat similar in outline but with its center developed to a looped diamond. In this chair we

10

First type of Philadelphia pierced splat, baluster form (detail from fig. 69).

also find pendant tassels and drapery swags, usually associated with New York chairs; but this is one of the many cases of basic English motifs available to anyone (fig. 74) proving attractive to more than one region. Another variation of the pierced baluster form (fig. 78'), exploiting the possibilities of free-flowing strapwork, again has a direct English source, figure 77.

The most decorated of the three forms is the first, which is sometimes enriched with curved leafage, especially on the outside of the lower scrolls, and with carved rosettes or volutes, which sometimes mark the crossing of straps or termination of scrolls. The other two forms show little decoration, what there is being confined mostly to the top rail (figs. 82 and 91, although fig. 95 is certainly an exception).

All the Philadelphia splats are based on English patterns, both in their general design and form of decoration.

In England it was common, though not the rule, to house the back splat directly in the back rail, passing behind the shoe (compare figs. 13 and 14). The shoe merely appears from the front to hold the splat. Probably the idea was to have a nonstructural member on chairs upholstered on the rear seat rail. The loose shoe could be used to cover the back edge of the upholstery and yet remain easily removable for re-upholstering. In Philadelphia, however, the seat rails were rarely over-upholstered (fig. 87 is an exception); rather, the chairs had removable slip seats and the shoe was fixed, permanently fastened to the back seat rail, with the splat housed into the top of it. The flared base of the shoe provides structural and visual unity between the back rail and splat; the curves on the sides of the shoe bring the eye from the seat rail up onto the splat and the curve on the front carries the horizontal line of the seat up to the vertical movement of the

12

Third type of Philadelphia pierced splat, Gothic form (detail from fig. 91).

11

Second type of Philadelphia pierced splat, vase-baluster form (detail from fig. 80).

splat. The upper edge of the shoe was usually decorated only with a light molding that was one piece of wood with the shoe, but it was sometimes carved to complex patterns such as a daisy and dart pattern, or a leaf design (fig. 68).

The rear part of the arm, on Philadelphia arm chairs designed as such, was attached to the front of the back posts. However, in the eighteenth century it was cheaper to buy a side chair and have arms attached;[7] and since the side chairs were narrower than the arm chairs, the practice developed of attaching the arms of these "converted" chairs to the sides of the posts, rather than to the front, in order to give extra width. In all the chairs the arms

[7] Hornor, pp. 215–16.

13

Splat housed into top of shoe (detail from fig. 52).

cross-section. Leaving the arm in a backward, then forward, curve, it joins the seat rail close to the front to bring the visual and structural thrust near the front line, uniting the physical strain and eye movement down the front leg.

Another rare type of arm and support has been isolated. Figure 57 shows an arm and post combination which, when it does appear, is found on chairs from about 1750 to 1770. This rolled or looped arm was common in England but, possibly because of its inherently weak construction, never became popular in the colonies. The other types of arms and supports already discussed allow a large, strong, tenoned joint at their junction and the shape recognizes the strength of the wood's grain structure. In the looped arm, the lower member violates the grain structure where it suddenly moves forward into the loop. Here the vertical grain is reduced to such a small dimension that it is easily snapped by excessive pressure.

The seats of Philadelphia chairs were nearly always formed of two parts, the removable slip seat and the surrounding and supporting seat frame. The seat frame was notched on the inner upper edge to hold the slip seat, except at the back where it was often

were S- or reverse-curved, moving out from the back posts around the person seated and curving in again to be supported directly over the seat rails, thus giving a vertical solidity both visually and structurally. After the arm joins its support, it again curves outward with an intimation of open, inviting generosity; usually, it terminates in a scrolled handhold (fig. 49), and by the middle of the century the scroll was usually knuckled (fig. 66). The outer edge of the arm was often raised on these later, more elaborate chairs and a more sculptured quality developed.

Two basic types of arm supports were used. The most common throughout both periods was that of figures 47 and 66, which show its development from a simpler form where the front and inside faces are flattened and the rear is quarter-round in shape. By 1740–50, on the finer chairs, the front and inside faces were shaped to concave surfaces and the upper part thinned out to a distinctive Philadelphia form. The second and less common support (fig. 82) was in use during the Chippendale period and seems confined to chairs with the second and third type of splat. It repeats the reverse curve of the arm and usually is of rounded

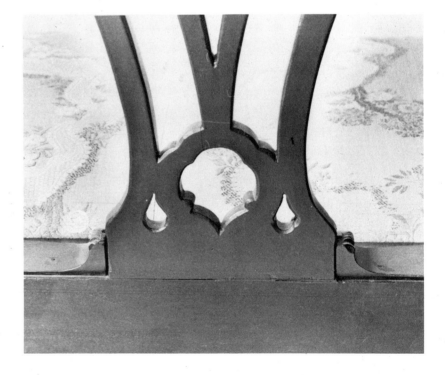

14

Splat seated in rear seat rail, passing behind shoe (detail from English settee, The Museum of Art, Rhode Island School of Design).

constructed with the front and side rails tenoning into the upper part of the cabriole front legs (fig. 15); but as the desire for all visible parts to appear thinner and curved became supreme, Philadelphia makers adopted another English technique of fastening the side and front rails to each other with a large horizontal mortice and tenon joint (fig. 16). The leg, which appears to stop at the seat, was actually reduced at that point to a dowel-like member that continued up through the seat frame; this "dowel" served an additional function of locking the mortice and tenon joint of the seat

15

Construction of front corner joints of squared seat frames (detail from The Museum of Art, Rhode Island School of Design).

left unsupported. Rare exceptions are the over-upholstered chairs (figs. 87 and 93).

The first Queen Anne seats were squared (really trapezoidal in shape) but, as the taste for curves dominated the style (1740–60), they became curved or horseshoe-shaped. To construct these seats, Philadelphia developed a special English practice found elsewhere only in Connecticut work. Earlier, the seat had been

16

Construction of front corner joint of Philadelphia-type horseshoe-shaped seat frames (detail from fig. 54).

17

Philadelphia-type of horseshoe-shaped seat frame (detail from fig. 54).

rail. To leave material enough to house this extension of the leg and to provide the strength lost when the seat was made vertically thinner, the inside edge of the seat was not cut to correspond to the outer edge but was left deep, in the shape of a square (this is different from the standard New England solution, compare figs. 17 and 27). Also peculiar to this way of constructing a seat and nearly always used with it is the applied rim, which is glued to the upper edge of the rail to enclose the slip seat (fig. 53). (On figure 56 the front rim is a solid piece with the seat rail but the side rims are applied.) The applied rim is the obvious answer when the wood is of so great a depth; otherwise much labor would have been expended to form a rim cut from the solid. At the height of its glory, the front of the rounded seat rail often had a decorated recess (fig. 57). With the coming of the Chippendale crest rail and the straight back posts, the seat returned to a squared form, providing the lower edge of the visual frame for the back splat as well as a

flatter background for the carved decoration then desired; sometimes a suggestion of the circular movement was continued by rounding the front corners of the seat rail (fig. 66).

From the beginning of the Queen Anne style it was a common practice to shape the lower edge of the seat rail horizontally on both the front and the sides; that is, to remove the central part of the lower edge of the rail. This allowed a wide member to enter the upper part of the leg and make a strong mortice and tenon joint, while at the same time keeping the rail from appearing too heavy in relation to the other members of the chair. The terminal pattern of the end of the shaping was commonly a C shape and a notch (fig. 45), which visually carries out the flow of curves set by the knee bracket. Taken together, the curves are the cyma curve of the knee bracket, then a fillet, then a cove and fillet. When a seat became horseshoe-shaped and the legs were pegged into the bottom of the seat frame, the joint, with its greater depth, was found strong enough with thinner (in height) members; thus the reduction in height at the corners terminated the need for horizontal shaping. When seats returned to the squared form, shaping reappeared.

Early Queen Anne chairs had no decoration on the straight seat rail except for the standard rounded top edge molding, sometimes distinctively quarter-round in shape. The only added interest was the form chosen for the horizontal shaping (fig. 47). The simple horseshoe-shaped seat was kept plain, the veneer enrichment on figure 50 is rare, while the recessed or re-entrant form usually carried an applied shell (fig. 57). Ordinarily, the shell on these rayed upward, but occasionally this was reversed. When the style shifted again to the squared seat frame and horizontal shaping reappeared, the front shaping was often interrupted in the center by some type of drop decoration. On the trifid foot chairs and the chairs with the first type of pierced strapwork splats, it was usual to apply a shell to the drop center of the seat rail in order visually to balance the shell on the crest rail. Some cabinetmakers developed an asymmetrical seat rail shell to relate more directly to the asymmetrical shell of the crest rail (fig. 68). Chairs with the second and third forms of splat were usually without decoration on the seat rail, which was simply horizontally shaped. The exceptions carried some raised ornament concentrated in the center; often it was in the form of leafage around a cartouche, and the shaping itself consisted of two scrolls with raised edges carved to form C scrolls (figs. 85 and 91). Here the leafage and scrolls were cut from the solid, in contrast to the shells of the first type, for they were not as deep. Gadrooning seldom appears on Philadelphia chairs, but figure 93, very English in detail, is a rare exception. This example shows the typical positive and negative carving, really a flute between each member of the gadrooning, and is like that found on Philadelphia case pieces, rather than the New York form of a simple undulating line (compare fig. 136).

When Philadelphia chairs were made with squared seats, without the great strength provided by the additional depth given the horseshoe-shaped seats, additional support was gained by using inner corner bracings or corner blocks. Philadelphia-type corner blocks, quarter-round in form, of vertical grain (they were made in two pieces, which fitted around the inside of the legs), were usually attached only with glue (fig. 18). This form of corner block is basic in Philadelphia for both the front and the rear of the seat, although the rear block is smaller and of one piece (fig. 19). Exceptions to this are the front half of the front blocks of figure 89, which are secured with wooden pins, and the original rear

block of figure 67, which is attached with two nails; otherwise these blocks are standard in form. The other form of corner block, which dominated Massachusetts, is triangular in shape, of one piece, with horizontal grain (fitting around the inside of the leg), and is applied with nails as well as glue (fig. 28). Many English chairs show a combination of these—that is, the "Philadelphia" form in the front and the "Massachusetts" form in the rear—and a similar combination is found on a few Philadelphia chairs. The reason for this variation in a single piece is not known; the fact that the inside of the front leg, the part enclosed by the corner block, is larger than that in the rear may be at least part of the logic.

It is, of course, a fallacy to believe that we can regionalize by relying entirely on the basis of such small details as corner blocks. The routine construction techniques, such as dovetails in case pieces and corner blocks in chairs, were probably often left to the apprentices or assistants, when the shop was fortunate enough to be thus supplied, and one shop in which several men worked might well have produced differences in these details. A man could have carried his former employer's method to another area,

18

Philadelphia-type of front corner block: two piece, quarter-round shape, vertical grain, no nails (detail from fig. 70).

causing a particular method to turn up in several locations. Connecticut, New York, and to some degree Rhode Island show both Massachusetts and Philadelphia corner blocks. Philadelphia and Massachusetts pieces have almost always appeared with their own peculiar form, and south of Philadelphia seems to have used the Philadelphia type, although an exception to so small and invisible a detail may appear any day. It should always cause raised eyebrows, however, as fakers have a passion for the "unique," and it might just as easily be a European example similar to an American piece except for this detail, which has been left unaltered.

Chairs are usually constructed with the rear seat rail thinner in depth than the side post into which it is tenoned. This leaves a shoulder, or projecting corner, on the inside of the chair. In Massachusetts, where the corner blocks are of one piece, they are cut to fit around the post. In Philadelphia, the one-piece, quarter-round rear block is not cut to fit around the protruding corner. Instead, the rear rail is padded out to bring it flush with the inner edge of the post. In some cases, the rail was made of extraordinary

depth to accomplish this; in others, a piece of wood was applied to the entire inside surface of the rail (fig. 91); in yet others, small pieces were glued between the inside of the rail and the corner blocks (fig. 19). The last practice is also found in a few New York chairs that have the Philadelphia form of corner block (fig. 141), and on some Southern chairs.

Perhaps the most famous feature of Philadelphia chair construction is the through tenon or exposed tenon (fig. 20). In this construction the rear tenon of the side seat rail, where it forms a joint, passes completely through the back post and is secured from behind with wedges. In a few cases where the tenon is very deep it is fashioned to two parts, an upper and a lower, making two superimposed tenons. It is commonly assumed that through tenons appeared only in Philadelphia; but they did, in fact, appear on many Connecticut examples and some Southern chairs, as well as on one of the most famous New York Chippendale chairs (fig. 139). After 1790, during the early Classical Revival period, other areas also used this form of construction. It is fair to say that the

19

Squared seat frame and Philadelphia-type corner blocks, front and rear (detail from fig. 70).

majority of Queen Anne and Chippendale chairs made in America with through tenons were of Philadelphia origin; on the other hand, we must remember that, contrary to popular belief, this feature does not appear on all Philadelphia chairs, some of which are constructed with hidden or blind tenons (figs. 80 and 92). In 1795, it cost sixpence extra to have chairs constructed with through tenons;[8] this extra cost was undoubtedly for the additional labor. The outline of the hole in the back had to be neatly chiseled and the tenon neatly cut so that the joint would be as nearly invisible as possible, and this took more time. The reason for wanting something not only more expensive but also visible from behind[9] was that the customer was hereby assured of a long, tight-fitting joint (at least where it showed!), and the maker could not cheat on labor by making a shallow joint that would weaken after use. That such a consciousness of strength was indeed the motive is supported by the fact that on Philadelphia straight-legged chairs, which usually were made with the additional strength of stretchers, through tenoning is less common (fig. 92).

It was long ago suggested that through tenons are found in the North Country in England, and this general statement has been proven true. Through tenons are found in chairs installed in the Wordsworth Museum near his home in Grasmere, Westmorland, chairs thought to have belonged to him during his life. In other ways, too, these Wordsworth chairs are like those made in Philadelphia, having a Philadelphia form of pad foot, and the solid, fretted splat similar to that seen on figure 52; a novice might accept them as Pennsylvania products. Other through tenon chairs, of much the same form as the Wordsworth chairs, were found in a nearby antique shop, and the proprietor considered them local products. In mid-Yorkshire, notably at Gainsborough Old Hall, through tenons were also discovered. Like the Wordsworth chairs, the general design of these examples is usually akin to Philadelphia products, particularly in the shaping of the Queen Anne splats and in the shape and piercing of the "Chippendale" splats, the latter being similar to the first strapwork form (fig. 69), and in the shape of their Queen Anne feet. The Wordsworth chairs are made entirely of oak, a practice rarely adopted in America, where walnut and other local woods were as easily obtained, far easier to work, and more in accord with the fashionable taste. In fact, this prevalence of oak in England conditioned, to a great

20

Through tenons of side seat rails (back view of fig. 52).

degree, the difference between their "country furniture" and ours.[10]

Another method of strengthening the chair was the bracket respond, which was more common in New England than in Phila-

---

[8] Hornor, p. 207.

[9] The back view of chairs must have been considered unimportant, since trial carving is sometimes observable there.

[10] In the colonies there was an abundance of maple, a wood not standard in English work. Maple was more easily turned and adaptable to thin, light forms, making possible more delicate, graceful country pieces.

delphia. Filling the lower corner between the seat rail and the back leg, these pieces usually respond in design to the knee bracket of the front leg, and, despite their smallness, add great additional rigidity (fig. 21). The separate piece was applied with glue and sometimes with nails as well; in rare cases, they tenon through the leg and are visible from behind, looking like a downward extension of the seat rail tenon. Often, to achieve the same visual effect without either increased labor or increased strength, the rear terminal of the side horizontal shaping is cut like a bracket respond; that is, to a reverse curve (fig. 68).

The cabriole front legs of Philadelphia chairs, regardless of the way they were united with the seat frame, always appeared to be a separate unit from it. The cabriole sprang from below the rail level, curving out and down, returning in again to the ankle, then moving outward to the foot, making a complete reverse curve. The movement was always away from the chair on a line drawn from the opposite back post. On early Queen Anne chairs, the knee of

21

Bracket respond, junction seat rail and back post (detail from fig. 52).

the leg was cut with a flat front and side, with a rounded corner between (fig. 45). But with the introduction of the horseshoe-shaped seat, this corner disappeared and the leg became rounded and sculptured to follow the curve of the seat (fig. 48). Various modifications were introduced to carry special carvings, such as on figure 52 where the leg swells to provide a flattened surface for the carved leaf. With the return of the squared seat, the earlier form of flattened sides reappeared, but the ridge between remained well rounded.

The knee brackets were made of a separate piece of wood (fig. 22), attached with glue, although in many cases nails were used for additional security, some with large heads and some with small. The earlier knee brackets were a simple reverse curve in form (fig. 45). Soon the lower edge was carved to a scroll to recall the scroll on the crest rail (fig. 53). With the coming of the Chippendale style, the knee bracket, though retaining a basic reverse curve, developed forms that provide backing to various kinds of carved leafage. These developments, the knee bracket and leg decorations, must be treated together because they were conceived of as one visual unit. Throughout the Queen Anne and Chippendale periods, the knee area was often left uncarved. The earliest form of knee decoration was the convex shell carved from the solid, with the base downward, often, though not always, recalling a shell on the crest rail (fig. 53). Another form of early knee bracket decoration, rarely found in Philadelphia, is the C scroll (fig. 58). Sometimes rudimentary leafage appears, as on figures 62 and 66, and this simple edging of the bracket remained popular throughout the Chippendale period.

Carving was a matter of economics; each area of additional carving was charged for separately. We must not, however, rule out the choice of plainer objects for personal, aesthetic reasons. Plain Philadelphia objects cannot be assigned only to Quaker simplicity: Quaker simplicity as it has become known is in large part a nineteenth-century idea, just as much of our concept of Puritan plainness is due basically to nineteenth-century misinformation. The richest Rhode Island Queen Anne and Chippendale furniture was made by the Quaker Goddard and Townsend families. In any case, for whatever reason, chairs with widely divergent amounts of carving remained popular simultaneously, and many chairs continued to have certain areas richly carved and others not carved at all.

The carved leafage of the knee develops in elaboration from about 1750 (fig. 55). In Philadelphia, its source is handled principally in two ways on the fully developed knees. In figure 23 it they each have their own source of origin. The one springing in from the base of the knee bracket decorates only the bracket itself. The secondary leafage spills down from the junction of the leg with the line of the seat frame. A variation of these two is seen in figure 68, where the stem of the secondary leafage springs from behind the upper part of the primary leafage. The relationship of the units varies continually, but usually within these limits. A rare exception is figure 89, where the primary unit begins at the top of the bracket to curve downwards, the secondary unit beginning under it. In many cases the knee, between the secondary leafage of the

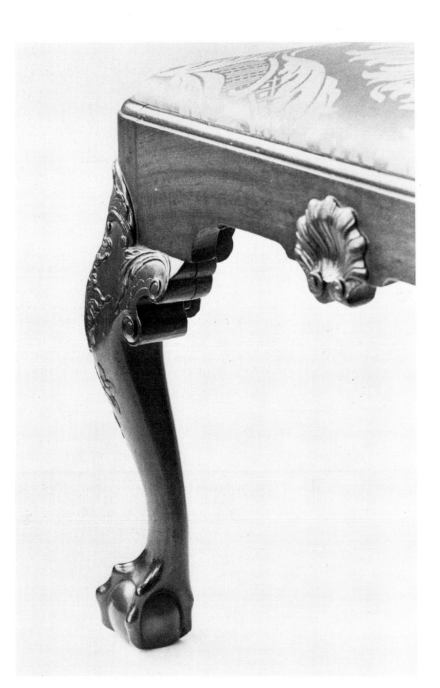

22

Knee bracket between leg and seat rail (detail from fig. 70).

springs from one source, which is at the base of the bracket. Beginning in a scroll, it moves upward toward the center of the chair. A small part outlines the edge of the bracket (we will call this the primary leafage), and the majority (the secondary leafage) continues from under a leaf toward the knee to curve down to its ridge; a like carving from the side bracket meets it there. The second basic form has the same two units of leafage (fig. 75), but

23

Two-part knee leafage typical of Philadelphia (detail from fig. 69).

front and sides, is filled with additional leafage, particularly in chairs with variations of the second and third basic splat (fig. 89). But often the first type of knee allows an open area at the top of the leg which is usually filled with a nonleafage decoration. A popular motif for this spot is the daisy (fig. 23), although infinite variations exist. To unite the leg and the seat visually, the carving between the secondary leafage is sometimes continued onto the rail (fig. 71); this was a popular English-Irish trick, but never became common in this country. Figure 66 shows a chair with a matting or punched background for the knee carving; this form of background decoration rarely appeared on Philadelphia chairs, and is much more common in Massachusetts.

A different form of knee bracket and related seat rail decoration, popular during the Chippendale era, appears on many Massachusetts examples, but in Philadelphia is limited almost exclusively to the Gothic splat chair. It usually appears with the seat rail shaped on its lower edge to two scrolls flanking central leafage (fig. 91).[11] Repeating the form of the seat rail and its raised edge, the knee bracket is simply curved with a raised edge that fades into the leg; the leg decoration is usually leafage, centered around a cartouche on the knee. This form of knee decoration is more logical here since there is no base of a reverse-curve bracket from which to spring the primary leafage.

The feet of the front legs developed during our two periods from a pad form (fig. 1) to a trifid form (fig. 3) and its related claw and ball foot (fig. 4), all of which show many variations. On the earliest chairs (fig. 48), the feet are distinctly pad in form. The foot is completely round, with a groove above and below the pad, which rests on a thin, round shoe or sole. Though it appears carved, this foot was usually lathe turned. It is distinct in form from the Massachusetts club foot of the same period (fig. 6). From about 1735 to 1740 a carved variation developed, the elongated club or slipper foot, usually with a raised or tongued center (fig. 49). About 1740–5 the many varieties of trifid feet appeared, to remain in use until at least 1795 (fig. 50). One variation (seldom seen) is usually thought of as found only in New York (see fig. 128), but it also appears on Philadelphia pieces (see note 4, p. 45). The basic trifid is a three-toed foot: figure 62 shows this with three raised tongues, figure 61 a related form with a single tongue. Although such feet appeared mostly on the economical "plain"

chair[12] with a solid splat, they did occur on a few pierced splat chairs.[13]

The claw and ball foot appeared at about the same time, and around 1755 became firmly identified with the Chippendale style. In Philadelphia, fully developed Chippendale chairs with pierced splats almost invariably carry the claw and ball foot.

The claw and ball foot does not appear in Chippendale's influential *Director* except on a tea caddy. Instead, he suggested scroll feet, but the scroll form never really caught on in America. (Despite Chippendale's disregard for the claw and ball foot, much of the noncourt work of the English Chippendale school uses it.) The claw and ball foot moves out of the leg into four claws. The front three are in deep relief and consist of heavy members, which move out and down to upper knuckles where they leave the web (often pronounced) to continue as rounded claws, curving down and out to the second kunckle. They then move downward again to the third knuckle, which is usually directly below the second, to end in a brief talon. The fourth or inner claw is without pronounced knuckles and is straight (fig. 69) or curved (fig. 68) in profile, terminating in a talon like that of the other claws. The ball grasped by the claws is not round but flattened slightly on top and completely so below, and bulges out between the claws—particularly the back and side claws. It is, in fact, formed rather like a tomato, with the claws covering the creases down the sides. There are a few exceptions to this foot. The retracted claw foot described under Massachusetts, with the two side claws raking backwards, sometimes appeared here in a modified form, and like other forms has an English precedent (figs. 72, 82, 85, and 90).[14] But the basic shape of the parts is always similar, without the Massachusetts elongated talons (compare with those of fig. 122). One of the Philadelphia chairs included here has hairy paw feet (fig. 93), but it is exceptional.

The back posts below the seat always sweep down and back in a curve and in some examples this curve is extremely pronounced. They continue the line of the posts above, converging toward each other at the base. In the earliest Queen Anne chairs,

---

[11] Joseph Downs, *American Furniture: Queen Anne and Chippendale Periods* (New York: The Macmillan Company, 1952), fig. 50, shows a vase-baluster splat arm chair with this knee bracket, though not the related seat rail shaping.

[12] See the Introduction, p. 7, for a discussion of the dating of this foot.

[13] Downs, fig. 39, the famous labeled William Savery chair; although it has a pierced splat, this chair is very simple.

[14] This form of the retracted claw foot is known also on a Philadelphia dressing table, the Hayloft advertisement, *Antiques,* 13 (February 1928), inside back cover. Feet similar to the Philadelphia retracted claw form are found not only in England but also on the continent; for example, in Holland: Dr. Anne Berendsen, *Antick in Nederland* (Antwerp, 1952), fig. 192; see also note 3 on p. 40.

they are usually chamfered; that is, the corners are cut flat, making an eight-sided leg (fig. 45). With the development of the rounded seat, the chamfer becomes a smooth curve leaving only the sides flat (fig. 55). The back posts of the Chippendale chairs are usually ovoid in cross-section but sometimes continue the flat sides. Sometimes the posts, particularly in the most fully developed Queen Anne style, terminate in a squared foot, following one of the popular English fashions, with the leg thin just above (fig. 50).

During this entire period, stretchers between the legs of a Philadelphia chair were never common. From the first, Philadelphia followed the contemporary English fashion of removing this extra support, with a resulting dependence on the joining of leg and seat frame to stabilize the chair. On our earliest example, the stretcher is of the flat variety which curves horizontally (fig. 45); it is thinner than the Newport and New York interpretations, with strong reverse curves. Figure 55 shows a fully developed Philadelphia Queen Anne chair, with horseshoe-shaped seat and tongued trifid feet. This chair is one of an extremely rare Philadelphia group that has turned side, medial, and rear stretchers of the type usually found in New England (fig. 103), although the baluster turning of the side stretchers is closer to that of figure 161. In form, both the turned and flat stretchers are of English origin. Figure 48 shows the retention of a back stretcher only, a practice common in rural England (fig. 46) and Ireland that also appears in Connecticut (fig. 190). Hornor reports finding documents that record stretchers on claw foot chairs,[15] and while none are now known it would not be too surprising to find a few examples with this mingling of styles. Although used in England during this period, straight stretchers of rectangular section with the narrow side up, such as appear on Philadelphia Chippendale straight leg chairs and later on Classical Revival chairs, were not used here on a cabriole leg chairs.[16] (Another English practice not known in Philadelphia is the straight-turned, dowel-like stretcher.)

We tend to expect certain woods to dominate in certain areas during certain style periods. We must, however, remember that countless varieties of woods were imported into one area from another; Connecticut imported cherry from upper New York State[17] and, after the Revolution, Charleston, South Carolina, imported white pine from New England. Walnut had been the basic wood of the English William and Mary, Queen Anne, George I, and George II furniture; mahogany had been used only where it would make the best show, usually as veneers, where fine grain patterns would work to the best advantage.[18] A new influx into England of mahogany around 1730 coincided with, as well as made possible, the desire for lighter, more delicate furniture, richly carved to fine detailing, as exemplified by the elaborate ribbon-back chairs of Thomas Chippendale. Philadelphia, as usual, took its clue from London, and in its early Queen Anne chairs, walnut dominated. The forests around Philadelphia were thick with walnut trees and even after 1745, when mahogany became the stylish wood in Philadelphia as elsewhere in America, Philadelphia continued to make a large percentage of its finest furniture from this local, easily obtainable material; indeed, most of its Chippendale highboys are of walnut. By mid-century, however, much furniture was made of mahogany. At best, walnut is difficult to carve; it tends to splinter, often producing rough surfaces that are difficult to smooth. Working close-grained mahogany is more like carving hard soap, and smooth surfaces are readily produced under the sharp tool of a skilled carver. Yet walnut still appeared in Benjamin Lehman's list of prices in 1786 as the basic alternative to mahogany; a chair with claw and ball feet but solid splat costing £2.0s. in ma-

[15] Hornor, p. 193. James James's bill to Thomas Wharton in 1758 includes " '½ Doz Chears Claws & Stretchers.' "

[16] These often appear on continental and English chairs related to American ones such as Wallace Nutting, *Furniture Treasury* (1928; reprinted, New York: The Macmillan Company, 1954), figs. 2223 and 2242.

[17] Letter from Houghton Bulkeley, Sept. 9, 1965, "There are several 'ads' in Hartford papers, and I also think in New London papers, of cherry or cherry-wood from Whitestown, New York."

[18] Many authors have given the following reasons to account for the change in England from walnut to mahogany: first, the heavy frost of 1709 killed much of the continental walnut, which led to hoarding, eliminating export to England, and thus to shortages; secondly, the repeal of 1733 of an import duty on mahogany made it cheaper and thus more popular. Edward T. Joy, however, in an important article, "The Introduction of Mahogany," *Country Life* (Nov. 12, 1953), pp. 1566–7, notes of the first that the annual importation of walnut from France fell from £845 in 1719 to £17 in 1722, but Holland and Spain supplied large amounts and "Italy, Turkey, Portugal, Madeira and 'The Streights' (Morocco)" sent varying amounts, and that "Virginia and Maryland at times sent well over £2,000. Moreover, other American colonies, including Pennsylvania, Carolina, New York and New England, sent some." As for the second reason, there appears to have been no repeal act of 1733. Rather, the act of 1721 "to allow timber from any British plantation . . . 'free from all customs and importations whatever,' " which was to encourage wood needed for ships, had the effect of raising the importation of mahogany from £277 in 1722 to £6,430 in 1735, and by 1750 to nearly £30,000.

hogany, cost £1.10s. in walnut.[19] Some of the mahogany chairs had minor parts such as stretchers made of walnut. Some high-style furniture was made of cherry, but this wood was more popular amongst the country workers. During the William and Mary and Queen Anne periods, cedar was sometimes used as a primary wood, but it was found to fade in color. Curly or tiger maple was also sometimes used because of its extraordinary grain pattern, but was far more difficult to work even than walnut. Gum, or "bilsted" as it was then called, was seldom used, for it " 'must not be brought near the fire, because it warps.' "[20]

Because secondary woods—those not immediately visible—are usually the least expensive, locally obtainable, soft wood, they are often far more helpful in establishing origin. There are, however, very few parts of a side or arm chair that are not visible: usually only the corner blocks and slip seat frame and, where the seat is over-upholstered, the seat rail. In Philadelphia, the basic secondary wood was pine, although tulip poplar was common and oak, cherry, white cedar, and other local woods were also used.[21]

It has become a standard rule to accept that objects made of American woods are necessarily American in origin. However, England had burned most of its oak to make charcoal in producing iron and already had a long tradition of purchasing wood from various parts of the continent. One of the first commodities exported by various newly established colonies was wood, and there are countless bills of lading that record large shipments of American woods to England and the continent. It is, then, safe to assume that furniture made of European woods is of European origin; but it need not be true that objects which include American woods were made on the American side of the Atlantic.

The only other materials used for chairs were the textile or leather for the seat, its stuffing and webbing, the glue for the joints, and iron for nails and screws. During this period nails were hand-made,[22] and they were used, in addition to glue, to attach many knee brackets, the Massachusetts form of corner block, and some

of the bracket responds. Screws were used, generally from the inside, to fasten the arm supports to the side seat rails.[23]

2. Massachusetts

AN EXAMINATION of Massachusetts high-style chairs must center chiefly on Boston and Salem. Although the "North Shore" was active, the present state of research makes impossible a separate study of that area, or the definite separation of Salem from Boston, or even a clear distinction between the Salem-Boston chairs and the North Shore chairs. Therefore, these areas will be treated as one, though some differences will be suggested in the text and in the captions to the photographs.

The chairs fall into a logical progression similar to that of Philadelphia, so we will take as a simplifying and clarifying division Queen Anne (1730–60) and Chippendale (1755–95), ignoring the fact that in a few cases both styles continued into the nineteenth century, probably because of the purchasers' particular tastes.

The Queen Anne chairs are akin to the earliest Philadelphia chairs we have seen (compare figs. 45 and 97). Parallel back posts are spooned to correspond to the splat, but they do not develop the reverse curve on the frontal plane as found in later Philadelphia, Rhode Island, and New York chairs. The back posts flow into a simple crest rail, with a scooped or saddled center that does not develop a central decoration, although its direct English sources, such as figure 98, often carried a central shell. Visually, the crest rail is one piece with the splat, which is of a simple baluster form which in Philadelphia seems to have occurred only on rush-seated chairs (fig. 44), with the base of the splat shaped to a fillet above a cyma curve (fig. 97). Restrained in outline and harmonizing with the gentle curves present in the rest of the chair, this is the standard splat. However, the ear-accented splat of figure 102 may be a standard variant as yet seldom recognized as Massachusetts,

[19] Lehman's list, Hornor, p. 210.

[20] Hornor, p. 41.

[21] For detailed lists of wood, see Plumley's inventory of 1708, Hornor, pp. 7–9; for woods exported to England, Hornor, p. 42; for use of oak in 1786, Hornor, p. 208; for choice of mahogany, Hornor, pp. 87 and 208; and for the use and importation of cedar, Hornor, p. 45.

[22] In 1786, the first patent for a "cut-nail machine" was granted to Ezekiel Reed, Bridgewater, Massachusetts (Henry H. Taylor, *Knowing, Collecting and Restoring Early American Furniture* [Philadelphia: J. B. Lippincott Co., 1930] p. 122).

[23] Screws of this period were hand-made, thus the threads are irregular and the points blunt, unlike the sharply pointed, evenly threaded screws of today. A patent (No. 4704) for pointed screws was granted to T. J. Sloan, of New York, in 1846 (Henry C. Mercer, *Ancient Carpenters' Tools* [Doylestown, Pa.: The Bucks County Historical Society, 1929], p. 256).

24

Philadelphia-type Chippendale crest rail with richly molded ears (detail from fig. 68).

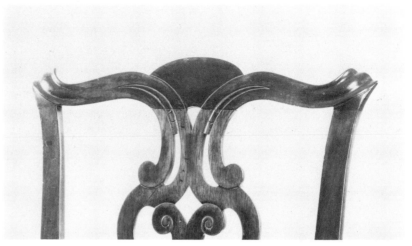

25

Massachusetts-type Chippendale crest rail with blunt-ended ears (detail from fig. 103).

since unless there is direct evidence to the contrary such chairs have been classified as Rhode Island.

We will begin by studying the form that constitutes the biggest group of related Chippendale chairs made during this period, and then investigate separately examples that (for reasons to be seen in Part III) stand apart from the majority. In the basic group, all of the chair backs, unlike Philadelphia backs, are completely straight vertically, without bow. The back posts are usually left undecorated. (Figs. 113 and 114, however, show a rare use of molded front surfaces.) The back posts diverge upward to a bow crest rail, usually related to the first type of Philadelphia rail (compare figs. 24 and 25). However, the ears are blunt-ended and carved to a simple serpentine curve, different from those of Philadelphia in that they do not have the large roll or swell in the center; they simply continue the movement of the crest rail. At the end of the rail, they appear to bend backwards as if doubling up on themselves to spill down the back of the back posts. Usually, the light center swell is not grooved in the middle as we will find in New York; figure 104 is an exception. At the center of the top rail each side flows in and down to form the top of the splat, leaving a "V" opening in the middle capped by a central raised ornament, normally a shell form (fig. 104), which is often left with an uncarved surface (fig. 25). Figure 107 shows a common variation edged with three C scrolls and decorated with leafage on a punch-decorated ground. As the top rail flows into the baluster splat, it divides to form two straps on either side, and the filled area be-

tween is sometimes chip carved (fig. 106). The outermost straps end by resting on the inner. The latter, after moving downward, spring sideways, then down again and in to make a complete circle, ending back at themselves. The ends of these straps are often decorated with volutes (fig. 106) and in rare cases rosettes (fig. 108). Contrary to the Philadelphia and New York practice, the scrolled strapwork is contained in the upper half of the splat and is not a visual unit with the lower part. The bottom half, separated from the top by a carved line, is pierced to vertical straps which act visually as a supporting column; the base of the lower part drops in a straight line to the shoe, without the cyma curve of the Queen Anne period. A standard variation of this splat also employs the same vertically pierced base, only the upper scrolls are arranged differently (fig. 111). The outer scrolls are much the same, but the inner straps continue their downward movement from the crest rail and, swinging in large C scrolls, make a half circle to meet the outer scroll. This back usually appears on less ornate chairs, and is related to the Rhode Island back (fig. 174), and is an English idea (fig. 110). The splat is seated in the shoe, except when the chairs are upholstered over the seat rail; then the splat rests directly in the rail, with the detachable shoe fitting around it over the rear edge of the upholstery. The exception to this in the Massachusetts slip seat chairs is figure 111, where it enters the rail, passing behind the shoe. The shoe is left simple and undecorated.

Massachusetts arm chairs are extremely scarce. Two of the

three shown (figs. 100 and 109) have similar arms which are simple in design. The first terminates in a flat C scroll and the second scrolls downward. The arm supports of a simple C shape are like those on New York chairs, figure 136. The third arm chair (fig. 123) has retracted arms and reverse-curve arm supports. These are decidely English in design, as is the whole upper part of the chair.

The shape of the seat, as in Philadelphia, moves from the squared effect of early Queen Anne to the horseshoe shape in late Queen Anne, returning to the squared with the adoption of the pierced splat. It is possible, although exceptional, to find a horseshoe-shaped seat on a Chippendale chair (figs. 103 and 104). Contrary to the Philadelphia custom, the manner of constructing both seat forms is the same. The upper part of the leg forms the member into which the side and front rails are tenoned (fig. 26); the leg is never pegged into the bottom of a frame. The horseshoe-shaped frame never achieves the depth of the Philadelphia example but goes in a straight line from inside the tenon in the rear post to inside the front tenon (fig. 27). Horizontal shaping, simple and developed, is common on Queen Anne chairs, and is continued on the horseshoe-shaped seats during the Chippendale period. The back rail of figure 104 has the unusual feature of being horizontally shaped like the front and side rails. The squared Chippendale seats, however, were usually very narrow in height, so that the cabinetmaker did not need to lighten the rail visually, and horizontal shaping is not present (fig. 106). Shaping of the seat rail is perhaps the only form of seat rail decoration developed in Massachusetts, except for the ornamental brass nails used on over-upholstered seats.

Over-upholstery, which was extremely rare on Philadelphia chairs, appears often in Massachusetts in the second half of the eighteenth century and is probably more common there than elsewhere in America. It may have resulted from the desire for the more lavish color and richness made possible by increasing the amount of textile, or because a part of England that liked this look was affecting Massachusetts.

The Massachusetts form of corner block, already discussed under Philadelphia, is made of one piece of wood, triangular in shape, of horizontal grain. It is notched around the inside of the leg, and is attached with nails as well as with glue (fig. 28); the same form and size was used in the front and rear corners.

So far no Massachusetts chair has appeared with through tenons. Applied bracket responds, usually with vertical grain, appear on about half of the Chippendale chairs, usually those without stretchers; and they are found at the rear as well on figure 104, probably to relate to the unusual horizontal shaping of its rear seat rail.

The cabriole front legs, during the Queen Anne period, were rounded at the knees (fig. 97) but the squared Chippendale seat had extremely sharp front corners and this sharpness was carried down onto the leg, giving way to a circular section at midpoint. A feature found on some known Salem furniture is a no-

26

Construction of front corner joint of Massachusetts-type horseshoe-shaped seats; front and side rails tenon into upper extension of front leg (detail from The Museum of Art, Rhode Island School of Design).

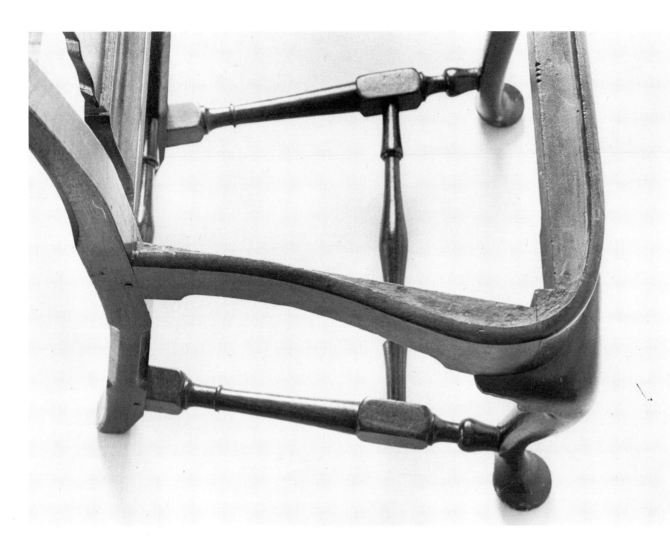

ticeably sharp break at this point, from the ridge or arris of the knee to the round of the leg (fig. 107). The legs of Chippendale horseshoe-shaped seats usually reinforce visually the roundness of the seat by retaining the rounded knee. Throughout both Queen Anne and Chippendale chairs with horseshoe-shaped seats the knee bracket was cut to a cyma curve, which forms a small projection where it meets the leg, and this same knee bracket was used on the Queen Anne square-seated chairs (fig. 97). Those of the Chippendale square-seated, arrised-knee chairs appear as one line with the leg, and are a simple reverse curve, having no projecting point where they meet the leg (fig 106). They are rather like the simpler knee brackets found on some Gothic back Philadelphia chairs (fig. 91). Usually, carved decoration appears only on these legs with the simpler knee bracket. The flat sides of these legs and brackets are often carved with leafage which spills down directly from the seat rail, leaving the arris between the two

faces plain, although sometimes the background or the arris ridge is textured with punchwork (fig. 106).

It was standard practice to use club feet on chairs with unpierced splats. The Holyoke family chairs (fig. 101) show the developed foot which is like a golf club, resting on a light pad or shoe (this form differs from the thin ring or pad foot of Philadelphia); many feet that are now thinner probably were of this thickness originally. The club foot sometimes appears with a very thick, heavy lower member (fig. 111), and it is almost always found on chairs with pierced, or Chippendale, splats. In Massachusetts, the heavier foot was the equivalent of the trifid foot of Philadelphia, since visually it suggested the same weight mass made fashionable by the claw and ball foot; but as it could be lathe-turned and not carved, it was far less expensive.[1]

The first mention in Massachusetts of a claw and ball foot was set by Irving W. Lyon in 1737; it may have been a Massachusetts or an imported chair.[2] As with other areas, Massachusetts has its own peculiar form of this foot. The purely round ball, flattened on the bottom, is lightly clasped by a crowlike foot which does not press into the ball as in Philadelphia, and the two side claws are yanked backward to form the famous "retracted claw" (fig. 30). In the eighteenth century, such a foot was sometimes called a "crowfoot" or "eagles foot"[3] and it is easy to see why these names were used. The knuckles are generally enlarged and the talons usually long and slender. Notice how far forward the three front talons on figure 29 begin; they appear bunched together at the front of the ball.[4]

Throughout both styles the back posts, below the seat, are

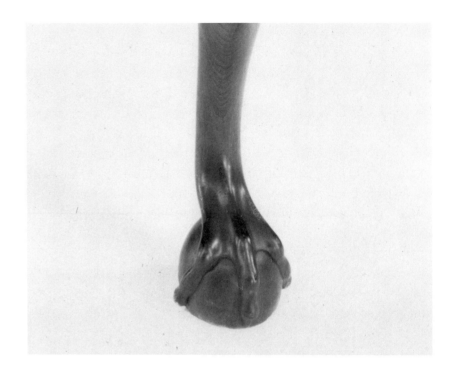

29

Massachusetts-type claw and ball foot, with the side claws raking backwards (detail from fig. 117).

square in section and much thinner than in Philadelphia; and when stretchers are present, the posts are chamfered on four sides between the seat and the stretcher and, on the front of the back posts, below the stretchers. When they are without stretchers the back post terminates in a flared square foot, often as pronounced as in Philadelphia and New York (fig. 104).[5] Stretchers are found on all early chairs and on the majority of the later ones. The Massachusetts cabinetmaker, always conservative, seems to have been hesitant to remove them and lessen the chair's stability. The stretchers were, as far as is known, always baluster turned rather than flat, and are found with the medial stretcher ending in a square die, as well as in a turned point (figs. 109 and 108).

A second group of Massachusetts Chippendale chairs is closely related in feel to the first but these pieces differ in their strapwork and the emphasis on richness. The strapwork often moves from shoe to crest rail without the division into upper and lower parts found in the first group, and it is more complicated. They are represented here by figures 113–125. Figure 114 from

[1] Richard H. Randall, Jr., *American Furniture* (Boston: Museum of Fine Arts, 1965), figs. 151 and 152, shows identical Chippendale chairs except that one has heavy solid club feet and the other claw and ball feet.

[2] Irving Whitall Lyon, M.D., *The Colonial Furniture in New England* (1891; 2nd edition, Boston and New York: Houghton Mifflin Company, 1924), p. 163.

[3] Lyon, p. 163. A similar foot was used in England and is known on a table made in China in the English taste. Ole Wanscher, *Møbelkunsten* (København: Thaning og Appels Forlag, 1955), pp. 422–3. Different photographs of this piece occur in the English translation by David Hohnen, *The Art of Furniture* (London: Allen and Unwin, 1968), pp. 308–9; see also note 14 on p. 34.

[4] One Chippendale chair with scroll feet (Randall, fig. 148) has been assigned to Massachusetts, possibly the Hingham area. The strapwork of the splat uses four, interlaced C scrolls that drop in a long curve, as found regularly in related English provincial chairs but not on the more standard Massachusetts ones. The straightness of the front legs is also like provincial English work. Analysis of the woods (the primary and part of the secondary wood is black walnut and part of the slip seat frame is red maple) suggests a Massachusetts origin. The chair is probably the product of a man trained in rural England working in rural Massachusetts.

[5] The squared foot is an English feature extensively used in this country, as we have seen, and is not confined to New York as has been suggested.

the Pickman family of Salem is famous for its direct borrowing of plate 9 of Robert Manwaring's pattern book (*The Cabinet and Chair-Maker's Real Friend and Companion,* published in London in 1765); however, the basic movement of the strapwork is not unlike the basic Massachusetts splat, with the four active scrolls above, the inner ones first supporting the outer and then scrolling in on themselves, and the lower straps acting as a separate supporting member. The thinness of seat rail, legs, and knee carving is akin to those discussed first and although the cabinetmaker was directly dependent on an English source he was sufficiently detached to disregard Manwaring's suggestion of straight legs which appear on so many of the English chairs included here. The new Massachusetts taste had established itself to such an extent that the maker was unwilling to update the lower half of the chair to meet English standards even though he accepted them for the upper half.

Figure 115 has a standard Massachusetts base but an unusual husk crest rail, although that feature appears again on the following chair (and in a related way on figs. 122 and 125) and the acanthus-carved splat and ears depend directly, as do so many of this group, upon English sources, as can be seen by studying figures 121–122 and 124–125.[6] Many parts of figures 116, 117, 118 are like those of the first Chippendale group. They have the same crest rails, with standard ears and center accent; also alike are the back posts, seat rails, knee carving, legs, and feet. Two are over-upholstered and one is with stretchers and two without. The movement and attitude of design are essentially the same as those of the first Massachusetts group; but they stand apart in that there is a consistency in the splat from crest rail to shoe, without the break into two parts discussed earlier.

Figures 119 and 120 represent another group of Massachusetts chairs that are often considered to be from the North Shore, for related chairs have been reportedly found in that area. But there are in fact five paintings by John Singleton Copley of men who are sitting in a chair with this back, and at least four were probably painted in Boston.[7] In figure 119 we find the standard

Massachusetts crest rail, ears, center accent, thinness of seat rail, front legs, rear legs, and rear feet. As in the two preceding chairs, the basic stance and attitude is what we have come to expect. Paw feet are more common in Massachusetts than elsewhere in America and appear on an arm chair similar to figure 123,[8] but they are still rare on Massachusetts chairs, being more prevalent on the case pieces of that area. (Many paw feet were recarved to standard claw and ball feet in the first half of this century when the latter were more saleable.) The crest rail and knee brackets of figure 120 are unlike the Massachusetts products we have seen so far; but the feet, stretchers, and chamfering of the back posts, as well as its general attitude, relate it to the earlier group. Here again the splat is one continual movement from seat rail to crest rail without the horizontal break noted earlier; the movement of the splat is

[8] Downs, fig. 55. This chair has been called English by some scholars because it has a beech seat frame and richer carving, but this is not proof of English origin.

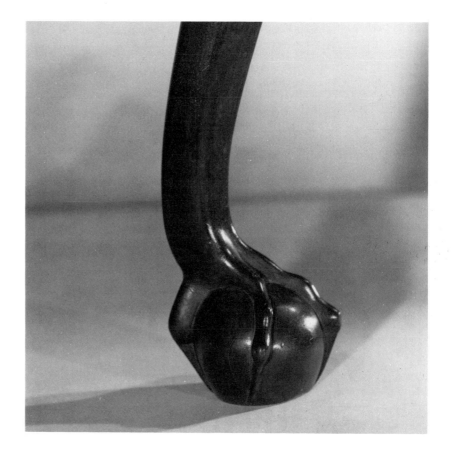

30

Massachusetts-type claw and ball foot, with side "retracted" claws and elongated talon (detail from fig. 123).

[6] J. P. Blake and A. E. Reveirs-Hopkins, *Old English Furniture* (London: B. T. Batsford Ltd., 1930; reprinted, 1944), fig. 63, shows three different English chairs; they reflect the source of figs. 111, 115, and 125.

[7] Jules D. Prown, *John Singleton Copley* (2 vols., Cambridge, Mass.: Harvard University Press, 1966), plates 218, 277, 318; also plate 217 uses the same chair but the sitter has not been identified and other sitters may be using the same chair. The chair could have been a fixture which Copley chose to re-use regardless of the sitter's origin.

much like the vase-baluster splat of the second type of Philadelphia Chippendale chair. Again we are working with a chair that has a direct English source for its crest rail, splat, leg, knee bracket, and horizontally shaped seat.

According to tradition, figure 122 was used by the Swan family of Boston and Dorchester. The base has the standard slender, active front legs with crowlike feet, crisply carved to precise delineation of parts. The seat rail is narrow, and the back is flat, without bow or spooning, with the splat showing a two-part division. Figure 121 shows the typical English source with its two-stage Gothic back, its acanthus and central husk crest rail, and its back posts with molded front faces. Here again England is dominating directly.

Figures 124 and 125 demonstrate again the derivative character of Massachusetts design, and this splat appears again in New York (fig. 145). Figure 123, except for its front feet, is line for line a copy of English chairs. Its splat, stop-fluted back posts, arms, and knee carving seem initially unrelated to American products. It is really only in its front legs and feet (fig. 30) that we first see the connection. Then we note that the crest rail, the thin seat rail, and back legs and feet, and the thin, spare quality of the carving, as well as the front legs and feet, are all of Massachusetts character. And this, plus the secondary woods, the construction, and the history of its having been at least used in Boston by Governor Belcher, ties it down to that area.

As in Philadelphia, woods are only a general help, and infinite variations and exceptions to any rules can be found. The standard primary woods are walnut for Queen Anne and mahogany for Chippendale. Maple slip seat frames are more frequent than pine, but both are common, the Massachusetts pine being less striped than that of Philadelphia. Corner blocks are nearly always made of maple. Round-headed nails, rather like small upholstery tacks, are found in some Massachusetts chairs; these appear also in Rhode Island and Canada.

3. New York

NEW YORK CHAIRS remained in relative obscurity until the Sack sale of 1932, when a Chippendale chair catalogued as Philadelphia (primarily because it had through tenons, rounded back legs, and acanthus carving in the Philadelphia manner) was found to be signed in pencil, "Made by Gilbert Ash in Wall street. Warranted sold April 2 1756." In addition, it was marked number three of a set (fig. 139). (This writing is now considered to be a recent addition and it is not yet clear where the information came from or whether it has any basis in fact.[1]) Following this sale, a group of articles appeared on newly discovered New York chairs; but as late as 1950, Sack included in his book over forty from Philadelphia and only five from New York. This scarcity of published examples is explained in part by the fact that New York was much smaller than Philadelphia during the period, its prosperity and importance developing after the Revolution, and in part by the fact that New York furniture has not been as popular among modern collectors. It is possible that other forms from New York are still to be recognized, and probably many simple chairs now overlooked will be found to have been important in furnishing the homes of New York's eighteenth-century citizens. Also, much richly developed, as well as simple, furniture was imported into New York from New England, as we have already seen in the case of the early nineteenth-century Salem pieces labeled by Phyfe. Some of the imported New England work was branded by its New York owners and this now causes confusion, since evidence of a New York owner has frequently been held as evidence of a New York maker.[2] The absence of a broad variety of high-style chairs in the period is one of the reasons why it is impossible to show any simple progression like those we can see in Philadelphia and Massachusetts. There are simply not enough objects known to give the panorama necessary for developing a logical sequence, if indeed one ever existed. A second factor that makes it difficult to develop a logical date sequence is that where Philadelphia and Massachusetts used early and late Queen Anne and early and late Chippendale forms, New York did not. New York, with a few exceptions, used only the middle two. These, although termed late Queen Anne and early Chippendale in America, are in England seen as

[1] I am indebted to Charles F. Hummel for confirming this uncertainty. A chair, perhaps from the same set, was included in Joseph Downs and Ruth Ralston, *A Loan Exhibition of New York State Furniture* (New York: The Metropolitan Museum of Art, 1934), the catalogue of a loan show, as fig. 76. The catalogue reads ". . . inscribed: *Made by Gilbert Ash in Wall Street.*" Some who saw this inscription remember it as having been in ink. It may or may not have been the origin of the pencil inscription on fig. 139.

[2] See [Norman S. Rice], *New York Furniture Before 1840*, Introduction by Milton W. Hamilton, Description by Benjamin Ginsburg (Albany, N.Y.: Albany Institute of History and Art, 1962), p. 20, for a chair probably made in Boston and branded by the Van Rensselaer family.

one style, George II, which includes both the late, broad, un-pierced splat chairs and those with the early, heavy pierced splats. In New York, the earlier unpierced splats continued in favor even when later pierced splats came into fashion, and both were made simultaneously after 1755. While it has been said that New York is extremely Dutch in feel, because it reflects the great breadth and heaviness associated with Dutch furniture, there are English George II prototypes for most of the developed New York chairs.

In spite of these difficulties, it is possible to separate New York chairs into groups by using a modified form of the traditional distinction between Queen Anne and Chippendale, and further to subdivide each group according to special features.

The chairs of Group i are related in the following ways: crest rails with rounded shoulders; back posts, in all but one case, shaped to reverse curves above the seat on the frontal plane; usually an unpierced splat; and, except for one example, a horse-shoe-shaped seat (figs. 126–134). Those of Group ii have bowed crest rails; straightened back posts; pierced splats (except for fig. 135, but its splat's outline is like those of figs. 146–148); and, on most examples, squared seat frames (figs. 135–152). The difficulty about this division is that it does not take into account overlaps in other features; for instance, figure 129 of Group i and figure 136 of Group ii have similar arms and arm supports, placing them close to each other in date. In other words, these groups do not correspond to the traditional Queen Anne-Chippendale dates; although Group i is related to "Queen Anne," it seems to cover both periods, just as the trifid foot chair with solid splat, studied under Philadelphia, covered the second half of the Queen Anne period and all of the Chippendale. Group ii might be set in the second half of the eighteenth century because of the pierced splats, and is called Chippendale.

Queen Anne (probably 1740–1790)

Group ia (figures 126–128)

The back posts move out and down from the crest rail, with which they are visually of a piece, then move in and out in a reverse curve to about one-third of the way above the seat; there they break, to drop to the seat rail. The hoop-top rail drops at the center to a convex shell ornament, which rises higher than the flanking

rail, generally with supporting leafage or a scrolled lower edge. The line of the inner edge of the top rail continues its curve to a baluster splat, usually with ears. The splat follows nearly the same line as the posts. The innermost part of the back posts is often a separate piece of wood applied to the main piece. Sometimes the splats are made of figured walnut veneer backed by another wood. Figure 127 has caused regionalizing problems in the past. The question is not where in America it was made, but whether it is from New York or England. It is included here as New York.[3] Its splat is pierced to the initials of the original owners, possibly a unique instance. The weight mass of the splat is fairly evenly distributed, with some emphasis given to the top third.

In most New York slip seat chairs, the splat seats into the shoe. The two exceptions are closely related, figures 127 and 146. On a few New York chairs, the shoe is one piece with the back rail (fig. 131).

The horseshoe-shaped seat, which is nearly flat in front, is

[3] Those who know New York chairs will realize the problem caused by the Livingston family chairs. The reasons for their inclusion here are as follows: (1) The New Hampshire dealer who purchased the set from the descendant of the original owner was told by her that while the Livingstons had their own wharves and boats and could have bought them in England, the chairs were always known in the family as American, even during the period when an English origin was considered more prestigious. (2) The evidence of the pierced monogram is ambiguous. The initial M could refer either to Margaret Beekman, who married Robert Livingston in 1742, or to Mary Stevens, who married Robert Livingston, Jr., in 1770. There is as yet no information that tells for which of these families they were made. The style of the chairs is George II and, if made in New York, they could have been made throughout our two style periods except for the piercing of the splat, which suggests a date after 1750 at the earliest. If they are English chairs of 1742 they are by a lesser English maker, for the finer ones had progressed to eared crest rails and more generous splats. If they are England 1770, they are the work of an even more *retardataire* maker. Why then in either case bring them from London when they could have been made here at either date, except for the piercing of the splat? (3) The method of construction does suggest an English rather than American origin, but the beech of the back rail is a wood used here although it was more common in England. The seat is braced by corner cross braces instead of corner blocks, a practice known in English examples and as yet undocumented here prior to the 1780's. The cross-braces are of oak, more standard in English examples although known in New York. A related cross-tie of oak from front to rear appears in the slip seat of fig. 133. However, there are other reasons to relate them to the New York group. Their general all-over design was the prevailing taste of New York, while only one of many modes found in England. The broad seat, heavy knees, narrow ankle, and heavy foot are like those of fig. 146. The crest rail shell shows the undulating line of New York gadrooning rather than delineating the positive and negative lines as common elsewhere. The weight of the evidence seems to be that these are New York examples made in 1770 or later. This would confirm the family history, affirm the New York attitude of the general design pattern, and eliminate the necessity to justify the importation of chairs that are, except for their piercing, of simple design, and explain their strong relationship to fig. 146.

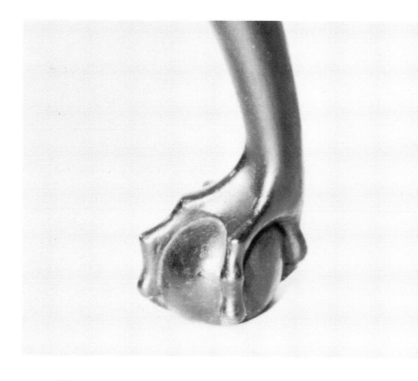

31

First form of New York claw and ball foot (detail from fig. 143).

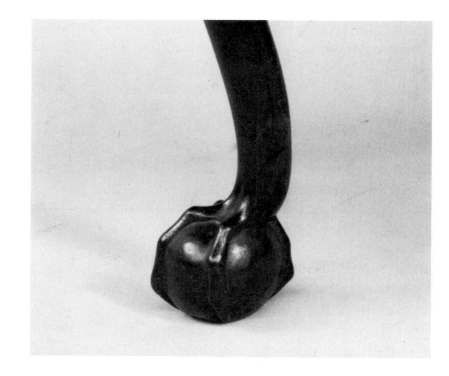

32

Second form of New York claw and ball foot (detail from fig. 146).

horizontally shaped on the front and sides. The front joint of the seat frame always remained the same, with the seat rails tenoned directly into the front legs; it did not have the pinned-in leg of Philadelphia nor did the side rails ever reach Philadelphia's thickness in depth. As in the Massachusetts horseshoe-shaped seat, the inside line did not follow the outer curve; instead, it remained straight from the inside of the tenon in the back post to the inside of the tenon in the front leg. The squared seat is made as in Philadelphia and Massachusetts.

Corner blocks are rare in horseshoe-shaped seats, but when found they are generally of quarter-round section, with vertical grain, similar to the Philadelphia blocks but smaller and one piece as there is often no projecting inner corner to the leg. The squared seat is generally braced by either a "Philadelphia"-type block, quarter-round, with vertical grain and held only by glue, or by a typical "Massachusetts" triangular block, with horizontal grain, attached by glue and nails. It is not customary for the side rails to tenon through the back posts as in Philadelphia, although this did occur (figs. 137, 139, etc.). In New York, bracket responds are the rule rather than the exception. Usually, they are of reverse-curve

shape; about half have vertical grain and half horizontal. Figure 146 demonstrates the consciousness of the response: the scroll carved on the front knee bracket is echoed on the bracket respond. Occasionally on horseshoe-shaped seats without horizontal shaping the bracket is placed under another applied extension of the seat rail, which is cut to appear like the rear part of horizontal shaping (fig. 130). It must be noted that many of the bracket responds found today are replacements since often they were attached only with glue; it is probable that most of the New York chairs originally had them.

In this, the first Queen Anne group (figs. 126–128), the knees of the front legs are usually decorated with convex shells and pendant husks, which, as in every region, are cut from the solid. The knee brackets, undecorated, are a distinct reverse curve. New York cabriole legs show two basic movements; most are stocky and straight but some—figures 127, 133, 143, 146, 148, and 152— show the undercut knee that makes them appear more fluid, and they tend to thrust the foot out beyond the knee.

All but three of the New York chairs shown have claw and ball feet. Figure 135 has club feet but it and its mate are the only known New York chairs with this form. Figure 128[4] shows a typical English foot (fig. 151), known also on a few Philadelphia and Southern chairs. Figure 134 shows the pointed club foot used as rear feet on some New York chairs.

There are four basic forms of New York claw and ball feet. The first is like that of Philadelphia although it shows variations (fig. 31). In the second form the ball is large, with wiry, webless talons (fig. 32). The third form has nondescript talons like heavily pronounced ridges, continuing to undefined claws, often with a heavy uniting web (fig. 33). The fourth appears blocklike, as if the foot were using the full limits of a cube of wood (fig. 34).

Turned stretchers, as on figure 128, with the medial stretcher having two ball accents and ending in square dies at the junctions with the side stretchers, are typical of New York. Although this form is found in New England as well (fig. 112), the other New England form (fig. 108) is not found here. The back posts on

---

[4] It may be that some of the Philadelphia feet normally considered trifid in form are really of this form, or based on it; see a chair by Joseph Armitt, Hornor, plate 23, pp. 192, 200, and 202.

figures 126 and 127 are rounded below the seat, terminating in small feet. Since there are stretchers, the back posts of figure 128 are square, and chamfered between the seat and the stretchers, and on their inner faces below the stretchers as in Massachusetts.

Group i*b* (figures 129-131)

The top rails are visually the continuation of the unspooned or bowed back posts, rising into shoulders and dropping to a dominating central shell, which is generally raised high and pierced to an elaborate full relief, supported by some ornamentation and flanked by leafage. In figure 131, a simple shell decorates the center and is only elaborated by a scrolled line at its base. The back posts above the seat curve out and down from the crest rail, breaking at midpoint to a lower reverse curve, then back in again above the seat to a line straight down. This is one more curve than on Group i*a*, and the extra outward movement past the edge of the back posts makes it follow more faithfully the shape of the splat. As in Group i*a*, the inner part of the posts is often applied so that lighter stock could be used. The top of the splat appears as a con-

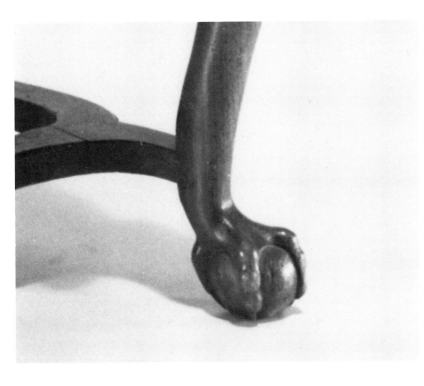

33

Third form of New York claw and ball foot (detail from fig. 130).

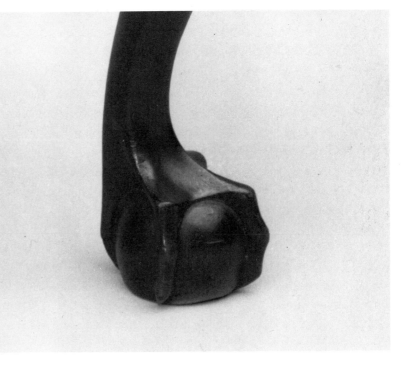

34

Fourth form of New York claw and ball foot (detail from fig. 136).

tinuous line from the lower edge of the crest rail, and the base of the splat narrows drastically to leave the weight mass at the top. Usually, the splat is spooned, although the posts are straight on the side plane, and are made with walnut veneer applied to a backing, sometimes of hard and sometimes soft wood. The splat houses into the shoe, which is molded and shaped to a "cupid's bow" on its upper edge, a standard English form of decoration. One of these chairs (fig. 129) is an arm chair.

In New York, as in Massachusetts, arm chairs are rare. Only three have been included. The arms consist of a reverse-curve-shaped form that moves around the seated person, back over the arm support, and out again into scrolled handholds carved to eagle heads. The arm supports, always kept vertical above the seat rail for structural purposes, have a simple C-curve movement similar to that found in Massachusetts.

The horseshoe-shaped seat, nearly flat in front, is heavily braced at the junction with the back posts, both by applied pieces like the rear part of horizontal shaping and by bracket responds. The seat construction is standard throughout the period. The knees of the front legs are decorated with simple shells, usually holding pendant husks. Starting at the seat rail, the knee brackets are cut to a heavy, circular drop curve, which breaks and curves to a point and breaks again to curve to the leg. This form is undecorated and has so far been found outside New York only on rare Massachusetts chairs (fig. 120), although it is better known in England (fig. 51). Here it recalls the roundness of the focal point of the splat. The leg terminates in a nearly broken ankle, projecting the foot forward. The foot is one of the four characteristic New York feet. The back posts are square, with rounded corners below the bracket responds, and taper to small squared feet. Stretchers are not common on these chairs. Figure 130 shows the only known New York flat stretcher, heavier than we saw in Philadelphia and closer to the type used in Newport.[5]

Group ic (figures 132-133)

This group is also high-shouldered, with the unspooned or bowed splats and crest rail visually one. The crest rail is ornamented with a shell and leafage but this is not raised so as to over-dominate. The back posts show the double or "Flemish" curve on

[5] This is the first New York chair with flat stretchers to come to light. It and the rest of the set were found in 1962; it makes us realize again that we are far from knowing all American work.

the front plane, as in the preceding subgroup, except that the lower break does not curve out beyond the outer face of the back legs, and the splat lacks the corresponding bulge. Again, the inner edge of the crest rail flows into the eared-baluster splat, which has its weight mass in the upper half, with a thin waist below shaped to relate to the back post. Carving is sometimes introduced into the splat (fig. 133) and its base is housed into the shoe. The horseshoe-shaped seat, nearly flat in front, is given extra support by bracket responds. This is the only Queen Anne subgroup that has acanthus-carved knees, which suggests that it could have been made in the second half of the eighteenth century. The carving on the leg springs from the upper part of the knee bracket, which is cut to a drop curve as in the preceding group. In figure 132, the area on the knee between the leafage is filled with cross-hatching, a form of decoration more commonly, but not exclusively, found in New York. The leafage of figure 133 springs from a rosette as on the splat and the junction of the leafage from each bracket holds a central leaf carving. The cabriole leg, wider, particularly at the knee, than a Philadelphia leg, terminates in a claw and ball foot, closely allied in character to those of Philadelphia. The back posts of figure 133, rounded below the seat, taper to pointed club feet.

Figure 134 is discussed in detail in Part III, 3, on New York, as it is an unusual piece for that region.

Chippendale (1755–1795)

Group iia (figures 135–148)

These chairs, although they show marked differences, are related and undoubtedly cover the same time span. Most of the backs are unbowed. The back posts, without decoration, diverge upward to a bow crest rail, which usually terminates in flat ears which are, except for a few, slightly scrolled at the sides. The ears are treated in three basic ways. Sometimes, they are left plain; more often, they are treated with leafage which springs forward from the rear of the ear; and thirdly, the ear may be raised in the center and at the edges as in Philadelphia, but the central rise is grooved, dividing the ear in half, as we saw in Massachusetts and will find again in Connecticut (fig. 194). The center of the top rail is generally accented by a shell form. In figures 136–138, the shell movement is only suggested by the central carving, which becomes part of a general decoration or carved leafage; but the center of the rail is raised in shell outline. The crest rail of figure 138 resembles that of figure 123. Figures 135 and 139–143 have raised shells or leafage in shell form, but not as prominent as on the Queen Anne Group *ib*, except for figure 143 where the shell is stylized, a fea-

ture possibly unique in America to this famous set of chairs.[6] The raised shells are generally also flanked by leafage or some form of carving. Figures 145–147 have no central shell, but a central accent is created by the shaping or carving of the top rail. Typical of New York, and possibly passed to Connecticut from there, is the strong backward roll given to the central top part of the crest rail (fig. 146). In the other colonies, the back rather than the front of the rail is cut away to lighten the top line. Here the front plane rolls, adding a feeling of depth and weight.

If we divide each splat into four parts, the weight mass and main action occur in the fourth just above center. In all cases, the outline is a baluster form, with the inner area (except on figs. 135 and 145) pierced to one of three basic forms of strapwork. The first is popularly called the "tassel and ruffle" pattern (figs. 136–138). The second is pierced to scrolls and a diamond, the lower half acting as a base supporting the upper scrolls (figs. 139–144). This is related to the equivalent New England pattern (fig. 112). The third (figs. 146–148), like the second, is pierced to strapwork but not shaped to form a lower part supporting scrolls; the scrolls continue nearly to the shoe to form a single unit. This splat appears in Rhode Island (fig. 182 with the same notch carving as 147) and England (fig. 181). A related Philadelphia splat has a somewhat different source, figures 77 and 78. The tassel and ruffle is also not confined to New York,[7] and figure 145, a rare splat for New York, is like the Massachusetts splat, figure 125, with an English source, figure 124.

Though squared seats dominate this subgroup, one-third of the chairs have horseshoe-shaped seats, and the squared seats have slightly rounded front corners. Both forms usually have bracket responds. Many of the chairs in this group have ornamentation along the base of the front seat rail; usually it is a wavy gadrooning peculiar to New York, rather than the positive and negative (convex and fluted) pattern of Philadelphia (compare figs. 136 and 93).[8] A rare variant of this is the leaf-carved band of figure 138. Both forms of decoration, of course, resemble the skirt carving applied to the famous New York Chippendale gaming tables. These

35

New York knee carving (detail from fig. 143).

[6] The shell is carved with the "Philadelphia peanut," often held to be proof of Philadelphia origin, as is the center of the crest rail of fig. 137.

[7] The "tassel and ruffle" back is similar in form to the Philadelphia back, Nutting, no. 2191; Sack, *Fine Points,* p. 39 (center of page); or Hornor, plate 334.

[8] Nutting, no..2232, shows an exception where the "Philadelphia"-type of gadrooning is used. Although its crispness of carving may imply a restoration, it is impossible to tell from the photograph.

decorations are carved on a separate piece of wood and applied to the bottom of the seat rail with glue and nails. Other chairs of this group have simple horizontal or patterned shaping. Some are constructed with through tenons (figs. 137, 139, 141, and 144), despite the tradition that these *ipso facto* indicate Philadelphia.

The knees are generally broad and decorated. Most carry a leafage decoration which springs from only one source, on the knee brackets. In figure 136, its source is the lower edge of a reverse-curve knee bracket; springing up and out, it spills down the leg. In figure 140, it spills as if its source were under the seat rail; though on figure 35, with a knee bracket related to those on the Queen Anne Group i*b*, we see a combination of these two methods, as in the English example, figure 59. Figure 139, like Philadelphia, has primary and secondary leafage. On other chairs only the center of the knee carries decoration, and it is of various forms: leafage, flowers, or a shell with pendant husk. Figure 146 shows an unusually broad knee related to that of figure 127 (as are the feet), which is carved to appear as if it had an applied, scrolled plaquage, with the bracket respond carved to a related scroll.[9] In this group, the ankle is generally nearly broken. Here we find three of the four forms of New York feet. Five of the fourteen chairs of this group have back posts below the seat that are thin and squared, with rounded corners tapering to small square or pointed club feet. The other nine are mostly chamfered; figure 139 is like the so-called stump leg of Philadelphia; these posts have no special form of foot. Stretchers seem not to appear on chairs of this group.

Group ii*b* (figures 149–152)

This group is united by some similarity of splat outline, by the similar piercing of the upper half of the splat, and by a relationship in the handling of the crest rail and back posts above the seat. The back posts diverge upward more than is normal just below the crest rail. Above the seat, they are sometimes decorated on the front face; in figure 149, they are molded as in a related English chair back, figure 242; and in figure 150, they are stop fluted (the latter form of decoration rarely appears on chairs in New York, or in America for that matter). The crest rails undulate in a seemingly pointless manner, though their relation to

the outline of other standard forms can be found (fig. 147); usually, they do not have dominant ears, but rather there is some decoration in the form of carved leafage or scrolls. Basically the splats are baluster forms, the lower part being narrow and the upper flaring out to the crest rail. The dominant piercing is vertical in movement, opening to some form of a fanned top. Figure 150 is more complex in piercing, but is related to figure 149 in being pierced to Gothic forms in its lower section. The seats are squared or horseshoe-shaped and usually have bracket responds. Figure 149 shows typical New York gadrooning on its lower edge, which, as always, is carved separately and applied. Figure 150 is another exception to the rule that New York does not have primary and secondary leafage on its knees, and is an example of the way specific details crop up now and again in all areas. Two of the basic kinds of feet are found in this subgroup. The back posts below the seat are also treated in the variety of ways we have seen.

As in Philadelphia and Massachusetts, the primary woods in New York are walnut and mahogany. It seems to have been a matter of preference, or perhaps date, in the Queen Anne group as to which wood was used; in chairs with pierced splats, mahogany was preferred. As elsewhere it would not be particularly useful to name all of the woods found here. However, it is again of some help to name those secondary woods which are uncommon in other areas: cherry, oak, beech (this has often been incorrectly regarded as indicating an English origin), red gum,[10] chestnut, and ash were all popular, but not much more so than the pine, tulip poplar, and so on, found elsewhere.

It is particularly interesting to note the features not found in New York chairs but present in Philadelphia and Massachusetts examples. Most of these were mentioned in passing, but they are enlightening when brought together. We found only one pair of chairs with simple club feet; rarely are seats horizontally shaped; the horseshoe-shaped seat is constructed as in Massachusetts; few of the backs are spooned or bowed, whereas in Philadelphia this is the rule; triangular corner blocks are sometimes used, but the quarter-round ones are more common. As in Philadelphia, there are no simple baluster splats although they were common in New England. New York chairs are just as common without back feet as with, at least when they have bow crest rails and pierced splats; square, blocklike feet are not the rule and through tenons are infrequently used.

---

[9] This more developed response is found on many English George II chairs, and is often carried to the extreme of having the rear leg, below the seat, repeat the form of the front leg.

[10] Red gum was called bilsted in eighteenth-century inventories.

4. *Rhode Island*

The focus on Rhode Island has, until recently, been on the work of Newport, and the products of the Goddard and Townsend families are so important that they have overshadowed all other men. Only now are we realizing that other Newport men and other Rhode Island towns, particularly later in the century, produced important, developed forms. To a great degree the concentration on Newport is justified, for the best case pieces made by those two intermarried Quaker families are among the finest furniture produced anywhere. It would, however, be as inaccurate to consider all of the fine Rhode Island or even Newport work to be by these cabinetmakers as it was in the 1930's to consider all fine Philadelphia work to be the product of William Savery.

The Rhode Island chairs have been grouped according to the traditional differentiation between "Queen Anne" and "Chippendale," those with solid splats and those with pierced splats. Although there does seem to be a progression from one form to another, as we saw in Philadelphia, there are many chairs that continue the earlier style into the second half of the century. The first three Queen Anne chairs (figs. 154–156) are grouped together because of similarly shaped back posts or crest rails. Strongly spooned back posts rise to break outward to rolled-shoulder crest rails, which have a simple scoop above the splat. In figures 154 and 155, the straight-edge splats recall the source of so much of the Queen Anne design, Chinese furniture. The chair design with the straight splat (fig. 153) and rolled-shoulder crest rails became popular in England during the latter years of the seventeenth and the first years of the eighteenth centuries. Other areas of America seem not to have used these two features. These first two chairs are like English work in other ways: the splats are veneered and they are made with detachable shoes. The first chair needs this construction so that a detachable shoe can cover the rear edge of the upholstery, but it is not necessary on the second, which has a slip seat. This construction is rarely found on American chairs and a greater knowledge of the circumstances under which it does occur may eventually lead us to a fuller understanding of regional traits and particular makers' work. In figure 156 we find a baluster splat of the simple form we know in Massa-

chusetts and in simpler chairs of Pennsylvania. Here, however, it is formed with a different feeling for design. Compared with figure 97, the crease in the upper part of the splat is more heavily accented: the splat dropping from the crest rail breaks further inward, producing a heavier curve, and it swells out again in a more full-blown motion, to move in again at midpoint down the splat to a narrowed waist. The weight of the splat seems forced upward toward the top.

Figure 157 is very like the Massachusetts chair, figure 102, except that the splat appears pinched in at the base because the upper part is broader.

Figures 158 and 159 show the back posts with a reverse curve on the front plane; they rise to break either side of a central unscooped crest; one is pieced on the inner edge so that lighter stock could be used. The break to re-entrant upper corners, seen on figure 159, recalls the similar form of figure 45, which has the same Oriental origin. In figure 158, this is altered to seem like an applied plaquage that flows down into the splat. This plaquage recalls an English George II form: it is known on a tiger maple Rhode Island chair[1] and is related to the New York knee plaquage on figure 146. The scrolls on the crest rail of figure 158 appear on figure 159 as small accents. On these two, the crest rails move down into standard splats—one the basic baluster form, the other recalling the cupped baluster form seen in Philadelphia (fig. 45) and in New York (fig. 134), which is a standard English form.

The maple chair, figure 160, has a back with unusual parts. The top of the splat is a simple inward curve as on figures 158 and 167, and several of the pierced splat chairs, but here it accents the slenderness of the main body of the splat.

The majority of the solid splat or Queen Anne chairs have spooned backs, with both the splat and the back posts above the seat formed to reverse curves on the side plane, though on a few only the splat is shaped, the posts remaining straight, and on figure 167 both are straight. From the front, most of the Queen Anne chairs have either back posts shaped to reverse curves above the seat or rolled-shoulder crest rails; only six are completely straight on the front plane, and of these, four have rounded posts.

Figures 161–166 form a group because of their rounded back posts, continuing into rounded crest rails, and because of the shape of their splats. Though the rounded post was fairly common in England, this form was not as popular elsewhere in America ex-

---

[1] Israel Sack, advertisement, *Antiques,* 73 (February 1958), p. 108 [illustrated].

cept on a few highly developed Philadelphia Queen Anne chairs. In two cases the splat is of the simple form and three are scroll-eared. Figure 161 shows an attenuated form, with the line of the upper section curving in further as it drops from the crest rail, then dropping in a long slender curve to the shoe. Here, there is a feeling of the upper part of the splat being scooped away unlike anything we have seen before. In figures 162–164 we see another practice found before only on one Massachusetts chair (fig. 102) and New York chairs such as figure 128. The inner line of the crest rail moves down to a tight reverse curve as it joins the top of the splat, then breaks straight downward to a point or corner, then makes a sharp curve inward to the inner point of the ear of the splat. This sharp break or notch is observed also in figures 168–170, while on figure 172 the upper reverse curve is missing and only the sharp point and downward curve remain. In other words, this variation occurs only on the eared baluster splats north of Philadelphia, since it is not necessary on the more standard baluster forms. It is interesting that Massachusetts, Rhode Island, and New York used this solution for their eared splats, but Philadelphia designed eared splats in other ways, figures 50 and 52. It has been thought that all scroll-eared splats of the simple form are of Rhode Island origin. This however seems too simple, and although the Massachusetts chair, figure 102, seems a rare occurrence, further research will probably increase the number of known scroll-eared splats of non-Rhode Island origin.

The backs of figures 165 and 166 seem to fit into this group, yet these chairs stand apart in many ways. They are like other Rhode Island chairs in having reverse-curve posts, and the knee decoration suggests such chairs as figure 158; but they are unusual in having rear legs of a cabriole form, something rarely seen in America. These two chairs have so much in common in detail and general feel that they suggest one maker.

The backs of figures 167–172 are much alike in feeling and general handling of design. Two have spooned splats flanked by back posts that are straight on the side plane but shaped on the front. Several of the posts are pierced out where they break inward. The line of the back post continues into the crest rail, which is ornamented in the center by a simple shell of positive and negative gadrooning, supported below by a serpentine line terminating in scrolls. The shells on figures 168 and 172 show interesting variations; that of figure 168 is unusual in that its base is carried onto the splat and that this part is composed of only positive statements. This acts as a support to the upper, more standard part, rather like stop fluting, and the whole appears more like the traditional husk

motif than a shell. The shell of figure 172 has a C-shaped cutout center which recalls the shells on Goddard and Townsend case pieces, as does the carving of the knees and feet.

The splats of this group show a variety of forms. Figures 169 and 170 show splats with more fully developed shaping and have a close counterpart in New York (fig. 126). In the Rhode Island examples the parts are leaner, the movement of the lines is more lively, the swing of the shoulder is freer.

It is certain that, as we have found elsewhere, solid splat chairs continued to be made in the second half of the century. Several of them appear with claw and ball feet which, though they were probably known in Rhode Island by 1745, suggest that these chairs may well be later. Note the basic similarities of figures 165 and 166 or figures 169 and 170; it seems unjustified to consider one of each pair as necessarily earlier than the other because of feet designs; all could have been made any time between 1745 and 1795.

On the majority of the Chippendale chairs, the splats and back posts are not spooned or even bowed when viewed from the front or side. They are simply raked backward above the seat, recalling the straightness of so much Massachusetts and New York work.

Figure 172 shows the beginning of the pierced splat forms, although its back posts and crest rail repeat those of the earlier chairs. Its splat is really a simplified version of the bottom half of what became the standard strapwork splat of Rhode Island. Figures 173–176 show this standard splat (see fig. 36 for detail), which is similar to the basic variant of the standard Massachusetts pierced splat (fig. 111), with four interlaced C scrolls dropping from the crest rail, supported on four vertical straps. In figure 173, in the Ewing Collection, it is organized in a way found so far only in Rhode Island. The strapwork does not simply drop from the crest rail but is a part of it. The slip seat frame is signed in eighteenth-century script, "Prov." The mate to this chair, at Yale University, is signed "Providn"; a related low or "slipper" chair, with a script "P," is also in the Ewing Collection; and another related chair has a Providence history.[2] It seems fair to say that chairs with this active upper scrolling, integrated with the crest rail, are at least in large part of Providence origin. The standard Rhode Island shell is not usually associated with this group; rather, the

[2] Ralph E. Carpenter, Jr., *The Arts and Crafts of Newport Rhode Island 1640–1820* (Newport, R.I.: The Preservation Society of Newport County, 1954), p. 40, fig 14.

36

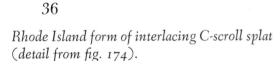

Rhode Island form of interlacing C-scroll splat (detail from fig. 174).

center of the crest rail rises in an arch (fig. 175) closer to some of the arch shells of Massachusetts, with the enclosed area carved to cross-hatching and small dots at the center of each diamond. Sometimes the area at the top of the scrolls is solid, figure 176, and sometimes open, figure 175; the chair with the Providence history, related to figure 173, has the crest rail piercing only suggested by shallow carving. The ears on the majority of this group have a simple roll backward at the ends, with small scrolls on either side. The central ridge is often notched, a standard practice in New York, though it rarely appeared in Massachusetts and Philadelphia. A few of the ears are simply straight and undecorated, and are related to the basic New York ear (fig. 140).

A type of Rhode Island splat found almost only on simple, rush-seated Chippendale chairs is like the most common Massachusetts pierced splat (fig. 103).

Figures 178 and 179 show a pierced splat which is found on many unelaborated Rhode Island examples, a form not popular elsewhere in America although it has an English precedent, figure 177, and was used to some degree from Massachusetts southward (fig. 96).[3] It is a simple baluster form pierced to three vertical straps, the outer two marked at the center with dots. Figure 178 has projecting ears with their bottom edge cut to a curve. This is found on many simple Rhode Island chairs, particularly the more countrified examples with trumpet-turned front legs, and on bannister backs. Figure 180 is in many ways an exception to any list of features associated with Rhode Island. It has a splat associated with Massachusetts (fig. 115) and known in Philadelphia.[4] The feet, with retracted claws, are like those associated with Massachusetts. However, the breadth and general stance, the back posts breaking to reverse curves to support a high-shouldered crest rail, the central Rhode Island-type shell, and the shell and husk carving of the knees all suggest a Rhode Island origin. Here, individual features of one area have been transplanted to another, and it is mostly the general character of the chair that reveals its origin.

Figure 182 represents a common Rhode Island form. Its back, particularly in the carving, has a clarity of drawing and simple delineation of outline typical of much Rhode Island work. The basic scrolling and shaping of the splat we have seen in Philadelphia (fig. 78) and New York (fig. 148), with an English source (fig. 77). Here there is chip carving at the top and base of the splat, as seen also on another New York version (fig. 147) and on an English chair, figure 181. The cross-hatching of the crest rail is like that of figure 176, though expanded to cover a larger area. The legs of figure 182 show the surface decoration of stop fluting usually associated only with Rhode Island. This is an oversimplification, however, since other areas do use stop fluting on furniture, though to a lesser extent. We have already seen it on the back posts of Philadelphia, Massachusetts, and New York chairs (figs. 72, 123, and 150); it is known on case pieces from all major areas, and is common in Europe.

Figure 183 is of particular interest because the Gothic back

---

[3] Massachusetts, Randall, fig. 147.

[4] Sack, *Fine Points*, p. 28.

is usually associated, in this country, with Philadelphia and a few Connecticut chairs but again an English source for the back (fig. 86) was available to all. This chair has the lean, clearly delineated look of New England and a preciseness found particularly on Rhode Island chairs such as figure 182. Its notched ears are related to other Rhode Island ears, and similar ears are included here on only one Massachusetts chair (fig. 104). Like the Providence chair, figure 173, the tenons of the slip seat frame are pinned.

The majority of the seats shown are horseshoe-shaped, though most of those from the Chippendale period and figures 166 and 167 show an extremely flat front, often considered a New York characteristic. Only seven of the cabriole leg chairs have squared seat frames (straight leg chairs as a rule have squared seats), and there seems to be no rationale as to the time of their appearance, except that figures 154 and 155 are probably early.

The horseshoe-shaped seats are fashioned like those of New York and Massachusetts, with the inner edge a straight line from the inside of the back tenon to the inside of the front tenon. These do not follow the curve of the outer edge, nor are they made with great depth as in Philadelphia. In all cases the rails are tenoned into the top of the front legs instead of in the Philadelphia manner. An unusual feature of figures 167, 173, and 183 is that where the sides of the slip seat frame meet in a tenon, there is a peg running vertically through the joint to secure it; this appears also on a few Southern chairs, figures 212 and 214.

The standard Rhode Island corner block is like that of Massachusetts: horizontal grain, triangular in shape, and secured with nails as well as glue. There are some exceptions to this, but not the mixture we found in New York; a few are constructed with the Philadelphia-type block; figure 176 has both types, and figure 168 is of two vertical-grain pieces, but the two pieces do not overlap to form a quarter-round. Rather, each piece is a triangular section of vertical grain that merely fills the space between the leg and the seat rail. Though through tenons appear on Rhode Island chairs after the Revolution,[5] they are not as yet known to have been made there during our period. The majority of the chairs do not have bracket responds although they exist, and on several of the chairs the rear of the horizontal shaping is made to a reverse curve in order to respond visually to the reverse curve of the knee

brackets. Figure 168 has bracket responds on the rear seat rail as well, as found elsewhere. Two chairs, figures 156 and 161, have the curious feature that the seat rail and stretchers slope toward the front. This is perhaps caused by the front feet having been cut or greatly worn, but a similar sloping is found on a set of bannister-back chairs in the Garvan Collection at Yale University and on that set the front feet are intact.

Two of the cabriole leg chairs are designed without horizontal shaping (the over-upholstered one is also straight). The rest are about equally divided between simple shaping (used also on the rear of fig. 165) and more developed shaping (fig. 162); the latter has been considered a Rhode Island characteristic although it occurs on the square-seated Massachusetts Queen Anne chairs. The basic form for the developed shaping of the Rhode Island skirt seems to be a central circular drop, flanked by reverse curves (fig. 162), though this shows many variations: figure 161 shows only the double reverse curve, and in figure 166 the central drop is more developed. It is often supposed that Rhode Island chairs have sharply ridged or arrised knees. So far, no such chair has appeared. Arrised knees are, however, common on Rhode Island case pieces and it would not be surprising if a Rhode Island chair appears with this particular feature.

On figures 155, 156, 158–161, and 165–166, the knees are outlined by C scrolls which continue, in many cases, to outline the knee brackets; this decoration is cut from the solid and reflects a feature well known in England. Though we have seen C-scrolled knees elsewhere in America, their appearance in Rhode Island is far more common. Here lambrequin knee decoration often accompanies the C scroll (fig. 166). This combination has been considered a sure proof of a Goddard and/or Townsend origin, since it appears on chairs known to be by these great cabinetmakers.[6] However, if one considers the variety of chairs included with this combination, it is clear that they are by more than one hand or single school of cabinetmakers.

Shell-carved knees appear on four of our chairs: three are of similar form, and are outlined below by a serpentine line terminating in scrolls like the shells on the crest rails. The chairs with shell-

---

[5] [Joseph K. Ott], *The John Brown House Loan Exhibition of Rhode Island Furniture* (Providence, R.I.: The Rhode Island Historical Society, 1965), fig. 16.

[6] Sold in the Flayderman sale, American Art Association, Jan. 2–4, 1930, lot 492, and later sold in the Sack sale, American Art Association, Jan. 9, 1932, lot 80; the Sack catalogue reports that Job Townsend made these for the Eddy family in 1743 and that a related piece, with a Job Townsend label, is still in the Eddy family. See also the wing chair, lot 81. The wing chair, with side chairs mentioned, appears in Albert Sack, *Israel Sack: A Record of Service 1903–1953* (no publishing data), p. 37.

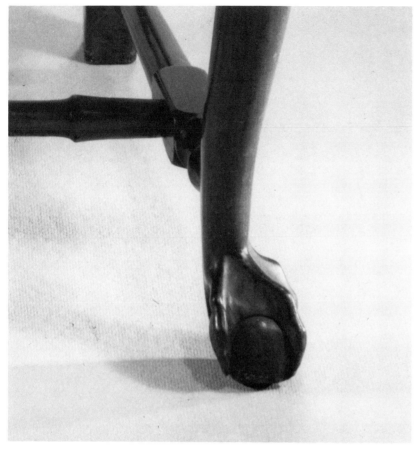

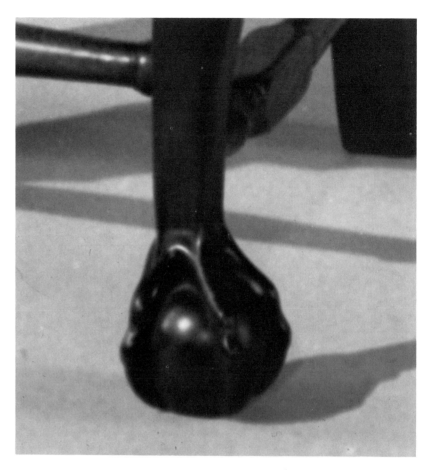

37

First form of Rhode Island claw and ball foot
(detail from fig. 171).

38

Second form of Rhode Island claw and ball foot
(detail from fig. 172).

carved knees all have shell-accented crest rails, and the knee shells have pendant husks. The majority of the knees, however, are undecorated, with only simple reverse-curve brackets. These help create the boldness often associated with Rhode Island cabriole legs; for example, figure 175 shows the heavy outward movement of the knee, down a rather full-blown leg, to a foot pushed well forward.

The form of the earlier club foot, which continues into the later part of the period, is much like the early Massachusetts foot. The pierced splat back chairs, figures 174–176, are so alike that the presence of club feet on one and claw and ball feet on the other two is not sufficient evidence to place one in the first and two in the second part of the century; rather, the difference was a question of economics or preference or both. There are two well-known forms of Rhode Island claw and ball feet, and they are best seen in figures 37 and 38. On the former, the foot is formed to

bold, nondelineated claws, appearing as though the skin of the web covered all the members completely, to the ends of the claws. This is carried to an extreme on figure 166 where, though the knuckles seem prominent, there is a smoothness and largeness of web we have not seen elsewhere except on the New York chair, figure 131. The resemblance between these feet and the New York form causes constant problems as to regional origin. The second foot (mentioned in relation to the Goddard and Townsend school) is one of long claws and talons, seemingly webless, with prominent knuckles; this foot grasps a large round ball flattened only on the base, easily seen in figure 176. On this chair we see also the flat inner sides of the cabriole leg again associated with the Goddard-Townsend school, which often produced the well-known "square cabriole" leg, that is, flat on all four sides.

The majority of the back posts below the seat are squared when stretchers are present, with the corners between the seat rails and stretchers chamfered, except on the group formed by figures 172–176 where they are left squared. Almost limited to Rhode Island is the English back leg with a tubular member between the seat rail and the stretcher (fig. 155), which perhaps introduces a rather awkward note, except in figure 161 where it appears with a related post, round above the seat. In this study, this rounded member is found outside Rhode Island only on the Massachusetts chair, figure 99. Another unusual feature we have noted is the back leg shaped to a cabriole form. And a further variation from the standard of other areas, except New York (fig. 130), is the squared rear leg tapering to a small foot when stretchers are present (figs. 158 and 159).

Rhode Island is famous for its flat, reverse-curve stretchers that recall the movement of the seat frame; they appear on five of the chairs included here. (It must be said that some chairs were originally made with turned stretchers, which have since been removed and replaced by flat stretchers. This alteration raises the price of the object for the unwary, and typifies the danger of buying that centers on rarity rather than quality.) The flat stretcher is heavier than the Philadelphia version, and more akin to the New York pattern. Three of the flat stretcher chairs have a rear stretcher of the simple, turned form known in Massachusetts, and figure 158 shows the Anglicized straight rear stretcher. Figure 155, like the Connecticut chairs figures 187, 188, and 191, has only side and rear stretchers, perhaps attempting an open feeling while keeping some additional bracing. The majority of the turned stretchers are of the standard form we saw in Massachusetts, with the medial stretcher ending in a point where it meets the square die of the side stretchers. But in figure 180, the point of junction is made with squared blocks, a feature seen in Philadelphia, New York, and Massachusetts. The shape of the baluster turning of the side stretchers of figure 161 occurs on another chair illustrated here (fig. 55). Behind the square die formed to hold the medial stretcher, the rear part of the stretcher bulges to a reverse-curve line instead of maintaining the straight columnar form known elsewhere (fig. 160). Both of these forms strongly reflect English practices.

A discussion of the woods is moderately helpful here. About half of the chairs with solid splats are mahogany and half walnut, again suggesting that this form was continued until the end of the century; most of the pierced splat chairs are mahogany. Secondary woods tend to emphasize maple above pine or tulip poplar, though both soft woods were used, particularly for corner blocks. One chair has mahogany corner blocks, which appear original and are extremely unusual in America; maple was also, though rarely, used for corner blocks, and chestnut, a wood associated particularly with Rhode Island though used elsewhere, appears in only one chair. The slip seat frame was usually of maple, though again other woods were used, and cherry, birch, and beech are found. The nails used to hold the corner blocks were usually of the large "rose-headed" form, though two other patterns are known, one with a smooth, round head also used in Massachusetts and Canada, and another with a very small head looking more like a brad than a nail.

5. Connecticut Valley

THE CONNECTICUT STYLE covers an area larger than the present state boundaries suggest. The underlying factor of a style area is an easy means of communication, and where communication is swiftest the taste is more nearly the same; as it becomes increasingly difficult, styles are less unified. The swiftest means of communication during this period was by water, and the Connecticut Valley, up through the middle of Massachusetts, must be seen as one style center, although it is formed of many small towns. It is true that each town shows its own peculiarities, but the total region has much in common.[1]

This proved the region for which it was hardest to assemble a body of chairs large enough to permit a valid generalization, except for the South, and the seventeen chairs included represent the types that could be found. Undoubtedly, other variations exist and will appear in time, but as will be seen in Part III, the rural craftsman reflected his environment as much as the city cabinetmaker, and since his rural approach to life differed, his design differed, so that much of Connecticut's work falls outside the developed forms included here. There is a good deal of variation among the seven Queen Anne chairs represented. But of the nine bowed crest rail chairs, seven are closely related and may be by the same man, Eliphalet Chapin, or by Chapin and his cousin, who was at one time apprenticed to him. This lack of a cross-sec-

[1] The same conclusion is apparent in the dialect studies of the same area; see Appendix.

tion of material should be remembered, for certainly other men must have made full-blown Chippendale chairs.

The backs of just over half of the Queen Anne chairs are straight. All the back posts are straight on the front plane and flow into undecorated saddle-hoop top rails. Most of the splats are simple in form, using the basic baluster shape known in Massachusetts and Rhode Island high-style chairs, in the simple rush-seated chairs of Philadelphia, and elsewhere. Figures 185 and 186 add a ring silhouette at the necking of the splat, which seems almost confined to these related chairs. It is known on a pair of simple New York chairs but as yet no English source has been discovered (this rash statement means, of course, that one will turn up immediately). The splats of figures 187–188 add the fret so popular in Philadelphia and Ireland. On the seven related Chippendale chairs (figs. 193–199), the back posts above the seat bow backwards, diverging sharply to a bow top rail with a central shell ornament, similar in placement to that of Philadelphia chairs. In figure 194, it is carved to undulating lobes (see fig. 39 detail) like the New York shell, figure 127; in figure 196, it is more like Philadelphia. The ears are notched in the center as in New York and Rhode Island, and the sides retreat in small scrolls. The front of the top rail rolls to the rear in the New York manner, and is carved to flow visually into the C scrolls of the bowed splat, which resembles the strapwork of a Massachusetts and a Rhode Island splat (figs. 111 and 174). The scrolls rest on a base of vertical strapwork, and are visually divided from it by a carved line reflecting another Massachusetts idea, that of upper and lower parts, rather than having the top and bottom interwoven as in Philadelphia. The diamond form of figures 197 and 198 is found in Massachusetts (fig. 112) as well as in New York, where it is a standard design. The splat of figure 199 seems to be unique to one closely related group of chairs. The "X" motif is known on the plinth of a highboy by the same school of workers,[2] whose best-known figure, Eliphalet Chapin, worked in Philadelphia where this "X" appears on the central plinths of many case piece pediments[3] and in the backs of a few chairs based on a design in Chippendale's *Director*.[4] The basic design of this splat, without the "X," combines elements from the Philadelphia Chippendale Gothic splats and from the standard Massachusetts Chippendale chair (compare it with figs.

[2] Nutting, fig. 370.

[3] Hornor, plate 134.

[4] Downs, fig. 136.

39

Connecticut back with lobed shell, notched blunt ears, backward rolling crest rail, and interlacing C-scroll splat (detail from fig. 194).

90 and 103). The splats, except for those of the over-upholstered chairs, figures 196–198, rest in the shoe. The splats of figures 191 and 201 are similar and their histories place them both in Norwich.

The arms and arm supports on the three Chippendale arm chairs are like those on the Philadelphia chair, figure 82. The arms on figure 188 are set on C-shaped supports as found in Massachusetts, New York, and Norwich, England (fig. 192).

Figures 185 and 186 are probably of the same period and yet have different shaped seats, which suggests that in the earlier part of the period squared and horseshoe-shaped seats were used interchangeably as personal preference dictated. It is typical of Connecticut that there is no single type of construction for Queen Anne seats. The early chairs with squared seats (fig. 184) show the method common in Massachusetts and early Philadelphia chairs (fig. 19). The construction of the horseshoe-shaped seat, figure 186, is like the fully developed Philadelphia Queen Anne seat, with its pegged-in legs and applied seat rim surrounding the slip seat frame (fig. 17). Figure 187 is like Massachusetts, New York, and Rhode Island horseshoe-shaped seat construction (fig. 27). Chippendale squared-seat chairs are made like those of the other areas. The seat rails of both styles are generally horizontally shaped; figure 186, constructed in the late Philadelphia Queen Anne manner, is visually light and thus left unshaped; and figure 189, which is left straight, appears heavy.

None of the Queen Anne chairs retains its original corner blocks, and those of the Chippendale chairs are made in the Philadelphia manner, quarter-round of two pieces, with vertical grain; but they are somewhat larger and bolder and some are secured with nails. In Connecticut, it is as common to find through tenons as not. Only one of the Connecticut chairs has bracket responds, and they are applied with large-headed nails and glue.

The knee brackets on the Queen Anne examples show strong, active lines but no standard form, and figure 185 has none at all. A practice known elsewhere in Philadelphia and the South is the application of the knee brackets onto the seat rail, figures 40, 184, and 190 (as they are applied to the skirts of tables). It is widely used on English chairs. C-scrolled knees are known on at least one Connecticut Queen Anne lowboy and may someday be found on chairs. The legs of the Queen Anne chairs are sometimes arrised and sometimes rounded. They show the same simple club foot as Massachusetts. All the claw and ball chairs have identical knee brackets, legs, and feet, which is one of the reasons they are considered the work of one man (see the caption to the key Chapin chair, fig. 193). The back posts, below the seat, are chamfered on all but one of the Queen Anne chairs; one shows a distinct break or backward flare at the foot (fig. 186). This is an English trick to obtain a broader base support and seems to be restricted in this country to the Connecticut Valley, though perhaps it appears in some regions of the South. The lower back posts of the Chippendale chairs are shaped to an oval section as in Philadelphia.

Stretchers were sometimes used but they were kept to a turned form. Figure 184 shows the retention of an early form with the double baluster-turned medial stretcher, with a central ring accent, and a straight rear stretcher of rectangular section. Both of

40

Construction detail showing how a knee bracket (removed in photo) may be glued to a downward extension of the seat rail rather than glued under the seat rail as is more normal; see fig. 22 (detail from English chair, Victoria and Albert Museum).

these are found on early bannister-back chairs. Figures 187, 188, 190, and 191 continue simple turned stretchers after a less functional placement has minimized their usefulness; this reflects an English practice seen also in Philadelphia and Rhode Island. The use of three stretchers on the first two and the shape of their backs, front legs, and feet suggest the same maker. Figures 187 and 191 are related to a roundabout by the shape of its front leg and foot and by a similar history which places them both in Norwich.[5]

A mixture of construction methods has been described, but none occur which are not used in some other area as well and the noticeable mixture is important since it tells us much about the dependence of Connecticut's style.

[5] [John T. Kirk], *Connecticut Furniture, Seventeenth and Eighteenth Centuries* (Hartford, Conn.: Wadsworth Atheneum, 1967), fig. 234.

Of the seventeen chairs, all but three are made of cherry; figure 184 is of maple painted red with black streaks, and looks like cherry. Cherry dominates all eighteenth-century Connecticut high-style furniture, both as a primary and a secondary wood; in fact, there was such a demand that it was imported from upper New York State in preference to other woods that could as easily have been obtained.[6] Maple, the second most common wood, was also used as a secondary wood and for less developed, usually painted pieces. In addition, pine, poplar, chestnut, ash, and oak were used as secondary woods, probably in this order of decreasing frequency.

6. *The South*

No DISCUSSION of American design in the Queen Anne and Chippendale periods is complete without a consideration of Southern furniture. But any attempt to provide a systematic analysis of Southern design and construction comparable to that of Northern style centers, or even general areas like the lower Connecticut Valley, presents great difficulties. The first is that the major exploratory scholarship which brings the range of design types and achievements into the public domain and begins the survey of construction, details, and woods, comparable to the landmark scholarship carried on in the twenties and thirties for Northern areas, is only now being done. For those not directly involved in this first-hand exploration, comparatively little information is available. Such groundbreaking studies as E. Milby Burton's *Charleston Furniture,* plus the catalogues of major shows of the furniture of particular areas, such as the two important Baltimore shows,[1] and the commentary on a few Southern pieces appended to discussions whose focus lies north of the Mason-Dixon line are as much awareness of this area as most discussion of American furniture reflects. Collections, like that of the Museum of Early Southern Decorative Arts, are now being formed, and studies of local

areas, on which any fundamental advance beyond the level of generally accepted "rule of thumb" generalizations depends, are under way. The knowledge that individuals working in depth on the furniture of given locales have accumulated is already far beyond that reflected by general surveys of the field; these studies will ultimately have to be synthesized by scholars whose long experience of distinctively Southern problems will permit them to balance the findings of one area with another.[2] In the meantime, generalizations must necessarily be confined to noting certain major factors that set the whole problem of Southern craftsmanship off from the situation in other regions.

Another difficulty in studying Southern furniture, and undoubtedly part of the reason there is still so little published scholarship, is the lack of material to be studied. For a combination of reasons, comparatively little Southern furniture exists.

It should be made clear at the outset that this lack is not primarily the result of the Civil War, as is often said, but ironically enough of the economic prosperity of the South prior to that time. From the earliest times, the Southerner who would have purchased the type of high-style furniture we are studying prospered handsomely through the exportation of indigo, rice, tobacco, and later cotton. This left him, unlike his counterpart in the North, with capital in England which made it natural for him to purchase goods there. In the South, the economic class that in other American regions provided the patrons of high-style American craftsmen thought of itself as representing something like an English squire-archy. It followed English concepts of the dignified life more closely, down to the custom of the "grand tour" as the completion of one's education. Besides purchasing English furniture,[3] men of this class tended when possible to follow the English pattern of refurnishing and redecorating with each generation, whereby the furniture of one generation was relegated to secondary settings in the next and ultimately used up in plantation cabins or given away to dependents of the family. A surprising number of key Southern pieces have been found by dealers in swamp cabins or island homes and brought out by boat.

---

[6] See note 17, p. 35.

[1] *Baltimore Furniture* 1760–1810 (Baltimore, Md.: The Baltimore Museum of Art, 1947); William Voss Elder, III, *Maryland Queen Anne and Chippendale Furniture of the Eighteenth Century* (Baltimore, Md.: The Baltimore Museum of Art, 1968).

[2] I am particularly grateful to Miss Conover Hunt, Mrs. G. Dallas Coons, William Voss Elder, III, E. Milby Burton, Graham Hood, Berry Greenlaw, and particularly Frank Horton for their generous help and guidance in the study of Southern furniture in general and in the preparation of this section in particular. Without their knowledge and help it would not exist.

[3] Frank Horton, in a letter of January 31, 1972, reports that Peter Mongault, of Charleston, wrote, about 1774, that having lived in a very poor house he was now building a new one and, needing furniture, he was ordering it from England and enclosed a list.

Because those who would naturally patronize superior cabinetmakers purchased abroad, comparatively little high-style furniture was made. As Carl Bridenbaugh's study of colonial craftsmen demonstrates, surprisingly little cabinetwork was ever done in the South, and what was made seldom represented the fully developed high-style furnishings with which the Southern equivalent of a Philadelphia or Boston mansion was supplied. According to Bridenbaugh, it was nearly impossible for a cabinetmaker to make a living at his craft without exercising other functions as well, except in Charleston. After the Revolution, Philadelphia cabinetmakers came south to Charleston and were successful,[4] and Baltimore produced a considerable body of fine Classical Revival furniture (it is significant that two of the great Southern shows have been Baltimore ones). Even before the Revolution, Annapolis and Charleston produced first-rate furniture. Annapolis made pieces closely akin to Philadelphia, often with over-elaboration found in dependent centers[5]; and Charleston's work closely reflects the English taste of the mid-eighteenth century. The elaborate furniture that does exist below the level of the first-rate work of Baltimore and Charleston shows a degree of provinciality which suggests it was never intended to be the finest furniture in a fine urban household; rather, if it was for an elegant house it probably was part of the "second-string" furniture, but it was naturally found in lesser city houses or rural settings.

It is in this set of objects which were not directly inspired by elegant English examples and were not high style that we begin to see a distinctively Southern design aesthetic. But as soon as we attempt to study such pieces, we find ourselves faced with another element that has no parallel in the Northern centers included here, with the possible exception of Connecticut. The South has no dominant style center to play the role for a whole region that Philadelphia or Boston or Newport play for their respective areas. As a result, distinctive provincial schools of simpler furniture have grown up from region to region, differing from each other and making it almost impossible, at this stage at least, to identify "Southern" as distinct from local elements. The state of research is perhaps analogous to that on Connecticut up through the 1940's. There, such diversity existed among the few pieces known that

students of furniture fell back on rule of thumb formulas—Connecticut furniture is all cherry, Connecticut furniture is all eccentric—or else acknowledged its diversity by giving up hope of discerning coherent patterns. Just as a sharper awareness of the contribution of each Connecticut subregion laid the foundation for a new understanding of Connecticut, which led to the formation of new collections like the Barbour one and ultimately to more general scholarly discussion, so the study of these local Southern schools will ultimately provide the basis for a redefinition of our ideas on Southern furniture.

In this connection, one of the most revealing bodies of material available to the student of Southern Queen Anne and Chippendale is provided by a group of simple Virginia and North Carolina chairs, a number of which are now at Colonial Williamsburg and MESDA. By examining this group, which is extensive enough to provide a basis for analysis, we can begin to identify factors which may prove generally characteristic of Southern work.

Because of the necessarily general nature of this section, each chair will be discussed separately rather than taking all the parts in sequence; that is, the total design of each chair will be considered rather than first discussing all crest rails, then all splats, and so on. The chairs have been arranged by groups that show some similarities, particularly in having similar splats, rather than by attempting an arrangement in date order. When chairs have similar features, that feature will be most fully discussed under the chair in which it first appears.

The chair, figure 202, is included despite its unusual form as a speaker's chair because it includes rarely found Queen Anne feet and scrolled arms on turned supports that recall the William and Mary period. The legs are necessarily heavy, but their flow into the feet and the nonturned shape of the feet are important characteristics, for they are the result of design rather than structural ideas. The feet are not turned forms; they were shaped to this outline. Although not at first apparent, there is horizontal shaping, for the knee brackets are applied to the face of the seat rail, which drops behind them, a feature found also on figure 215. This practice is more common in England than northern America. Colonial Williamsburg has found no precedent or prototype for the form of this chair, but its files report that the Second Master's seat at Winchester College, England, although crude and simple, does have a pediment top. The back of the pediment is complete with moldings and finish although the remainder of the back is unfinished.

Figure 203 is typical of a large group of English work usually

[4] Burton, pp. 79, 81, 98, 113.

[5] The dependence of Baltimore and its surrounding area on Philadelphia rather than on its more Southern neighbors during the second half of the eighteenth century was shown by Jane N. Garrett, "Philadelphia and Baltimore, 1790–1840: A Study of Intra-Regional Unity," *Maryland Historical Magazine*, 55, No. 1 (March 1960).

41

Standard Southern upward flaring splat pierced to four ribs connected at midpoint by dots (detail from fig. 205).

rural and often, as here, with a plank seat. This construction was common in England where "hall chairs" even by the most distinguished designers called for a plank seat—undoubtedly useful when halls were the waiting place for less welcome visitors who might arrive in damp clothing. In America, the Windsor chair took over this role. The shape of the crest rail, splat, seat, legs, and stretchers is closely akin to the simpler American chairs included in this section. The crest rail's simple top line and curved lower edges are like those of figures 204 and 220 and the splat is related

to those of figures 216–219. The medial stretcher is moved between the front legs, as found on figures 204–207, 216, and 221. Such a placement is rare in America outside this group. On this chair and the following, the splat passes behind the shoe and enters the rear seat rail, a practice usually confined in the North to over-upholstered chairs. As in most of these simple straight-legged chairs, there never were corner blocks and of course knee brackets are almost unknown except on elaborate straight-legged chairs such as figure 224, where open brackets are now missing. Probably they were thin and decoratively pierced rather than having structural significance.

Related to figure 203, figure 204 has a slip seat made of Southern pine. This chair, like figures 205, 206, 207, 209, 215, and 216, has a simple rounding on the top edge of its seat rails rather than being finished with a molding. As in figure 203, the splat passes behind the shoe rather than entering it, and like figure 209, on the inside of the rear seat rail there is an additional support for the shoe. Figure 218 has an extra-deep rear seat rail that serves the same purpose. Like so many of these simple Southern chairs, figure 41 (detail of fig. 205) has a simple upward flaring splat pierced to four ribs connected at midpoint. Here the crest rail is simply arched and flanked by scroll ears that appear as extensions of the back posts although they are one piece of wood with the crest rail. Scroll ears are found in Pennsylvania and are common in England (fig. 59). This and figure 217 are the only chairs in this simple straight-legged group to be made without a rear stretcher. One other Southern chair with this feature, figure 212, probably lacks one because the designer did not wish to interrupt the outward curves of its rear legs. The Roanoke history that accompanies figure 41 has possible significance in focusing its special features on that area.

Long considered a Virginia chair, figure 206 has much in common with this group: seat rails with round top edges, scroll ears, fanned splat, front stretcher, and a lack of corner blocks. The splat is slightly more complex and its stance is wider.

Figure 207, similar to many in the group, has a different crest rail. It is shaped like those found on a few Rhode Island chairs, which also use this shape of splat although in Rhode Island they are unpierced. No such chairs are included in this study but a set belonged to John Brown of Providence.[6] Unusual as this splat is in America it was common in England. An almost identical

[6] Now in the collection of Normal Herreshoff, Bristol, R.I.

Southern chair but with an over-upholstered seat is in Colonial Williamsburg's collection.[7]

The more elaborate side chair, figure 208, introduces further features for study. The ears of the crest rail are rounded, the center of the crest rail scooped. The splat is as we have seen on the simpler chairs; the front corners of the seat frame are chamfered and fluted, a feature not found elsewhere in this study; and it has original rear corner blocks. The other chairs to have this last feature or evidence of early blocks are figures 209, 211, 214, 215, 218, 219, 222, and 223, and all the original blocks or remaining parts of them are in the Philadelphia manner except for figure 223. Another "Philadelphia" feature is the use of through tenons, found also on figures 212–214. Many people from Pennsylvania migrated down behind the Virginia mountain range to settle in the fertile valley, so that the transference of such structural features is not surprising. Most of the Southern chairs included here are of walnut. Probably because mahogany was difficult to obtain outside major seaports, the rear seat rail of this mahogany chair has a heavy mahogany veneer on a pine base. There is no horizontal shaping; the rail is kept relatively slender. The front feet are of an English club foot design. Their outline is softer than the usual New England club foot and the ankle is nearer to the center of the foot.

The straight-legged side chair, figure 209, like the other simple chairs, has a flared splat. But it has five rather than four vertical straps, which produces a more massive effect, and it is unique in this study in that the splat is constructed of two pieces. There is a seam down the middle of the center strap. Also unusual in the Southern group is the bowed back, which occurs here and on figures 218, 220, 223, and 224. The crest rail is scooped to three curves. This is one of the Southern chairs with original corner blocks and one of those with an extra inner support for the shoe. As on most of the medial stretcher chairs, that stretcher is dovetailed into the side stretcher, but here at the top of the joint the end of the medial stretcher is cut to a "V." It had been hoped that whether medial stretchers were either dovetailed or morticed and tenoned into side stretchers would prove to indicate a difference between American and English origin. Both, however, are found in both places.

Related in general design to a chair with an Essex County, Virginia, history,[8] figure 210 is light in appearance, which sug-

gests a late eighteenth- or early nineteenth-century date. Unlike many of these simple chairs, it has an edge molding on top of the seat rails and a similar molding down the outer edge of the front legs. A further detail that helps to create the light appearance is the heavy chamfering on the inner edge of the legs.

Figure 42 shows the splat of figure 211 which has a history of having been used in Williamsburg. This would account for its more developed design and makes it of real importance in any understanding of Southern work. Somewhat surprising, at least in the present state of research, is its use of cherry as a primary wood. Perhaps, however, a group of more elaborate walnut or mahogany Williamsburg-made chairs will emerge. On the other hand, an individual patron may have preferred this wood, or it may have been a lesser chair among English ones. More developed than the other vertical ribbed chairs, it uses a bowknot to unite the ribs below midpoint, suggesting, as do similarly developed English chairs, that a ribbon was the original connecting design and that the simple dots found as connectors on other chairs are a stylization from this.

It is important that this key chair is one of the few that retain at least part of their corner blocks. Another unusual feature when considering all American chairs is that this and three other chairs—figures 212, 215, and 216—have their shoe and rear rail made out of one piece of wood. (A feature that was found in Massachusetts and New York on figs. 122, 130, and 131.)[9] Such a method of construction does not make it impossible to insert the splat after the main assemblage of the chair if the crest rail is left until last. The crest rail is decorated to a contained unit by seven C scrolls, the outer two with leafage, and two S scrolls. The background of the anthemion carving of the crest rail and the bow of the splat are matted with punchwork. The anthemion is a design most often connected with the Classical Revival styles that began in America after 1795, and although Adam and others used them from about 1765, this feature suggests a late date for this chair.

Surprising is the presence of horizontal shaping on a straight leg chair, but more surprising is its use on the rear seat rail when it is not present at the front or sides.

Figures 212 to 214 form an interesting group. They are related by the shape and piercing of their splats and in their attempt at sophisticated designs. Fortunately, two have histories or similar-

---

[7] Accession number 1960.24.

[8] Helen Comstock, *American Furniture* (New York: The Viking Press, 1962), fig. 278.

[9] Frank Horton reports that "the use of a one-piece back rail (no separate shoe) seems to be common to the entire Tidewater, Virginia, area and down into Albemarle, North Carolina." (Letter of January 31, 1972.)

42

Back developed in detailing; bowknots such as those at midpoint of this splat are probably the design origin of the connecting midpoint dots found on the simplified, almost stylized, backs such as fig. 41 (detail from fig. 211).

ities to regionalized chairs that suggest a Virginia origin. Figures 212 and 213 are possibly from the Winchester area of the upper Valley. One has a history that records it there. And the use of white pine, rather than the more common yellow pine, is found in that area. Another feature found in the Winchester area is that in some chairs the back posts through tenon the crest rail.[10] Both use crude versions of Pennsylvania shells; that of the side chair is less

[10] Frank Horton, letter of January 31, 1972.

crude but not necessarily by a different hand. The arm chair has scooped arm supports that are probably a simplified version of those associated with Pennsylvania. Further, all three have through tenons (found on another developed Southern chair, fig. 208) and the bracket responds of figure 214 have through tenons as found on some Philadelphia chairs. Since the upper valley was settled from Pennsylvania, this migration of features is not unexpected. The ears have moderate scrolls and are not knuckled in the Philadelphia manner, and the shape of the splat with four interlocking C scrolls is not of Pennsylvania origin.

The rear legs of figure 212 curve outward, are rounded on the inner corner, and do not hold a rear stretcher. The top edge of the seat frame has a recessed rounding which carries down the outer corner of the front legs. The same areas of the related chair (fig. 213) show a more distinctive quarter-round molding; on both, the molding is as always cut into the solid.

The original slip seat frames have pegs through their mortice and tenon joints, a feature so far recorded elsewhere only in Rhode Island, particularly Providence.

Unlike the two preceding chairs, the Pennsylvania feature of figure 214, through tenons, is a constructural and not a visual part of the design. Also, the chair is of mahogany. Like the two preceding straight-legged chairs, it has no horizontal shaping of the seat rail. Its feet, of a type found on some New York chairs (fig. 128) and a few Philadelphia pieces, are common in England (fig. 151).

The two most elaborate Southern chairs included have claw and ball feet. A few other Southern chairs with claw and ball feet are known and undoubtedly others will appear. Figure 215—like the related and better-known arm chair at Shirley Plantation which has leaf-carved knees—shows an interesting if somewhat naïve use of English and perhaps Irish designs. Its crest rail is in three design parts, the scooped center is raised, and the ends have the backward-rolling scrolls common on fine English chairs. The outline of the splat is related to those of the following chairs, as well as to the vase-baluster designs of Philadelphia and splats such as the Massachusetts design, figure 120, and the New York back, figure 152. Figure 215 uses the piercing to four ribs that was obviously enjoyed in the South, interlacing them with a diamond. The base is edged with stylized leafage and like the splat of the following chair is pierced to a heartlike shape. The seat frame is horizontally shaped, but the ends or dropping parts of the shaping on the front rail and on the front of the side rails are covered with knee brackets that are glued onto the face of the rail. This is common on tables, rare although not unknown on other American chairs, but quite common in England. (The English also use knee brackets placed between the leg and seat rail.) The rear of the side horizontal shaping is a reverse curve like a bracket respond, and on the rear rail the "horizontal shaping" is made by adding two bracket responds at each end.

The shell and husk pendant knees are like those of New York, Newport, and England; the rather pudgy front feet are like some provincial English feet; and the back posts end in squarish feet as found elsewhere in America and England. There are no stretchers. The shoe and the back rail are one piece of wood. There are traces of corner blocks which may or may not have been original.

Figure 216 is another simple straight-legged chair which has scrolled ears, as found on figures 205 and 206, and a splat that relates it to the preceding chair and the two that follow. In its lack of moldings, placement of front stretcher, a lack of corner blocks, and use of walnut and yellow pine, it is like the other simple, possibly Virginia or North Carolina chairs. In most of its features, it resembles a chair with a North Carolina history.[11] In addition, its shoe is one piece with its rear seat rail. Figure 217 uses the same wood and simple design but has a medial stretcher and the splat's outline is more like that of the following chair, as is its shaping of the center of the crest rail to a raised arch flanked by small scrolls, and its "scrolled" or rolled ears.

The side chair, figure 218, shows a splat and crest rail best known in Philadelphia and widely used in England. The stance of this example is like the leaner of the related English chairs (fig. 79) rather than the broader English or Philadelphia examples (fig. 80). It has a history that could place it in Baltimore or South Carolina, although the former seems unlikely because of its leanness. Most of the developed Baltimore chairs appear broad, particularly the front seat rail, and the piece seems to fit more easily into this more Southern group.

The first of the more certain North Carolina chairs, figure 219, is possibly from the Edenton area. It uses a vase-baluster splat pierced to a figure eight under a broad, rolling serpentine crest rail, which ends in simple ears. There is a leanness about the parts of the back that carries through into the simple scrolled arms and their C-shaped supports. The lower horizontal and vertical mem-

43

Richly developed Southern back, possibly from the Edenton area (detail from fig. 222).

bers continue this feeling of leanness. The top of the seat rail and front corners of the front legs are molded. Unusual is the setting of the rear seat rail so that it is not flush with the back faces of the back posts. The corner blocks are in the "Philadelphia" manner.

Also possibly from the Edenton area is the commode chair, figure 220. It too is lean in parts, except for the necessarily deep seat rail. Paired reverse-curve shaping on the bottom edge of the crest rail flanks a flared splat with five straps, its back like the possibly Virginia, but perhaps North Carolina chair, figure 204. It also has the same boxy stance, this boxlike quality being

[11] *Southern Furniture 1640–1820,* compiled by the editors of *Antiques* (New York: *Antiques,* 1952), fig. 53. This chair is recorded as of apple wood, and has a history of being from Rocky Mount. It has reverse-curve shaping on the lower edge of the crest rail, as on fig. 204.

furthered by vertical arm supports and arms that move rather straight in their forward thrust. The seat rail is carved to a concave shell, which holds leafage in a rather Philadelphia and Maryland manner. But here the shell is stiffer and the leaves broader. The seat rail is horizontally shaped; on the side, it is cut to paired reverse curves. The medial stretcher is placed near the front legs. The back seat rail is of two superimposed pieces.

Just as we have included straight-legged chairs in this section because cabriole leg chairs from the South are so rare, so we include the unusual arm chair, figure 221. At first it appears to be a sort of roundabout, but it also resembles an arm chair with splats under the arms. Its history suggests the northeastern area of North Carolina and perhaps a Quaker maker. The top rail, like a roundabout, has a raised block which connects the arms. The outline and piercing of the splats are like some Rhode Island, English, and Philadelphia splats (figs. 177, 178, and 96), and the base is simple horizontals and verticals with a front rather than medial stretcher. The outer edges of the seat frame, front legs, and stretchers are molded. The seat rests on a ledge provided by shaped strips that cover the inside of the side and rear seat rails.

The second really elaborate chair, figure 43 (detail of fig. 222), with claw and ball feet, is thought to be possibly from the Edenton area. Here great sophistication has been attempted. Rounded back posts break twice in their movement, unlike those of Philadelphia (fig. 53). The crest rail has central and flanking leafage above a baluster splat related to that of the English and Philadelphia chairs, figures 74 and 75. Here the side scrolls frame a figure eight whose halves do not flow into each other: the diamond does not interlace the eight and its sides are not looped but carved to flowers. The figure eight is found in Massachusetts (fig. 118) but in a differently shaped splat. The arms and their supports have more shaping than is usual. The seat rails have shaped lower edges, the rear drop of the side rails has an additional ⅝-inch piece added before the bracket respond. The knee brackets have a stylized leafage and the leafage of the front knees is carved to appear as though it came from under that of the knee brackets. The claws of the feet are well defined. Unusual for America is the cabriole rear leg and its square cross-section, an English practice (fig. 153). Mahogany is the primary wood and the corner blocks are in the "Philadelphia" manner.

Before the Revolution, Annapolis had a more complex culture than Baltimore, and the arm chair, figure 223, may have been made there. It is included to make clear the even more rural quality of the preceding examples. In stance and motifs it is Philadelphia-like, but the ears are less knuckled. The center of the crest rail is a stylized shell over a ribbon-like band, above cross-hatching with the center of each diamond marked with a dot; the back is slightly bowed. The splat has ribs that move from shoe to crest rail with flanking C scrolls. The arms and arm supports have a central rope carving. The seat rail is deep, with a simple central shell with matted circular surround. The knees show stylized leafage on a matted ground. The corner blocks are Massachusetts-like in their shape, grain, and use of large-headed nails, but they are of hard pine.

Also included to set the Virginia–North Carolina chairs in context, and to act with the Baltimore chair as a kind of frame, is a Charleston chair, figure 224. The figure eight splat is similar to but more richly developed than the Massachusetts splat, figure 118. Here leafage flanks the figure eight and the hole in the crest rail is completely surrounded by it; on the Massachusetts chair, the lower half is edged with stylized drapery. On the Southern chair, the top edge of the crest rail and the ears are edge-molded. The leafage flanking the hole in the crest rail and the figure eight is gilded. The top of the seat rails and the outer edges of the front legs are molded. Knee brackets that were probably elaborately pierced are missing from the front and sides of the front legs and front of the rear legs. There are no traces of corner blocks.

Conclusion

WE HAVE EXAMINED six of the important American style centers, studying in detail what went into the designing of chairs of each given area. As stressed, one of the most damaging approaches to regionalized pieces is the use of shorthand, rule of thumb, or catch phrases, and it may perhaps be helpful to include a final list of normally accepted ideas which have been shown to be inadequate by the American examples we have seen:

The diamond motif appears only in New York splats:
   See figs. 112, Massachusetts; 197, Connecticut; 215, the South.
The looped diamond splat is the work of Thomas Elfe of Charleston, S.C.:
   See figs. 75, Philadelphia; 116, Massachusetts; 222, the South.

A tassel appears only in New York splats:
> See figs. 75, Philadelphia; 116, Massachusetts.

The tassel and ruffle splat is confined to New York:
> See footnote 7 on p. 47.

A "rope and tassel" carved crest rail appears only in Maryland:
> See fig. 67, Philadelphia.

Back posts rounded above the seat appear only in Rhode Island:
> See fig. 53, Philadelphia; 134, New York; 222, the South.

Heavily rounded corners on a squared seat appear only in New York:
> See fig. 66, Philadelphia. (They seem not to appear in New England.)

Connecticut Queen Anne chair seats are always squared:
> See fig. 186, which is ballooned.

Massachusetts Queen Anne seats are always ballooned:
> See fig. 97, which is squared.

Arrised knees appear only in Rhode Island:
> See figs. 106, Massachusetts; 184, Connecticut; 208, the South; in fact, they have *not* appeared in Rhode Island.

Retracted claws appear only on Massachusetts chairs:
> See figs. 90, Philadelphia; 180, Rhode Island; see also note 14 on p. 34.

The New York claw and ball foot is square and blocky:
> See figs. 31, 32, and 33, which show a variety of non-squared New York feet.

Flat stretchers usually designate Rhode Island and occasionally appear in Philadelphia:
> See fig. 130, New York.

Medial stretchers ending in squared dies appear only in New York:
> See figs. 55, Philadelphia; 103, Massachusetts; 180, Rhode Island.

Medial stretchers ending in turned, pointed ends appear only in Rhode Island:
> See figs. 97, Massachusetts; 184, Connecticut.

Medial stretchers with ring turnings do not appear in New York:
> See fig. 128, New York.

Back posts terminating in flared feet are standard on New York chairs:
> See fig. 139, a New York chair with no "back feet."

Back posts terminating in flared feet appear only in New York:
> See figs. 50, Philadelphia; 104, Massachusetts; 158, Rhode Island; 215, the South.

All Philadelphia chairs have through tenons:
> See fig. 92, a labeled Philadelphia chair without them.

Only Philadelphia chairs have through tenons:
> See figs. 139, New York; 186, Connecticut; 208, the South.

From this list, which could be lengthened, it is evident that such guidelines, although useful during the early period when interest in this field was developing, now distract far more than they help.

A PICTURE

PORTFOLIO

Philadelphia

FIGURES 44–96

44

Side chair, Philadelphia, 1740–90, possibly by William Savery
(1721–88). Courtesy of Henry Francis du Pont Winterthur Museum
(Acc. no. 67.793).

PRIMARY WOOD: *maple.*
DIMENSIONS: *height, 41 inches; width, 21½; height of seat rail,
17½.*
DESIGN AND CONSTRUCTION: *Back, spooned. Seat frame construction,
similar to fig. 19. Bracing of seat frame, stretchers below the seat.
No bracket responds. Horizontal shaping. No through tenons. Seating
of splat in rail above seat.*
NOTES: *Similar to several chairs carrying Savery labels (Hornor,
Blue Book, plate 462).*

53

Arm chair, Philadelphia, 1745–60. Courtesy of Henry Francis du Pont Winterthur Museum (Acc. no. 59.2500.2501).

PRIMARY WOOD: *walnut.*
DIMENSIONS: *height, 46 inches; width, 32¼; height of seat rail, 16½.*
DESIGN AND CONSTRUCTION: *Back, spooned. Seat frame construction, as fig. 17. Bracing of seat frame, the depth of the seat frame. Knee brackets, nailed. Bracket responds, horizontal grain, nailed. No horizontal shaping. Through tenons, seat rail and bracket responds. Seating of splat in shoe.*
NOTES: *Back posts pieced out on outer edge above seat. A history recorded inside the seat states that it was made in England in 1724, demonstrating the problem with recorded histories (Downs, American Furniture: Queen Anne and Chippendale, fig. 27).*

54

Side chair, Philadelphia, 1745–60. The Museum of Art, Rhode Island School of Design (Acc. no. 68.167).

PRIMARY WOOD: *walnut.* SECONDARY WOODS: *walnut and pine slip seat frame.*
DIMENSIONS: *height, 42½ inches; width, 20; height of seat rail, 17¼.*
DESIGN AND CONSTRUCTION: *Back, spooned. Seat frame construction, as fig. 17. Bracing of seat frame, the depth of the seat frame. Knee brackets, large-headed nails. Bracket responds, horizontal grain. No horizontal shaping. Through tenons, seat rail and bracket responds. Seating of splat in shoe.*
NOTES: *Rim of seat frame applied.*

55

Arm chair, Philadelphia, 1745–60. Courtesy of Henry Ford Museum, Dearborn, Michigan (Acc. no. 59.82.2).

PRIMARY WOOD: *walnut.* SECONDARY WOOD: *pine.*
DIMENSIONS: *height, 41 inches; width, 31⅛; height of seat rail, 15⅝.*
DESIGN AND CONSTRUCTION: *Back, spooned. Seat frame construction, as fig. 17. Bracing of seat frame, the depth of the seat frame. No horizontal shaping. Through tenons, seat rail and bracket responds. Seating of splat in shoe.*
NOTES: *Some of this information was provided by the Henry Ford Museum.*

56

Side chair, Philadelphia, 1745–60. Courtesy of Colonial Williamsburg (Acc. no. 1970.2).

PRIMARY WOOD: *walnut.* SECONDARY WOOD: *walnut slip seat frame.*
DIMENSIONS: *height, 41¾ inches; width, 20¾; height of seat rail, 17.*
DESIGN AND CONSTRUCTION: *Back, spooned. Seat frame construction, as fig. 17. Bracing of seat frame, the depth of the seat frame. Knee brackets, small-headed nails. Bracket responds, horizontal grain. No horizontal shaping. Through tenons, seat rail and bracket responds. Seating of splat in shoe.*
NOTES: *Back posts above seat pieced out on outer face at top and on inner face at base of reverse curve. Base of seat shell applied with glue. Rim of front seat rail cut from solid, rims of side seat rails added.*

57

58

Arm chair, Philadelphia, 1745–60. Courtesy of Henry Francis du Pont Winterthur Museum (Acc. no. 60.1037).

PRIMARY WOOD: *mahogany (Winterthur report)*. SECONDARY WOODS: *splat veneered on pine; walnut rear seat rail (Winterthur report)*.
DIMENSIONS: *height, 42½ inches; width, 25⅞; height of seat rail, 17*.
DESIGN AND CONSTRUCTION: *Back, spooned. Seat frame construction, as fig. 17. Bracing of seat frame, the depth of the seat frame. Knee brackets, medium-headed nails. Bracket responds, horizontal grain. No horizontal shaping. Through tenons, seat rail and bracket responds. Seating of splat in shoe.*
NOTES: *Base of seat shell applied with glue. New slip seat frame.*

Arm chair, Philadelphia, 1745–60. Courtesy of Henry Francis du Pont Winterthur Museum (Acc. no. 60.1039.1.2).

PRIMARY WOOD: *mahogony (Winterthur report)*.
DIMENSIONS: *height, 41¼ inches; width, 31¾; height of seat rail, 15⅝*.
DESIGN AND CONSTRUCTION: *Back, spooned. Seat frame construction, as fig. 17. Bracing of seat frame, the depth of the seat frame. Knee brackets, small-headed nails. Bracket responds, horizontal grain. No horizontal shaping. Through tenons, seat rail and bracket responds. Seating of splat in shoe.*
NOTES: *Back posts pieced out on outer edge above seat. New slip seat frame. Recorded as having been acquired from the descendants of Robert and Abigail Griffiths Smith, married in Philadelphia in 1760 (Downs, fig. 29).*

59

Arm chair, English, 1730–70. Present location unknown.

PRIMARY WOOD: *walnut*.
NOTES: *This chair not investigated personally*.

60

Arm chair, Philadelphia, 1745–95. Mabel Brady Garvan Collection, Yale University Art Gallery (Acc. no. 1930.2545).

PRIMARY WOOD: *walnut*. SECONDARY WOOD: *pine slip seat frame*.
DIMENSIONS: *height, 40¼ inches; width, 28⅛; height of seat rail, 17*.
DESIGN AND CONSTRUCTION: *Back, bowed. Seat frame construction, as fig. 19. Bracing of seat frame, corner blocks, new. Knee brackets, small-headed nails. No bracket responds, but rear of side horizontal shaping cut to reverse curve. Horizontal shaping. Through tenons. Seating of splat in shoe*.
NOTES: *Left rear leg shattered and repaired*.

61

Side chair, Philadelphia, 1745–95. Mabel Brady Garvan Collection, Yale University Art Gallery (Acc. no. 1930.2635).

PRIMARY WOOD: *walnut (Yale report).* SECONDARY WOOD: *pine slip seat frame.*

DIMENSIONS: *height, 40 inches; width, 23¼; height of seat rail, 17.*

DESIGN AND CONSTRUCTION: *Back, bowed. Seat frame construction, as fig. 19. No traces of any corner blocks. Knee brackets, large-headed nails. No bracket responds, but rear of side horizontal shaping cut to reverse curve. Horizontal shaping. Through tenons. Seating of splat in shoe.*

62

Side chair, Philadelphia, 1745–95, possibly by John Elliott, Sr. (1713–91). Courtesy of Henry Francis du Pont Winterthur Museum (Acc. no. 61.1526).

PRIMARY WOOD: *walnut.* SECONDARY WOOD: *pine corner blocks and slip seat frame.*

DIMENSIONS: *height, 40⅞ inches; width, 22½; height of seat rail, 17¼.*

DESIGN AND CONSTRUCTION: *Back, straight. Seat frame construction, as fig. 19. Bracing of seat frame, corner blocks, as fig. 18 in front; rear of vertical grain, square section with chamfered inner corner. Bracket responds. Horizontal shaping. No through tenons. Seating of splat in shoe.*

NOTES: *Elliott made a similar chair (Hornor, Blue Book, plate 68). Note that the chair lacks both through tenons and a bowed back.*

63

Low side chair, Philadelphia, 1745–95, possibly by William Savery (1721–88). Mabel Brady Garvan Collection, Yale University Art Gallery (Acc. no. 1930.2406).

PRIMARY WOOD: *walnut (Yale report).*
DIMENSIONS: *height, 36 inches; width, 23; height of seat rail, 13⅝.*
DESIGN AND CONSTRUCTION: *Back, bowed. Seat frame construction, as fig. 19. Bracing of seat frame, corner blocks, new. Knee brackets, large- and small-headed nails. No bracket responds. No horizontal shaping. Through tenons. Seating of splat in shoe.*
NOTES: *New slip seat frame. This chair has been attributed to William Savery because of similarity to the knee carving of Savery family pieces (lowboy in the* Pennsylvania Museum Bulletin, *no. 91, vol. XX, January 1925, p. 62 [illustrated]) and the pierced handhold in the top rail related to that in a labeled Savery chair (Downs, fig. 39).*

64

Side chair, Philadelphia, 1745–95. Mabel Brady Garvan Collection, Yale University Art Gallery (Acc. no. 1930.2411).

PRIMARY WOOD: *walnut.* SECONDARY WOODS: *white cedar and pine corner blocks; pine slip seat frame (Yale report).*
DIMENSIONS: *Height, 40½ inches; width, 22⅛; height of seat rail, 17⅜.*
DESIGN AND CONSTRUCTION: *Back, spooned. Seat frame construction, as fig. 19. Bracing of seat frame, corner blocks in front, as fig. 18. Knee brackets, large-headed nails. No bracket responds, but rear of side horizontal shaping cut to reverse curve. Horizontal shaping. Through tenons. Seating of splat in shoe.*

65

66

Side chair, Philadelphia, 1745–60. Collection of the Philadelphia Museum of Art (Acc. no. 40–19–1,2).

PRIMARY WOOD: *walnut.*
DIMENSIONS: *Height, 41⅜ inches; width, 21; height of seat rail, 16⅞.*
DESIGN AND CONSTRUCTION: *Back, bowed. Seat frame construction, as fig. 17. Bracing of seat frame, the depth of the seat frame. Knee brackets, medium-headed nails. Bracket responds, horizontal grain. No horizontal shaping. Through tenons, seat rail and bracket responds. Seating of splat in shoe.*
NOTES: *Back post pieced out on inner edge above seat, and of pointed-oval cross section. This is one of a pair of chairs owned by the museum; the information was recorded from Acc. no. 40–19–1 and the photograph was taken of Acc. no. 40–19–2.*

Arm chair, Philadelphia, 1755–95. Mabel Brady Garvan Collection, Yale University Art Gallery (Acc. no. 1930.2500).

PRIMARY WOOD: *walnut.* SECONDARY WOOD: *pine slip seat frame.*
DIMENSIONS: *height, 43⅛ inches; width, 30½; height of seat rail, 17.*
DESIGN AND CONSTRUCTION: *Back, bowed. Seat frame construction, as fig. 19. No traces of any corner blocks. Knee brackets, large-headed nails. No bracket responds. Horizontal shaping. Through tenons; arms also through-tenoned. Seating of splat in shoe.*
NOTES: *Downs, fig. 124, shows a similar splat with additional carving. Base or "foot" of back posts pieced out; this is the original construction, not a later repair.*

71

Side chair, Philadelphia,
Pont Winterthur Museu

PRIMARY WOOD: *mahoga*
blocks; tulip slip seat frai
DIMENSIONS: *height, 41*
17⅝.
DESIGN AND CONSTRUCTI
as fig. 19. Bracing of seat
complete; right front: on
Horizontal shaping. Thr
NOTES: *For Philadelphia*
59, see Stockwell adverti
This chair is recorded as
Lambert family in Phila

67

Arm chair, Philadelphia, 1755–95. Collection of the Philadelphia
Museum of Art, Cedar Grove (Acc. no. 28–7–7).

PRIMARY WOOD: *walnut.*
DIMENSIONS: *height, 42 inches; width, 35; height of seat rail, 17½.*
DESIGN AND CONSTRUCTION: *Back, bowed. Seat frame construction,*
as fig. 19. Bracing of seat frame, corner blocks, as fig. 18 in front,
and as fig. 28 in rear but with vertical grain. Additional pieces
applied at ends of inside rear seat rail to bring it flush with rear legs
and hold corner blocks. No bracket responds, but rear of side
horizontal shaping cut to reverse curve. Horizontal shaping; also on
rear seat rail. Through tenons. Seating of splat in shoe.
NOTES: *This chair is recorded as having belonged to Katherine*
Johnson (Jansen) Wistar (1703–86), at Cedar Grove (files of
the Philadelphia Museum of Art).

68

Side chair, Philadelphia, 1755–95. Mabel Brady Garvan Collection,
Yale University Art Gallery (Acc. no. 1930.2058).

PRIMARY WOOD: *mahogany.* SECONDARY WOOD: *white cedar corner*
blocks and slip seat frame (Yale report).
DIMENSIONS: *height, 40¾ inches; width, 23¼; height of seat rail, 17⅝.*
DESIGN AND CONSTRUCTION: *Back, bowed. Seat frame construction,*
as fig. 19. Bracing of seat frame, corner blocks, as fig. 19. Additional
pieces applied at ends of inside rear seat rail to bring it flush with
rear legs and hold corner blocks. No bracket responds, but rear of
side horizontal shaping cut to reverse curve. Horizontal shaping.
Through tenons. Seating of splat in shoe.

69

Side chair, [
Yale Univer

PRIMARY WO
frame.
DIMENSIONS
DESIGN AND
as fig. 19. B
responds. H
shoe.

73

Side chair, Pennsylvania, 1775–95. Collection of the Philadelphia Museum of Art (Acc. no. 55–63–1).

PRIMARY WOOD: *cherry.* SECONDARY WOOD: *tulip poplar corner blocks.* DIMENSIONS: *height, 40⅛ inches; width, 24; height of seat rail, 16¾.* DESIGN AND CONSTRUCTION: *Back, bowed. Seat frame construction, as fig. 19. Bracing of seat frame, corner blocks, related to those of fig. 19. Knee brackets, small-headed nails. No bracket responds, but rear of side horizontal shaping cut to reverse curve. Horizontal shaping. Through tenons. Seating of splat in shoe.*

74

Side chair, English, 1745–80. The Museum of Art, Rhode Island School of Design (Acc. no. 04.130).

PRIMARY WOOD: *mahogany.* SECONDARY WOOD: *mahogany corner blocks, beech cross-ties, mahogany plank slip seat.* DIMENSIONS: *Height, 37¾ inches; width, 23½; height of seat rail, 16⅞.* DESIGN AND CONSTRUCTION: *Back, bowed. Seat frame construction, as fig. 19. Bracing of seat frame, corner blocks, as fig. 19, but of small pieces that do not form a quarter-round section; also, old, possibly not original cross-ties. Knee brackets, glued to face of piece added like bracket responds to lower edge of seat frame. Bracket responds, made like end of horizontal shaping. No horizontal shaping. No through tenons. Seating of splat in shoe.* NOTES: *Slip seat is not a frame but a solid plank of mahogany.*

75

Side chair, Philadelphia, 1755–95. Mabel Brady Garvan Collection, Yale University Art Gallery (Acc. no. 1930.2105a).

PRIMARY WOOD: *mahogany.* SECONDARY WOOD: *pine slip seat frame.* DIMENSIONS: *height, 37½ inches; width, 23¾; height of seat rail, 16⅞.* DESIGN AND CONSTRUCTION: *Back, bowed. Seat frame construction, as fig. 19. Bracing of seat frame, corner blocks, new. Knee brackets nailed. No bracket responds, but rear of side horizontal shaping cut to reverse curve. Horizontal shaping. Through tenons. Seating of splat in shoe.*

76

Side chair, Philadelphia, 1755–95. Courtesy of Colonial Williamsburg (Acc. no. 1930.234.2).

PRIMARY WOOD: *mahogany.* SECONDARY WOOD: *pine slip seat frame.* DIMENSIONS: *height, 40¼ inches; width, 22¾; height of seat rail, 17.* DESIGN AND CONSTRUCTION: *Back, bowed. Seat frame construction, as fig. 19. No traces of any corner blocks. Knee brackets, glue only. No bracket responds. Horizontal shaping, also in rear. Through tenons. Seating of splat in shoe.*

77

Arm chair, English, 1740–70. The Old Hall, Gainsborough, Lincolnshire.

PRIMARY WOOD: *mahogany.* SECONDARY WOOD: *oak slip seat frame.*
DIMENSIONS: *height, 38½ inches; width, 26; height of seat rail, 17.*
DESIGN AND CONSTRUCTION: *Seat frame construction, as fig. 19 (seat rail thickness, ¾ inch). Bracing of seat frame, corner blocks, new. Knee brackets, thin in depth and backed with applied supports. Bracket responds, horizontal grain. No horizontal shaping. No through tenons.*

78

Arm chair, Philadelphia, 1755–95. Courtesy of Henry Francis du Pont Winterthur Museum (Acc. no. 60.1074).

PRIMARY WOOD: *walnut.* SECONDARY WOOD: *arbor vitae corner blocks (Winterthur report).*
DIMENSIONS: *height, 41½ inches; width, 30¾; height of seat rail, 17¼.*
DESIGN AND CONSTRUCTION: *Back, bowed. Seat frame construction, as fig. 19. Bracing of seat frame, corner blocks, as fig. 18 in front, rear blocks missing. Additional pieces applied at ends of inside rear seat rail to bring it flush with rear legs and hold corner blocks. Knee brackets nailed. No bracket responds but rear of side horizontal shaping cut to reverse curve. Horizontal shaping. Through tenons. Seating of splat in shoe.*
NOTES: *New slip seat frame.*

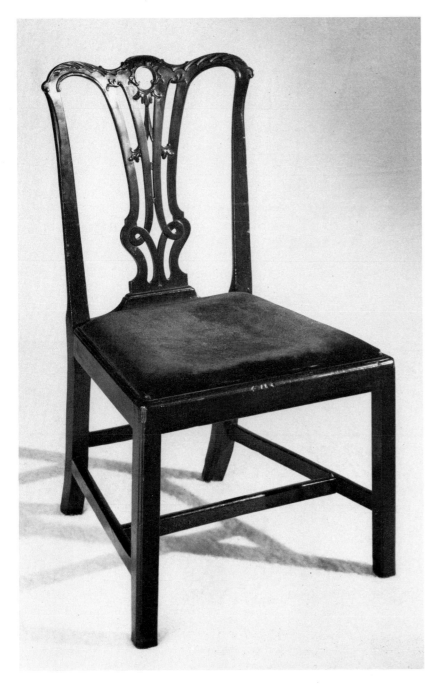

79

Side chair, English, 1750–80. Photo copyright, "The Council of Industrial Design, London, England." Formerly owned by M. Harrison & Sons (Neg. no. 508/83).

PRIMARY WOOD: *mahogany.*
NOTES: *This chair not investigated personally.*

80

Side chair, Philadelphia, 1755–95, possibly by Thomas Affleck (worked in America, 1763–95). Mabel Brady Garvan Collection, Yale University Art Gallery (Acc. no. 1930.2101b).

PRIMARY WOOD: *mahogany.* SECONDARY WOOD: *pine slip seat frame.*
DIMENSIONS: *height, 38¼ inches; width, 24¼; height of seat rail, 17⅜.*
DESIGN AND CONSTRUCTION: *Back, bowed. Seat frame construction, as fig. 19. Bracing of seat frame, corner blocks, new. Knee brackets, except right rear, replaced. Original block thin in depth and applied to face of drop of horizontal shaping. Bracket responds cut from the solid (see horizontal shaping) and shaped to reverse curve. Horizontal shaping, at sides and rear; front and front part of sides covered with knee brackets. No through tenons. Seating of splat in shoe.*
NOTES: *For attribution, see text, p.174.*

81

Side chair, Philadelphia, 1755–95, possibly by Thomas Affleck
(worked in America, 1763–95). Mabel Brady Garvan Collection,
Yale University Art Gallery (Acc. no. 1930.2104).

PRIMARY WOOD: *mahogany*. SECONDARY WOODS: *white cedar corner
blocks; pine slip seat frame; red gum inner face of rear seat rail (Yale
report).*
DIMENSIONS: *height, 39⅛ inches; width, 24½; height of seat rail,17⅛.*
DESIGN AND CONSTRUCTION: *Back, bowed. Seat frame construction,
as fig. 19. Bracing of seat frame, corner blocks, as fig. 19, front half
of front blocks original. Knee brackets re-attached with large-headed
nails, possibly in original holes. No bracket responds, but rear of
side horizontal shaping cut to reverse curve. Horizontal shaping.
Through tenons. Seating of splat in shoe.*
NOTES: *Left rib of splat partially replaced. Board applied inside rear seat
rail between it and corner blocks. For attribution, see text, p.174.*

82

Arm chair, Philadelphia, 1755–95, possibly by Thomas Affleck
(worked in America, 1763–95). Mabel Brady Garvan Collection,
Yale University Art Gallery (Acc. no. 1930.2103).

PRIMARY WOOD: *mahogany*. SECONDARY WOODS: *white cedar corner
blocks; pine slip seat frame.*
DIMENSIONS: *height, 37⅝ inches; width, 28¾; height of seat rail, 15¼.*
DESIGN AND CONSTRUCTION: *Back, bowed. Seat frame construction, as
fig. 19. Bracing of seat frame, corner blocks, as fig. 19; additional
pieces applied between corner blocks and rear seat rail. Knee brackets
attached with modern screws. No bracket responds. Horizontal
shaping in rear only. Through tenons. Seating of splat in shoe.*
NOTES: *For attribution, see text, p.174.*

83

83 *a*

Side chair. For date, see text, pp. 172–4. Courtesy of Museum of Fine Arts, Boston, M. and M. Karolik Collection (Acc. no. 41.602a).

Benjamin Randolph's label, on fig. 83.

PRIMARY WOOD: *mahogany.* SECONDARY WOOD: *oak slip seat frame.*
DIMENSIONS: *height, 38⅜ inches; width, 23¾; height of seat rail, 17.*
DESIGN AND CONSTRUCTION: *Back, bowed. Seat frame construction, as fig. 19. Bracing of seat frame, corner blocks, new. No bracket responds. Horizontal shaping; rear of side shaping applied. Through tenons, thin, 5⁄16 inch in width. Seating of splat in shoe.*

84

Side chair, English, 1754–80. Victoria and Albert Museum, London (Acc. no. W.8-1919).

PRIMARY WOOD: *mahogany.*
DIMENSIONS: *height, 38 inches; width, 21¼.*
NOTES: *This chair not investigated personally. Chippendale's pattern book source for this chair: 1754 and 1755 editions, plate XIII; 1762 edition, plate X.*

85

Arm chair, Philadelphia, 1755–95, possibly by James Gillingham (1736–81). Courtesy of Henry Francis du Pont Winterthur Museum (Acc. no. 57.666).

PRIMARY WOOD: *mahogany.* SECONDARY WOODS: *tulip and mahogany corner blocks (Winterthur report).*
DIMENSIONS: *height, 38¼ inches; width, 30¾; height of seat rail, 16⅞.*
DESIGN AND CONSTRUCTION: *Back, bowed. Seat frame construction, as fig. 19. Bracing of seat frame, corner blocks, as fig. 19. No bracket responds. Horizontal shaping. Through tenons; each side has a double tenon, one above the other. Seating of splat in shoe.*
NOTES: *Rear seat rail of same depth as back posts. Similar to labeled Gillingham chair in Taradash Collection, Antiques, 49 (June 1946), p. 359 [illustrated]. See also labeled chair, Antiques, 76 (November 1959), p. 394, and Lockwood, figs. 558 and 559. This back was also used by I. Duncan and others, probably including Thomas Tufft when he took over Gillingham's shop in 1773.*

86

Side chair, English, 1750–80. E. and D. Gibbs, London.

PRIMARY WOOD: *mahogany*.
NOTES: *This chair not investigated personally.*

87

Side chair, Philadelphia, 1755–95. Courtesy of Israel Sack, Inc., New York City, New York.

PRIMARY WOOD: *mahogany*. SECONDARY WOOD: *pine seat frame*.
DIMENSIONS: *height, 38⅛ inches; width, 24; height of seat rail. 15¾.*
DESIGN AND CONSTRUCTION: *Back, bowed. Seat frame construction, similar to fig. 19, although front legs are pinned through seat frame. Bracing of seat frame, the depth of the seat frame. No bracket responds. No horizontal shaping. Through tenons. Seating of splat in rear seat rail, passing behind shoe.*
NOTES: *This and its mate are the only over-upholstered horseshoe-seat Philadelphia Chippendale chairs yet discovered.*

88

88 *a*

Arm chair, Philadelphia, 1755–88, labeled by William Savery
(1721–88). Courtesy of Henry Francis du Pont Winterthur
Museum (Acc. no. 60.149).

William Savery's label, on fig. 88.

PRIMARY WOOD: *mahogany.* SECONDARY WOODS: *white cedar corner
blocks; pine and tulip poplar slip seat frame (Winterthur report);
pine inset.*
DIMENSIONS: *height, 38 inches; width, 30¼; height of seat rail, 15¾.*
DESIGN AND CONSTRUCTION: *Back, bowed. Seat frame construction,
as fig. 19. Bracing of seat frame, corner blocks, as fig. 19. No bracket
responds, but rear of side horizontal shaping cut to reverse curve.
Horizontal shaping. Through tenons. Seating of splat in shoe.*
NOTES: *Pine board applied to inner face of rear seat rail between
inner corners of rear legs.*

89

Side chair, Philadelphia 1755–95. Mabel Brady Garvan Collection, Yale University Art Gallery (Acc. no. 1930.2518).

PRIMARY WOOD: *mahogany.* SECONDARY WOODS: *tulip poplar corner blocks; pine slip seat frame; cherry inset.*
DIMENSIONS: *height, 38½ inches; width, 24½; height of seat rail, 16⅞.*
DESIGN AND CONSTRUCTION: *Back, bowed. Seat frame construction, as fig. 19. Bracing of seat frame, corner blocks, as fig. 19; front section of front blocks secured with wooden pin; left rear block replaced. Knee brackets of great depth, overlapping at inner corners. No bracket responds, but rear of side horizontal shaping cut to reverse curve. Horizontal shaping, also in rear. Through tenons. Seating of splat in shoe.*
NOTES: *Cherry board applied to inner face of rear seat rail between inner corners of rear legs.*

90

Side chair, Philadelphia, 1755–95. The Metropolitan Museum of Art, Sylmaris Collection; Gift of George Coe Graves, 1932 (Acc. no. 32.57.4).

PRIMARY WOOD: *mahogany.* SECONDARY WOOD: *pine corner blocks and slip seat frame.*
DIMENSIONS: *height, 38¼ inches; width, 24⅜; height of seat rail, 17.*
DESIGN AND CONSTRUCTION: *Back, bowed. Seat frame construction, as fig. 19. Bracing of seat frame, corner blocks, as fig. 19. Additional pieces applied at ends of inside rear seat rail to bring it flush with rear legs, and hold corner blocks. No bracket responds, but rear of side horizontal shaping cut to reverse curve. Horizontal shaping. Through tenons. Seating of splat in shoe.*
NOTES: *The feet show the retracted side talons usually associated with Massachusetts.*

91

Side chair, Philadelphia, 1760–87, labeled by Thomas Tufft (c. 1740–88). Courtesy of Henry Francis du Pont Winterthur Museum (Acc. no. 57.514).

PRIMARY WOOD: *mahogany.* SECONDARY WOOD: *white cedar corner blocks and slip seat frame (Winterthur report).*
DIMENSIONS: *height, 38½ inches; width, 23½; height of seat rail, 17.*
DESIGN AND CONSTRUCTION: *Back, bowed. Seat frame construction, as fig. 19. Bracing of seat frame, corner blocks, as fig. 19. No bracket responds, but rear of side horizontal shaping cut to reverse curve. Horizontal shaping. Through tenons. Seating of splat in shoe.*
NOTES: *The label is attached to ½ inch thick board, masking inner face of back rail. Tufft gave up business in 1787.*

91*a*

Thomas Tufft's label, on fig. 91.

92

Side chair, Philadelphia, 1760–92, labeled by Benjamin Randolph (worked c. 1760–92). Mabel Brady Garvan Collection, Yale University Art Gallery (Acc. no. 1930.2495).

PRIMARY WOOD: *mahogany*. SECONDARY WOOD: *white cedar corner blocks (Yale report)*.

DIMENSIONS: *height, 37 inches; width, 22⅞; height of seat rail, 16⅜*.

DESIGN AND CONSTRUCTION: *Back, straight. Seat frame construction, as fig. 19. Bracing of seat frame, corner block, as fig. 18, at front left. No bracket responds. No horizontal shaping. No through tenons. Seating of splat in shoe.*

NOTES: *It may be that the presence of stretchers here eliminated the need for the additional strength provided by through tenons and knee brackets. An unbowed back is unusual in developed Philadelphia work of this period. New slip seat frame.*

92 *a*

Benjamin Randolph's label, on fig. 92.

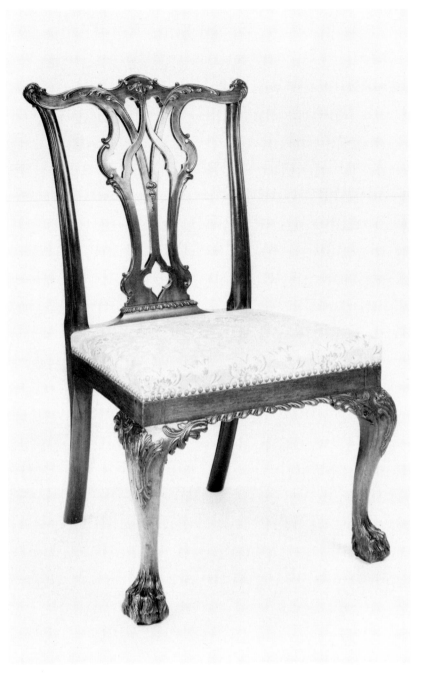

93

Side chair, Philadelphia, 1755–95. Courtesy of Henry Francis du Pont Winterthur Museum (Acc. no. 60.1066.2).

PRIMARY WOOD: *mahogany*. SECONDARY WOOD: *arbor vitae corner blocks (Winterthur report)*.
DIMENSIONS: *height, 38½ inches; width, 23½; height of seat rail, 17½*.
DESIGN AND CONSTRUCTION: *Back, bowed. Seat frame construction, as fig. 19. Bracing of seat frame, corner blocks, as fig. 19. Knee brackets, nailed. No bracket responds. No horizontal shaping. Though tenons. Seating of splat in shoe.*
NOTES: *The gadrooning is a separate piece applied with glue and nails. Rear seat rail of same depth as posts.*

94

Side chair, Philadelphia, 1763–95, possibly by Thomas Affleck (worked in America, 1763–95). Collection of the Philadelphia Museum of Art (Acc. no. 46-87-1).

PRIMARY WOOD: *mahogany*. SECONDARY WOODS: *pine corner blocks; tulip poplar inset*.
DIMENSIONS: *height, 39⅜ inches; width, 24⅜; height of seat rail, 17¼*.
DESIGN AND CONSTRUCTION: *Back, bowed. Seat frame construction, as fig. 19. Bracing of seat frame, corner blocks, as fig. 19 (rear with chamfered inner corner rather than quarter-round). No bracket responds, but rear of side horizontal shaping cut to reverse curve. Horizontal shaping. Through tenons. Seating of splat in shoe.*
NOTES: *Board applied to inside of rear seat rail between inner corners of rear legs. Hornor (Blue Book, plate 115) states that this chair was made by Thomas Affleck for the Fisher family of Wakefield. The design of its back was taken from Chippendale's pattern book (see fig. 228).*

95

Arm chair, Philadelphia, 1755–95. Courtesy of Henry Francis du Pont Winterthur Museum (Acc. no. 61.116).

PRIMARY WOOD: *mahogany.* SECONDARY WOODS: *tulip poplar, right rear corner block; white cedar, left rear corner block; pine slip seat frame (Winterthur report).*
DIMENSIONS: *height, 39 inches; width, 30½; height of seat rail, 16.*
DESIGN AND CONSTRUCTION: *Back, bowed. Seat frame construction, as fig. 19. Bracing of seat frame, corner blocks, as fig. 19, in rear. Knee brackets, nailed. No bracket responds. No horizontal shaping. Through tenons. Seating of splat in shoe.*
NOTES: *This chair is recorded as having belonged to Isaac Cooper Jones (1769–1865) (files of Henry Francis du Pont Winterthur Museum).*

96

Side chair, Philadelphia, 1755–95. Courtesy of Colonial Williamsburg (Acc. no. 30.241.1).

PRIMARY WOOD: *walnut.* SECONDARY WOOD: *pine corner blocks.*
DIMENSIONS: *height, 40 inches; width, 22½; height of seat rail, 16¾.*
DESIGN AND CONSTRUCTION: *Back, bowed. Seat frame construction, as fig. 19. Bracing of seat frame, corner blocks, as fig. 19. Knee brackets, small-headed nails. No bracket responds, but rear of side horizontal shaping cut to reverse curve. Horizontal shaping. Through tenons. Seating of splat in shoe.*
NOTES: *New slip seat frame.*

Massachusetts

FIGURES 97–125

97

Side chair, Massachusetts, 1730–60. Mabel Brady Garvan Collection, Yale University Art Gallery (Acc. no. 1930.2078).

PRIMARY WOOD: *walnut.* SECONDARY WOOD: *soft maple slip seat frame.*
DIMENSIONS: *height, 39½ inches; width, 21; height of seat rail, 16⅞.*
DESIGN AND CONSTRUCTION: *Back, spooned. Seat frame construction, as fig. 19. No traces of corner blocks. Knee brackets, probably originally attached with nails; right rear knee bracket replaced. No bracket responds. Horizontal shaping. No through tenons. Seating of splat in shoe.*

98

Side chair, English, 1715–40. Formerly Victoria and Albert Museum, London (Neg. no. 57411).

PRIMARY WOOD: *walnut.*
NOTES: *This chair not investigated personally. Recorded as having belonged to the Guild of the Apothecaries (files of Victoria and Albert Museum).*

99

Side chair, Massachusetts, 1730–60. Courtesy of Old Sturbridge Village (Acc. no. 5.1.756).

PRIMARY WOOD: *walnut.* SECONDARY WOOD: *maple slip seat frame.*
DIMENSIONS: *height, 40 inches; width, 20; height of seat rail, 16¾.*
DESIGN AND CONSTRUCTION: *Back, spooned. Seat frame construction, as fig. 19. Bracing of seat frame, no traces of corner blocks. Knee brackets, nailed. No bracket responds. Horizontal shaping. No through tenons. Seating of splat in shoe.*
NOTES: *According to tradition, this chair belonged to the Ellery family of Gloucester, Massachusetts.* J. LANGDON *is burned into rear seat rail and front stretcher of slip seat (Old Sturbridge Village files).*

100

Low arm chair, Massachusetts, 1730–60. Courtesy of Henry Francis du Pont Winterthur Museum (Acc. no. 58.2594).

PRIMARY WOOD: *walnut.*
DIMENSIONS: *height, 38 inches; width, 27⅞; height of seat rail, 12⅞.*
DESIGN AND CONSTRUCTION: *Back, spooned. Seat frame construction, as fig. 19. Bracing of seat frame, new small cross-ties. Knee brackets, nailed. No bracket responds. Horizontal shaping. No through tenons. Seating of splat in shoe.*

101

Side chair, Massachusetts, 1730–60. Mabel Brady Garvan Collection, Yale University Art Gallery (Acc. no. 1930.2626a).

PRIMARY WOOD: *walnut.* SECONDARY WOODS: *pine corner blocks; soft maple slip seat frame.*
DIMENSIONS: *height, 39¾ inches; width, 21½; height of seat rail, 16¼.*
DESIGN AND CONSTRUCTION: *Back, spooned. Seat frame construction, as fig. 27. Bracing of seat frame, corner blocks, as fig. 28, in front. Knee brackets, nailed. No bracket responds. Horizontal shaping. No through tenons. Seating of splat in shoe.*
NOTES: *This chair and its mates are recorded as having belonged to Edward Holyoke, president of Harvard College, 1737–69 (files of Yale University Art Gallery).*

102

Side chair, Massachusetts, 1730–60. Collection of the Philadelphia
Museum of Art; Charles F. Williams (Acc. no. 23-23-37).

PRIMARY WOOD: *walnut*. SECONDARY WOOD: *pine corner blocks.*
DIMENSIONS: *height, 39⅛ inches; width, 22; height of seat rail, 16⅜.*
DESIGN AND CONSTRUCTION: *Back, spooned. Seat frame construction,
as fig. 27. Bracing of seat frame, as fig. 28, in front, renailed. No
bracket responds. Horizontal shaping. No through tenons. Seating of
splat in shoe.*
NOTES: *New slip seat frame.*

103

Side chair, Massachusetts, 1755–95. Mabel Brady Garvan
Collection, Yale University Art Gallery (Acc. no. 1930.2116).

PRIMARY WOOD: *mahogany*. SECONDARY WOOD: *soft maple slip seat frame.*
DIMENSIONS: *height, 37¾ inches; width, 22¾; height of seat rail, 16⅞.*
DESIGN AND CONSTRUCTION: *Back, straight. Seat frame construction,
as fig. 27. No traces of any corner blocks. Knee brackets, small-headed
nails. No bracket responds. Horizontal shaping. No through tenons.
Seating of splat in shoe.*
NOTES: *For English chairs with retracted claw feet other than those
included here, see: Antiques, 3 (June 1923), p. 296, fig. 13; R. W.
Symonds, English Furniture, p. 36, fig. 15; Bulletin of the Museum
of Fine Arts, Boston, vol. XXXI, 1933, p. 14. For Dutch examples,
see reference on p. 34, footnote 14.*

104

Side chair, Massachusetts, 1755–95. Mabel Brady Garvan Collection, Yale University Art Gallery (Acc. no. 1930.2563).

PRIMARY WOOD: *mahogany*. SECONDARY WOODS: *white pine corner blocks; soft maple slip seat frame.*
DIMENSIONS: *height, 38 inches; width, 22¼; height of seat rail, 17⅛.*
DESIGN AND CONSTRUCTION: *Back, straight. Seat frame construction, as fig. 27. Bracing of seat frame, corner blocks, as fig. 28. Knee brackets, nailed. Bracket responds, also on rear rail, vertical grain, attached with nails. Horizontal shaping, including rear rail. No through tenons. Seating of splat in shoe.*

105

Side chair, English, 1750–80. Sold at auction, Brunn Rosmussen, Copenhagen, 1962 (Cat. no. 16.77).

PRIMARY WOOD: *mahogany.*
DIMENSIONS: *height, 37⅜ inches; height of seat rail, 16½.*
DESIGN AND CONSTRUCTION: *Seat frame construction, as fig. 19. No horizontal shaping.*
NOTES: *Made in England for Løvenborg Manor House, Denmark, and probably purchased through their London agent, John Collett (who died in 1759), and sold with other English pieces from the house. This chair not investigated personally, but it was studied in detail by the Nationalmuseet, Copenhagen.*

106

Side chair, Massachusetts, 1755–95. Mabel Brady Garvan Collection, Yale University Art Gallery (Acc. no. 1930.2127).

PRIMARY WOOD: *mahogany.* SECONDARY WOODS: *white pine corner blocks; soft maple slip seat frame.*
DIMENSIONS: *height, 37¾ inches; width, 23⅛; height of seat rail, 16⅜.*
DESIGN AND CONSTRUCTION: *Back, straight. Seat frame construction, as fig. 19. Bracing of seat frame, corner blocks, as fig. 28. Knee brackets, small-headed nails. No bracket responds. No horizontal shaping. No through tenons. Seating of splat in shoe.*

107

Side chair, Masachusetts, 1755–95. Mabel Brady Garvan Collection, Yale University Art Gallery (Acc. no. 1930.2478).

PRIMARY WOOD: *mahogany.* SECONDARY WOOD: *soft maple slip seat frame.*
DIMENSIONS: *height, 37⅝ inches; width, 23⅜; height of seat rail, 16½.*
DESIGN AND CONSTRUCTION: *Back, straight. Seat frame construction, as fig. 19. No traces of any corner blocks. Knee brackets, new nails. No bracket responds. No horizontal shaping. No through tenons. Seating of splat in shoe.*

108

Side chair, Massachusetts, 1755–95. Mabel Brady Garvan Collection, Yale University Art Gallery (Acc. no. 1930.2738).

PRIMARY WOOD: *mahogany*. SECONDARY WOOD: *soft maple seat frame (all four rails)*.
DIMENSIONS: *height, 37⅜ inches; width, 22¾; height of seat rail, 16¼.*
DESIGN AND CONSTRUCTION: *Back, straight. Seat frame construction, as fig. 19. Bracing of seat frame, corner blocks, new. Knee brackets, small-headed nails, some original. No bracket responds. No horizontal shaping. No through tenons. Seating of splat in rear seat rail, passing behind shoe.*
NOTES: *Rear rail not mahogany.*

109

Arm chair, Massachusetts, 1755–95. Courtesy of Henry Francis du Pont Winterthur Museum (Acc. no. 52.234).

PRIMARY WOOD: *mahogany*. SECONDARY WOOD: *maple seat frame (all four rails)*.
DIMENSIONS: *height, 38¼ inches; width, 26¾; height of seat rail, 18.*
DESIGN AND CONSTRUCTION: *Back, straight. Seat frame construction, as fig. 19. No bracing of seat frame. Knee brackets, new nails. No bracket responds. No horizontal shaping. No through tenons. Seating of splat in rear seat rail, passing behind shoe.*
NOTES: *Rear rail not mahogany. Repairs to rear seat rail.*

110

Side chair, English, 1750–80. Bolling Hall, Bradford, Yorkshire.

PRIMARY WOOD: *mahogany.*

DIMENSIONS: *height, 38½ inches; width, 23¾; height of seat rail, 17.*

DESIGN AND CONSTRUCTION: *Seat frame construction, as fig. 19 (thickness of seat frame, ⅞ inch). Bracing of seat frame, cross-ties in front; as fig. 28 in rear. Bracket responds, horizontal grain, tenoned into back leg and pinned through tenon, as is seat rail above. No horizontal shaping. No through tenons. Seating of splat in shoe, which is tenoned into back posts.*

NOTES: *Gadrooning: separate piece, applied with glue and nails.*

111

Side chair, Massachusetts, 1755–95 (see Notes below for possible attribution). Mabel Brady Garvan Collection, Yale University Art Gallery (Acc. no. 1950. 715).

PRIMARY WOOD: *mahogany.* SECONDARY WOOD: *soft maple slip seat frame.*

DIMENSIONS: *height, 37⅝ inches; width, 23½; height of seat rail, 17.*

DESIGN AND CONSTRUCTION: *Back, straight. Seat frame construction, as fig. 19. Bracing of seat frame, corner blocks right rear, as fig. 27. Bracket responds, vertical grain, right one replaced. Horizontal shaping. No through tenons. Seating of splat in rear seat rail, passing behind shoe.*

NOTES: *Back of rear seat rail stamped* D. AUSTIN, *possibly maker or owner.*

112

Side chair, Massachusetts, 1755–95. Mrs. Francis P. Garvan.

PRIMARY WOOD: *mahogany*. SECONDARY WOOD: *maple corner blocks*.
DIMENSIONS: *height, 36⅜ inches; width, 22⅛; height of seat rail, 17*.
DESIGN AND CONSTRUCTION: *Back, straight. Seat frame construction, as fig. 19. Bracing of seat frame, corner blocks, as fig. 28. No bracket responds. No horizontal shaping. No through tenons. Seating of splat in rear seat rail, passing behind shoe.*

113

Side chair, Massachusetts, 1765–95. Courtesy of Henry Francis du Pont Winterthur Museum (Acc. no. 56.52).

PRIMARY WOOD: *mahogany*. SECONDARY WOODS: *white pine corner blocks; maple and birch seat frame. (Winterthur report)*.
DIMENSIONS: *height, 37⅞ inches; width, 23¾; height of seat rail, 16½*.
DESIGN AND CONSTRUCTION: *Back, straight. Seat frame construction, as fig. 19. Bracing of seat frame, corner blocks, as fig. 28, re-attached with nails and screws. Bracket responds. No horizontal shaping. No through tenons. Seating of splat in rear seat rail, passing behind shoe.*
NOTES: *See Notes, fig. 114.*

114

Side chair, Massachusetts, 1765–95. The Metropolitan Museum of Art; Gift of Mrs. Paul Moore, 1939 (Acc. no. 39.88.2).

PRIMARY WOOD: *mahogany.* SECONDARY WOODS: *pine corner blocks; maple seat frame.*

DIMENSIONS: *height, 38¾ inches; width, 23¾; height of seat rail, 16⅝.*

DESIGN AND CONSTRUCTION: *Back, straight. Seat frame construction, as fig. 19. Bracing of seat frame, corner blocks, as fig. 27. Knee brackets, large-headed nails. Bracket responds, horizontal grain, tenoned into leg and secured with small-headed nails. No horizontal shaping. No through tenons. Seating of splat in rear seat rail, passing behind shoe.*

NOTES: *This back is copied from plate 9 of Robert Manwaring's 1765 pattern book. The chair is recorded as having originally belonged to Clark Gayton Pickman (1746–89) of Salem, in whose family it descended (files of the Metropolitan Museum of Art).*

115

Side chair, Massachusetts, 1755–95. Courtesy of Henry Francis du Pont Winterthur Museum (Acc. no. 51.64.8).

PRIMARY WOOD: *mahogany.* SECONDARY WOODS: *mahogany left rear corner block; bald cypress (Winterthur report) or birch slip seat frame; beech rear seat rail (Winterthur report).*

DIMENSIONS: *height 37⅞ inches; width, 23¾; height of seat rail, 17.*

DESIGN AND CONSTRUCTION: *Back, straight. Seat frame construction, as fig. 19. Bracing of seat frame, original rear corner block, small, quarter-round, of vertical grain. Bracket responds, original one of vertical grain, nailed. No horizontal shaping. No through tenons. Seating of splat in shoe.*

NOTES: *Unusual corner block wood for Massachusetts.*

116

Side chair, Massachusetts, 1755–95. Olivia Dann Collection, Yale University Art Gallery (Acc. no. 1962.31.1).

PRIMARY WOOD: *mahogany.* SECONDARY WOODS: *white pine corner blocks; soft maple side and front rails.*
DIMENSIONS: *height 37½ inches; width, 23½; height of seat rail, 17.*
DESIGN AND CONSTRUCTION: *Back, bowed. Seat frame construction, as fig. 19. Bracing of seat frame, corner blocks, as fig. 28, possibly original and re-attached. Knee brackets, small-headed nails. No horizontal shaping. No through tenons. Seating of splat in rear seat rail, passing behind the shoe.*
NOTES: *Note use of early Classical Revival twist to base of the rear posts. This is not simply an enlarged foot as in fig. 115.*

117

Side chair, Massachusetts, 1755–95. The Museum of Art, Rhode Island School of Design (Acc. no. 44.038).

PRIMARY WOOD: *mahogany.* SECONDARY WOOD: *maple slip seat frame.*
DIMENSIONS: *height, 37⅛ inches; width, 23; height of seat rail, 16⅜.*
DESIGN AND CONSTRUCTION: *Back, straight. Seat frame construction, as fig. 19. Bracing of seat frame, front corner blocks, and iron angle irons, new; no traces of rear corner blocks. Knee brackets, small-headed nails, perhaps some original. Bracket responds, horizontal grain at sides, vertical grain in rear; small-headed nails. No horizontal shaping. No through tenons. Seating of splat in shoe.*
NOTES: *Right rear knee bracket new.*

118

Side chair, Massachusetts, 1755–95. Courtesy of The Henry Ford Museum.

PRIMARY WOOD: *mahogany.* SECONDARY WOOD: *maple seat frame.*
DIMENSIONS: *height, 37 inches; width, 23; height of seat rail, 17¼.*
DESIGN AND CONSTRUCTION: *Seat frame construction, as fig. 19. Bracing of seat frame, evidence of former corner blocks. No bracket responds. No horizontal shaping. No through tenons. Seating of splat in rear seat rail, passing behind shoe.*

119

Side chair, Massachusetts, 1755–95. Courtesy of The Henry Ford Museum (Acc. no. 67.39).

PRIMARY WOOD: *mahogany.* SECONDARY WOOD: *maple slip seat frame.*
DIMENSIONS: *height, 36½ inches; width, 23; height of seat rail, 16¾.*
DESIGN AND CONSTRUCTION: *Back, straight. Seat frame construction, as fig. 19 (thickness of seat rail, ⅞ inch). Bracing of seat frame, corner blocks, as fig. 28, possibly original. Knee brackets, small-headed nails; side brackets thin in depth. Bracket responds, vertical grain, attached with small nails. No horizontal shaping. No through tenons. Seating of splat in shoe.*
NOTES: *For related, but more elaborate arm and side chairs with standard Massachusetts retracted claw, see Antiques, 11 (June 1927), p. 439 [illustrated].*

120

Side chair, Massachusetts, 1755–95. Mabel Brady Garvan Collection, Yale University Art Gallery (Acc. no. 1930.2562).

PRIMARY WOOD: *mahogany.* SECONDARY WOOD: *soft maple slip seat frame.*

DIMENSIONS: *height, 37 inches; width, 23; height of seat rail, 17⅛.*

DESIGN AND CONSTRUCTION: *Back, straight. Seat frame construction, as fig. 19. Bracing of seat frame, corner blocks, new. Knee brackets, large-headed nails. No bracket responds. Horizontal shaping. No through tenons. Seating of splat in shoe.*

121

Arm chair, English, 1750–80. Location unknown.

PRIMARY WOOD: *mahogany.*

NOTES: *This chair not investigated personally. For related English side chair, see Ralph Edwards,* The Shorter Dictionary of English Furniture, *fig. 116, p. 147.*

122

Side chair, Massachusetts, 1755–95. Mabel Brady Garvan Collection, Yale University Art Gallery (Acc. no. 1963.18.2).

PRIMARY WOOD: *mahogany*. SECONDARY WOODS: *white pine corner blocks; soft maple slip seat frame.*
DIMENSIONS: *height, 38⅛ inches; width, 25; height of seat rail, 17.*
DESIGN AND CONSTRUCTION: *Back, straight, with crest rail strongly concave. Seat frame construction, as fig. 19. Bracing of seat frame, corner blocks, as fig. 28, probably original and re-attached with original round-head nails. Knee brackets, nailed. Bracket responds, horizontal grain, tenoned into back posts and pinned through posts. No horizontal shaping. No through tenons. Seating of splat in shoe, which is one piece with back seat rail.*
NOTES: *This chair is recorded as having belonged to James Swan (1754–1830) of Boston and Dorchester (Randall, American Furniture, fig. 155).*

123

Arm chair, Massachusetts, 1755–95. Yale University Art Gallery, property of Sterling Library (Acc. no. 1967.26).

PRIMARY WOOD: *mahogany*. SECONDARY WOODS: *soft maple cross-braces and seat frame; birch rear corner blocks (Yale report).*
DIMENSIONS: *height, 37½ inches; width, 27; height of seat rail, 16⅝.*
DESIGN AND CONSTRUCTION: *Back, bowed. Seat frame construction, as fig. 28. Bracing of seat frame, cross-ties, and two types of corner blocks, as fig. 19 in front, as fig. 27 in rear, with round-headed nails. Knee brackets, new screws. Bracket responds, cut from the solid and over-upholstered. No horizontal shaping. No through tenons. Seating of splat in rear seat rail, passing behind shoe.*
NOTES: *This chair and its mates are recorded (on brass plaque attached to back of rear seat rail) as having been used by Governor Jonathan Belcher, descending in 1757 to his heirs. They were in the Sterling Library before 1904.*

124

Side chair, English, 1750–80. Victoria and Albert Museum, London.

PRIMARY WOOD: *mahogany.*
DIMENSIONS: *height, 36¾ inches; width, 22½.*
NOTES: *This chair not investigated personally.*

125

Side chair, Massachusetts, 1755–95. Courtesy of Museum of Fine Arts, Boston; Gift of Mrs. Carrington Weems (Acc. no. 60.1176).

PRIMARY WOOD: *mahogany.* SECONDARY WOODS: *pine corner blocks; maple slip seat frame.*
DIMENSIONS: *height, 37 inches; width, 23⅝; height of seat rail, 16⅝.*
DESIGN AND CONSTRUCTION: *Back, straight. Seat frame construction, as fig. 19. Bracing of seat frame, corner blocks, as fig. 28; secured with round-headed nails, and stained red as in England. Knee brackets, possibly new nails. No bracket responds. No horizontal shaping. No through tenons. Seating of splat in shoe.*
NOTES: *This chair recorded as having descended in the Lane family of Boston (Randall, American Furniture, fig. 150).*

New York

FIGURES 126–152

126

Side chair, New York, 1740–90. Courtesy of Albany Institute of History and Art.

PRIMARY WOOD: *mahogany.* SECONDARY WOOD: *oak rear seat rail and slip seat frame.*
DIMENSIONS: *height, 39 inches; width, 21¾; height of seat rail, 16.*
DESIGN AND CONSTRUCTION: *Back, splat spooned, posts straight. Seat frame construction, as fig. 27. Bracing of seat frame, corner blocks, new. No bracket responds, but rear of side horizontal shaping cut to reverse curve. Horizontal shaping. No through tenons. Seating of splat in shoe.*
NOTES: *Back posts pieced out on inner edge above seat.*

127

Side chair, New York, 1740–90. Mabel Brady Garvan Collection, Yale University Art Gallery (Acc. no. 1952.20.2).

PRIMARY WOOD: *mahogany.* SECONDARY WOODS: *white oak cross-ties and slip seat frame; white pine corner blocks in slip seat frame; beech rear seat rail. (Microanalysis of rear seat rail of chair from same set, at Winterthur, shows "American beech.")*
DIMENSIONS: *height, 41¾ inches; width, 22¾; height of seat rail, 17.*
DESIGN AND CONSTRUCTION: *Back, spooned. Seat frame construction, as fig. 27. Bracing of seat frame, cross-ties. Knee brackets, right rear replaced. Bracket responds, vertical grain, nailed. No horizontal shaping. No through tenons. Seating of splat in rear seat rail, passing behind shoe.*
NOTES: *Back posts pieced out on inner edge above seat; inner top edge of right seat rail pieced out.*

128

Side chair, New York, 1735–90. Courtesy of Museum of the City of New York (Acc. no. 53.150.8).

PRIMARY WOOD: *walnut.* SECONDARY WOODS: *tulip poplar corner blocks; maple slip seat frame; splat veneered on maple.*
DIMENSIONS: *height, 39½ inches; width, 21¾; height of seat rail, 17¼.*
DESIGN AND CONSTRUCTION: *Back, splat spooned, posts straight. Seat frame construction, as fig. 27. Bracing of seat frame, corner blocks, as fig. 28, right rear block missing. Knee brackets, nailed. No bracket responds. Horizontal shaping. No through tenons. Seating of splat* in shoe.
NOTES: *Back posts pieced out on inner edge above seat.*

129

Arm chair, New York, 1740–95. Courtesy of Henry Francis du Pont Winterthur Museum (Acc. no. 63.614.1).

PRIMARY WOOD: *walnut.* SECONDARY WOODS: *pine corner blocks; red gum slip seat frame (Winterthur report).*
DIMENSIONS: *height, 39⅜ inches; width, 26¼; height of seat rail, 16½.*
DESIGN AND CONSTRUCTION: *Back, splat spooned, posts straight. Seat frame construction, as fig. 27. Bracing of seat frame, corner blocks, as fig. 28 in front. Bracket responds, vertical grain; placed below rear applied "shaping." Horizontal shaping, applied "shaping" on rear of side rails only, as fig. 130. No through tenons. Seating of splat in shoe.*
NOTES: *Back posts pieced out on inner edge above seat.*

130

Side chair, New York, 1740–90. Courtesy of Ginsburg and Levy, Inc., New York City, New York.

PRIMARY WOOD: *walnut.* SECONDARY WOODS: *pine corner blocks; maple slip seat frame; splat veneered on maple.*
DIMENSIONS: *height, 38½ inches; width, 22; height of seat rail, 16.*
DESIGN AND CONSTRUCTION: *Back, splat spooned, posts straight. Seat frame construction, as fig. 27. Bracing of seat frame, corner blocks, as fig. 28 in front, probably original ones re-applied with screws. Knee brackets, small nails. Bracket responds, vertical grain, under applied rear horizontal grain "shaping." Horizontal shaping, applied "shaping" on rear of side seat rails only. No through tenons. Seating of splat in shoe, which is one piece with the rear seat rail.*
NOTES: *Interesting veneering of splat, and molding of outer edge of side stretchers. Back posts pieced out on inner edge above seat. According to tradition, this chair descended from the Apthorp family of New York (Comstock, fig. 161).*

131

Side chair, New York, 1740–95. Lent to the Museum of the City of New York by Anderson C. Bouchelle (Acc. no. L5234).

PRIMARY WOOD: *walnut.* SECONDARY WOODS: *pine corner blocks; maple slip seat frame; splat veneered on tulip poplar.*
DIMENSIONS: *height, 38½ inches; width, 21½; height of seat rail. 15¾.*
DESIGN AND CONSTRUCTION: *Back, splat spooned, posts straight. Seat frame construction, as fig. 27. Bracing of seat frame, corner blocks left front and right rear, as fig. 28; others replaced. Knee brackets, thin in depth and attached to applied backing. Bracket responds, vertical grain, under applied rear horizontal "shaping," also used on rear seat rail. Horizontal shaping, applied "shaping" on rear of side seat rail only. No through tenons. Seating of splat in shoe, which is one piece with rail.*
NOTES: *Back posts pieced out on inner and outer edge above seat.*

132

Side chair, New York, 1740–95. Courtesy of Israel Sack, Inc., New York City, New York.

PRIMARY WOOD: *cherry.* SECONDARY WOODS: *pine corner blocks; cherry slip seat frame.*
DIMENSIONS: *height, 39¼ inches; width, 22⅝; height of seat rail, 17.*
DESIGN AND CONSTRUCTION: *Back, splat straight, posts spooned. Seat frame construction, as fig. 27. Bracing of seat frame, corner blocks, as fig. 19; pieces glued between rear seat rail and corner blocks. Knee brackets, backed with added pieces. Bracket responds, horizontal grain. No horizontal shaping. No through tenons. Seating of splat in shoe.*
NOTES: *Back posts pieced out on inner edge above seat. Thin strip nailed to inside of rear seat rail on one of pair.*

133

Side chair, New York, 1740–95. The Metropolitan Museum of Art;
Dick Fund, 1940 (Acc. no. 40.100.2).

PRIMARY WOOD: *walnut.* SECONDARY WOODS: *pine corner blocks;
maple and cherry slip seat frame; oak cross-tie.*
DIMENSIONS: *height, 38¾ inches; width, 22¾; height of seat rail, 16⅞.*
DESIGN AND CONSTRUCTION: *Back, straight. Seat frame construction,
as fig. 27. Bracing of seat frame, corner blocks, as fig. 18 in front; rear
blocks replaced. Knee brackets, thin in depth, attached to applied
backing, small nails. Bracket responds, horizontal grain, small nails.
No horizontal shaping. No through tenons. Seating of splat in shoe.*
NOTES: *Board applied to inside of rear seat rail between inner corners
of rear legs. Back posts pieced out on inner edge above seat. Slip seat
frame has cross-tie from front to back. It is recorded that this chair was
acquired from a descendant of the original owner, Cornelius Willet,
and that this seems to be the chair mentioned in a will probated July
14, 1792 (files of the Metropolitan Museum of Art).*

134

Side chair, New York, 1730–60. Courtesy of Henry Francis du Pont
Winterthur Museum (Acc. no. 58.961).

PRIMARY WOOD: *cherry.* SECONDARY WOODS: *pine corner blocks; maple
slip seat frame.*
DIMENSIONS: *height, 39½ inches; width, 22¾; height of seat rail, 17.*
DESIGN AND CONSTRUCTION: *Back, spooned. Seat frame construction,
as fig. 19. Bracing of seat frame, corner blocks, similar to fig. 19, but
the two pieces are larger and not shaped to quarter-round. Knee
brackets, new, thin in depth and attached to seat rail that drops down
behind. Bracket responds, cut from solid. Very shallow horizontal
shaping. No through tenons. Seating of splat in shoe.*
NOTES: *New slip seat frame (Winterthur report).*

135

Side chair, New York, 1745–95. Courtesy of Ginsburg and Levy, Inc., New York City, New York.

PRIMARY WOOD: *mahogany.* SECONDARY WOODS: *pine corner blocks and slip seat frame; maple rear seat rail.*
DIMENSIONS: *height, 38⅞ inches; width, 22¾; height of seat rail, 17¼.*
DESIGN AND CONSTRUCTION: *Back, straight. Seat frame construction, as fig. 19. Bracing of seat frame, corner blocks, as fig. 19. Knee brackets, glued to backings. Bracket responds, horizontal grain. No horizontal shaping. No through tenons. Seating of splat in shoe.*
NOTES: *Back legs flat on front and rounded behind. Rear seat rail same depth as back posts. One row of punch work around shell of crest rail, two rows around knee shells.*

136

Arm chair, New York, 1755–95. The Metropolitan Museum of Art; Purchase, 1932 (Acc. no. 32.107).

PRIMARY WOOD: *mahogany.* SECONDARY WOODS: *pine corner blocks; maple slip seat frame; cherry rear seat rail.*
DIMENSIONS: *height, 39⅛ inches; width, 26½; height of seat rail, 17⅛.*
DESIGN AND CONSTRUCTION: *Back, straight. Seat frame construction, as fig. 19. Bracing of seat frame, corner blocks, as fig. 28 in front, and probably original. Bracket responds cut from solid. No horizontal shaping. No through tenons. Seating of splat in shoe.*
NOTES: *The gadrooning is a separate piece attached with nails. Back rail of extreme depth. This chair is recorded as having formerly belonged to Jeremias Van Rensselaer (files of the Metropolitan Museum of Art).*

137

Side chair, New York, 1755–95. Courtesy of Albany Institute of History and Art.

PRIMARY WOOD: *mahogany*. SECONDARY WOOD: *cherry slip seat frame*.
DIMENSIONS: *height, 38½ inches; width, 24; height of seat rail, 17.*
DESIGN AND CONSTRUCTION: *Seat frame construction, as fig. 19. No bracing of seat frame. Bracket responds, vertical grain. No horizontal shaping. Through tenons. Seating of splat in shoe.*
NOTES: *This chair is recorded as having been in the Van Rensselaer Manor House during the brief occupancy of Stephen Van Rensselaer, II. After his death in 1790 his widow, the former Catherine Livingston, married Domine Eliardus Westerlo, and this chair descended in their children's family (Rice, p. 27).*

138

Side chair, New York, 1755–95. Courtesy of Museum of the City of New York (Acc. no. 43.335.1a).

PRIMARY WOOD: *mahogany*.
DIMENSIONS: *38½ inches; width, 22⅝; height of seat rail, 17.*
DESIGN AND CONSTRUCTION: *Back, straight. Seat frame construction, as fig. 19. Bracing of seat frame, corner blocks, new. Knee brackets, thin in depth and attached with applied backing. Bracket responds, horizontal grain. No horizontal shaping. No through tenons. Seating of splat in shoe.*
NOTES: *The carved seat edging is a separate piece attached with glue and nails. Top 1½ inches of front and side seat rails replaced. New slip seat frame. This chair is recorded as having been made for Whitehead Hicks, mayor of New York (1766–76) and descending in his family (Miller, no. 66).*

139

140

Side chair, New York, 1755–95, possibly by Gilbert Ash (see Notes below). Courtesy of Henry Francis du Pont Winterthur Museum (Acc. no. 56.98.3).

PRIMARY WOOD: *mahogany*. SECONDARY WOODS: *hard pine slip seat frame; beach rear seat rail (Winterthur report)*.
DIMENSIONS: *height, 38¾ inches; width, 22¾; height of seat rail, 16⅞*.
DESIGN AND CONSTRUCTION: *Back, straight. Seat frame construction, as fig. 19. No traces of corner blocks. Knee brackets, large-headed nails. No bracket responds. Horizontal shaping. Through tenons. Seating of splat in shoe.*
NOTES: *The pencil inscription, which includes the name of Gilbert Ash, is not accepted by the Winterthur Museum as contemporary (see footnote 1, p. 42).*

Side chair, New York, 1755–95. Courtesy of Museum of the City of New York (Acc. no. 51.117.87).

PRIMARY WOOD: *mahogany*. SECONDARY WOOD: *pine corner blocks*.
DIMENSIONS: *height, 39 inches; width, 23½; height of seat rail, 16¾*.
DESIGN AND CONSTRUCTION: *Back, straight. Seat frame construction, as fig. 19. Bracing of seat frame, corner blocks, as fig. 28. Knee brackets, left front bracket replaced. Bracket responds, horizontal grain, one applied, one possibly cut from solid. No horizontal shaping. No through tenons. Seating of splat in shoe.*
NOTES: *The gadrooning is a separate piece applied with glue and nails.*

141

Side chair, New York, 1755–95. Courtesy of New Haven Colony Historical Society.

PRIMARY WOOD: *mahogany.* SECONDARY WOODS: *pine corner blocks; tulip poplar slip seat frame.*
DIMENSIONS: *height, 38¾ inches; width, 23; height of seat rail, 17⅛.*
DESIGN AND CONSTRUCTION: *Seat frame construction, as fig. 19. Bracing of seat frame, corner blocks, as fig. 19. Small pieces glued between inner face of rear seat rail and corner blocks. No bracket responds. No horizontal shaping. Through tenons. Seating of splat in shoe.*

142

Side chair, New York, 1755–95. Courtesy of Albany Institute of History and Art.

PRIMARY WOOD: *mahogany.* SECONDARY WOOD: *pine corner blocks.*
DIMENSIONS: *height, 38½ inches; width, 22⅝; height of seat rail, 17.*
DESIGN AND CONSTRUCTION: *Seat frame construction, as fig. 19. Bracing of seat frame, corner blocks, as fig. 19. Bracket responds, horizontal grain. No horizontal shaping. No through tenons. Seating of splat in shoe.*
NOTES: *This chair is recorded as having belonged to Philip and Maria Van Rensselaer (Rice, p. 25).*

147

Side chair, New York, 1755–95. Mabel Brady Garvan Collection, Yale University Art Gallery (Acc. no. 1963.11a).

PRIMARY WOOD: *mahogany*. SECONDARY WOODS: *red gum and mahogany corner blocks; red gum slip seat frame and rear seat rail.*
DIMENSIONS: *height, 39⅝ inches; width, 24¾; height of seat rail, 17¾.*
DESIGN AND CONSTRUCTION: *Back, straight. Seat frame construction, as fig. 19. Bracing of seat frame, corner blocks, as fig. 19. Small pieces glued between inner face of rear seat rail and corner blocks. Bracket responds, horizontal grain. No horizontal shaping. No through tenons. Seating of splat in shoe.*

148

Side chair, New York, 1755–95. Courtesy of Albany Institute of History and Art.

PRIMARY WOOD: *mahogany*. SECONDARY WOODS: *pine corner blocks; tulip poplar slip seat frame.*
DIMENSIONS: *height, 38⅝ inches; width, 22¼; height of seat rail, 17.*
DESIGN AND CONSTRUCTION: *Back, splat slightly bowed, posts straight. Seat frame construction, as fig. 27. Bracing of seat frame, as fig. 19. Bracket responds, horizontal grain. No horizontal shaping. No through tenons. Seating of splat in shoe.*
NOTES: *This chair is recorded as having belonged to General Philip Schuyler (1733–1804) (Rice, p. 43).*

149

Side chair, New York, 1762–95. Courtesy of Museum of the City of New York (Acc. no. 53.150.19).

PRIMARY WOOD: *walnut*. SECONDARY WOODS: *pine corner blocks in front, tulip poplar in rear.*
DIMENSIONS: *height, 38¼ inches; width, 25; height of seat rail, 17.*
DESIGN AND CONSTRUCTION: *Back, straight. Seat frame construction, as fig. 19. Bracing of seat frame, corner blocks, as fig. 28. Bracket responds, horizontal grain. No horizontal shaping. No through tenons. Seating of splat in shoe.*
NOTES: *The gadrooning is a separate piece attached with glue and nails. The date 1762 is provided by its ultimate design source (fig. 241).*

150

Side chair, New York, 1755–95. Courtesy of Henry Francis du Pont Winterthur Museum (Acc. no. 52.243).

PRIMARY WOOD: *mahogany*. SECONDARY WOODS: *soft maple (Winterthur report) front and side seat rails; rear, birch.*
DIMENSIONS: *height, 37⅞ inches; width, 24¼; height of seat rail, 17.*
DESIGN AND CONSTRUCTION: *Back, straight. Seat frame construction, as fig. 19. Bracing of seat frame, corner blocks, new; also new cross-ties, though they seem to be in early holes. Knee brackets, thin in depth, attached to applied backing. No bracket responds. No horizontal shaping. No through tenons. Seating of splat in rear seat rail, passing behind shoe.*

151

Side chair, English, 1745–70. Present location unknown.

PRIMARY WOOD: *mahogany.*
NOTES: *Splat, back posts above seat, and seat rail veneered. This form of foot is also known in Philadelphia and is often confused with the trifid form. This chair not investigated personally.*

152

Side chair, New York, 1755–95. Courtesy of Henry Francis du Pont Winterthur Museum (Acc. no. 59.2835).

PRIMARY WOOD: *mahogany.* SECONDARY WOOD: *tulip poplar corner blocks and slip seat frame.*
DIMENSIONS: *height, 39⅜ inches; width, 22¼; height of seat rail, 16⅝.*
DESIGN AND CONSTRUCTION: *Back, straight. Seat frame construction, as fig. 27. Bracing of seat frame, corner blocks, new. Knee brackets, thin in depth and attached to applied backing. Bracket responds, horizontal grain. No horizontal shaping. No through tenons. Seating of splat in shoe.*
NOTES: *It is recorded that this chair was made for General Samuel Blachley Webb and that Elizabeth Bancker made the seat covering before their marriage in 1779 (Downs, fig. 150).*

Rhode Island

FIGURES 153–183

153

Side chair, English, 1700–30. Victoria and Albert Museum, London (Acc. no. W.44–1938).

PRIMARY WOOD: *beech, japanned green and gold on a red ground.*
DIMENSIONS: *height, 45½ inches; width, 21½.*
DESIGN AND CONSTRUCTION: *Back, spooned. Seat frame construction, as fig.19. Bracing of seat frame, corner blocks, new. Bracket responds, horizontal grain; as rear leg repeats form of front they are really additional knee brackets. Horizontal shaping in front. No through tenons.*
NOTES: *The seat covering is original. Cheeks of rear cabriole legs pieced on.*

154

Arm chair, Rhode Island, Newport, 1730–50. Courtesy of Henry Francis du Pont Winterthur Museum (Acc. no. 59.69).

PRIMARY WOOD: *walnut*. SECONDARY WOOD: *maple*.
DIMENSIONS: *height, 43½ inches; width, 24½; height of seat rail, 16½.*
DESIGN AND CONSTRUCTION: *Back, spooned. Seat frame construction, as fig. 19. No traces of any corner blocks. No bracket responds. Horizontal shaping; early photograph shows pieces added to seat rail on either side of front knee brackets, now removed. No through tenons. Seating of splat in rear seat rail, passing behind shoe.*
NOTES: *Rear shaping of medial stretcher missing.*

155

Side chair, Rhode Island, Newport, 1730–60. Courtesy of Preservation Society of Newport County; Hunter House.

PRIMARY WOOD: *mahogany*. SECONDARY WOOD: *splat veneered on maple*.
DIMENSIONS: *height, 41 inches; width, 21¼; height of seat rail, 17½.*
DESIGN AND CONSTRUCTION: *Back, spooned. Seat frame construction, as fig. 19. No bracket responds, but rear of side horizontal shaping cut to reverse curve. Horizontal shaping. No through tenons. Seating of splat in rear seat rail, passing behind shoe.*

160

Side chair, Rhode Island,
Island School of Design (

PRIMARY WOOD: *maple.* s
DIMENSIONS: *height, 42 i*
DESIGN AND CONSTRUCTIC
as fig. 19. No traces of co
bracket responds. Horizo
the front of the side shap
the front shaping. No thr
NOTES: *Original under-u*
upholstery. Painted black

156

Side chair, Rhode Island, Newport, 1730–60. Mr. and Mrs. Ralph E.
Carpenter, Jr.

PRIMARY WOOD: *walnut.* SECONDARY WOOD: *maple slip seat frame.*
DIMENSIONS: *height, 41⅞ inches; width, 21¼; height of seat rail, 17⅞.*
DESIGN AND CONSTRUCTION: *Back, spooned. Seat frame construction,*
as fig. 27. Bracing of seat frame, corner blocks, new. No bracket
responds, but rear of side horizontal shaping cut to reverse curve.
Horizontal shaping. No through tenons. Seating of splat in shoe.
NOTES: *Seat and side stretchers slope forward.*

157

Side chair, Rhode Island, Newport?, 1730–60. The Museum of Art,
Rhode Island School of Design (Acc. no. 54.056).

PRIMARY WOOD: *walnut.* SECONDARY WOOD: *maple slip seat frame.*
DIMENSIONS: *height, 40⅜ inches; width, 22¼; height of seat rail, 17⅜.*
DESIGN AND CONSTRUCTION: *Back, spooned. Seat frame construction,*
as fig. 27. No traces of any corner blocks. Knee brackets, small-headed
nails. No bracket responds. Horizontal shaping. No through tenons.
Seating of splat in shoe.

158

Side chair, R...
Ewing.

PRIMARY WOO...
DIMENSIONS: ...
DESIGN AND C...
as fig. 27. Br...
small-headed...
through teno...
NOTES: Inne...

162

Side chair, Rhode Island, 1730–60. The Museum of Art, Rhode Island School of Design (Acc. no. 35.269).

PRIMARY WOOD: *maple*. SECONDARY WOOD: *maple slip seat frame*.
DIMENSIONS: *height, 39⅜ inches; width, 21¾; height of seat rail, 16¼.*
DESIGN AND CONSTRUCTION: *Back, spooned. Seat frame construction, as fig. 19. No traces of any corner blocks. Knee brackets, new small nails. No bracket responds. Horizontal shaping. No through tenons. Seating of splat in shoe.*
NOTES: *Cleaned of probably original black paint and stained dark. Left front and right rear knee bracket incorrectly replaced.*

163

Side chair, Rhode Island, Newport, 1763?, possibly by John Goddard. Courtesy of Moses Brown School.

PRIMARY WOOD: *walnut*. SECONDARY WOOD: *maple slip seat seat frame*.
DIMENSIONS: *height, 41¼ inches; width, 21¾; height of seat rail, 16⅞.*
DESIGN AND CONSTRUCTION: *Back, spooned. Seat frame construction, as fig. 27. No traces of any corner blocks. Knee brackets, large-headed nails. No bracket responds. Horizontal shaping. No through tenons. Seating of splat in shoe.*
NOTES: *This is possibly one of the "leather chairs" mentioned in a letter from Moses Brown to John Goddard, October 10, 1763 (Carpenter, fig. 11, p. 37).*

164

Side chair, Rhode Island, Newport, 1730–60. George Waterman, Jr.

PRIMARY WOOD: *walnut.* SECONDARY WOOD: *maple slip seat frame.*
DIMENSIONS: *height, 40½ inches; width, 21¾; height of seat rail, 16½.*
DESIGN AND CONSTRUCTION: *Back, spooned. Seat frame construction, as fig. 19. Bracing of seat frame, corner blocks, new. Knee brackets, small-headed nails. No bracket responds. Horizontal shaping. No through tenons. Seating of splat in shoe.*

165

Side chair, Rhode Island, Newport, 1730–60. Courtesy of Museum of Fine Arts, Boston (Acc. no. 63.1043).

PRIMARY WOOD: *walnut.* SECONDARY WOOD: *maple slip seat frame.*
DIMENSIONS: *height, 41 inches; width, 21½; height of seat rail, 17.*
DESIGN AND CONSTRUCTION: *Back, spooned. Seat frame construction, as fig. 27. Bracing of seat frame, corner blocks, new. Knee brackets, small-headed nails, one knee bracket replaced. No bracket responds, but rear of side horizontal shaping, and ends of same on rear rail, cut to reverse curve. Horizontal shaping, also on rear rail. No through tenons. Seating of splat in shoe.*
NOTES: *Cheeks of rear cabriole legs (as on the English chair, fig. 153) and inner edge of back posts above seat pieced out.*

166

Side chair, Rhode Island, Newport, 1740–70. Courtesy of Henry Francis du Pont Winterthur Museum (Acc. no. 58.960).

PRIMARY WOOD: *walnut.*
DIMENSIONS: *height, 40⅜ inches; width, 21¾; height of seat rail, 17⅛.*
DESIGN AND CONSTRUCTION: *Back, spooned. Seat frame construction, as fig. 27. Bracing of seat frame, corner blocks, new. Bracket responds, horizontal grain. Horizontal shaping. No through tenons. Seating of splat in rear seat rail, passing behind shoe.*
NOTES: *New slip seat frame. Cheeks of rear cabriole legs pieced to depth of bracket responds; the bracket responds are like knee brackets as they follow the cabriole form. Back posts pieced out above seat.*

167

Side chair, Rhode Island, Newport, 1740–70. Courtesy of The Rhode Island Historical Society.

PRIMARY WOOD: *mahogany.* SECONDARY WOOD: *maple slip seat frame.*
DIMENSIONS: *height, 38⅜ inches; width, 21¾; height of seat rail, 16½.*
DESIGN AND CONSTRUCTION: *Back, straight. Seat frame construction, as fig. 27. Bracing of seat frame, corner blocks, new. Knee brackets, small-headed nails, front left and part of right rear brackets replaced. No bracket responds. Horizontal shaping. No through tenons. Seating of splat in shoe.*
NOTES: *Repairs to ends of crest rail; joints of slip seat frame pegged.*

168

Side chair, Rhode Island, Newport, 1740–70. Mr. and Mrs. E. Ross Millhiser.

PRIMARY WOOD: *walnut.* SECONDARY WOODS: *mahogany corner blocks; pine slip seat frame.*
DIMENSIONS: *height, 38¾ inches; width, 20½; height of seat rail, 16½.*
DESIGN AND CONSTRUCTION: *Back, splat spooned, posts straight. Seat frame construction, as fig. 27. Bracing of seat frame, small corner blocks with vertical grain and triangular section filling in area between seat rails and corner of legs; also new cross-ties. Bracket responds, horizontal grain; also in rear, but vertical grain. Horizontal shaping. No through tenons. Seating of splat in shoe.*
NOTES: *Rear legs flare slightly at base. This chair is recorded as having originally belonged to Parson Thomas Smith of Newport (Ott, fig. 8).*

169

Side chair, Rhode Island, Newport, 1740–70. Mabel Brady Garvan Collection, Yale University Art Gallery (Acc. no. 1930.2712).

PRIMARY WOOD: *walnut.* SECONDARY WOODS: *pine corner blocks; maple and birch slip seat frame (Yale report).*
DIMENSIONS: *height, 39⅜ inches; width, 21⅞; height of seat rail, 17⅛.*
DESIGN AND CONSTRUCTION: *Back, splat spooned, posts straight. Seat frame construction, as fig. 27. Bracing of seat frame, as fig. 28 in front, rear blocks new. Knee brackets, small-headed nails, brackets at sides replaced. No bracket responds. Horizontal shaping. No through tenons. Seating of splat in shoe.*
NOTES: *Back posts are not pieced out at innermost curve, and are cut, on inner face below stretchers, to a sharp backwards rake.*

170

Side chair, Rhode Island, Newport?, 1740–70. Courtesy of Israel Sack, Inc., New York City, New York.

PRIMARY WOOD: *mahogany*. SECONDARY WOODS: *pine corner blocks; maple slip seat frame.*
DIMENSIONS: *height, 40⅞ inches; width, 22⅜; height of seat rail, 16½.*
DESIGN AND CONSTRUCTION: *Back, spooned. Seat frame construction, as fig. 27. Bracing of seat frame, as fig. 28, re-attached. Bracket responds, vertical grain, nailed, also in rear. Horizontal shaping, rear only. No through tenons. Seating of splat in shoe.*
NOTES: *Back posts pieced out on inner edge above seat.*

171

Side chair, Rhode Island, Newport, 1740–70. Courtesy of Wadsworth Atheneum, Hartford, Connecticut (Acc. no. 1918.1365).

PRIMARY WOOD: *walnut*. SECONDARY WOODS: *pine corner blocks; maple slip seat frame.*
DIMENSIONS: *height, 41⅜ inches; width, 21⅞; height of seat rail, 16½.*
DESIGN AND CONSTRUCTION: *Back, spooned. Seat frame construction, as fig. 27. Bracing of seat frame, as fig. 28, left rear block missing, right rear block replaced. Knee brackets, small-headed nails. No bracket responds. Horizontal shaping. No through tenons. Seating of splat in shoe.*
NOTES: *Rear legs cut on inner face below stretchers to sharp backwards rake.*

172

173

Side chair, Rhode Island, Newport, 1755–95. The Metropolitan Museum of Art; Rogers Fund, 1955 (Acc. no. 55.134).

PRIMARY WOOD: *mahogany*. SECONDARY WOOD: *maple slip seat frame*. DIMENSIONS: *height, 39 inches; width, 21¾; height of seat rail, 17⅛*. DESIGN AND CONSTRUCTION: *Back, straight. Seat frame construction, as fig. 19. No trace of any corner blocks. No bracket responds. Horizontal shaping. No through tenons. Seating of splat: splat enters shoe in two tenons, rather than as usual with one large tenon.* NOTES: *Back posts pieced out on inner edge above seat.*

Side chair, Rhode Island, Providence, 1755–95. Mr. and Mrs. Bayard Ewing.

PRIMARY WOOD: *walnut*. SECONDARY WOOD: *maple slip seat frame*. DIMENSIONS: *height, 38 inches; width, 21¼; height of seat rail, 17⅛*. DESIGN AND CONSTRUCTION: *Back, straight. Seat frame construction, as fig. 27. Bracing of seat frame, two new small corner blocks. No bracket responds. Horizontal shaping. No through tenons. Seating of splat in shoe.* NOTES: *Slip seat signed in ink* PROV; *three joints of slip seat frame pinned; repairs to back of crest rail, at center and at junction with back posts.*

178

Side chair, Rhode Island, 1755–95. Courtesy of Henry Francis du
Pont Winterthur Museum (Acc. no. 52.241.1).

PRIMARY WOOD: *walnut.* SECONDARY WOOD: *soft maple slip seat frame.*
DIMENSIONS: *height, 38¼ inches; width, 22; height of seat rail, 16¾.*
DESIGN AND CONSTRUCTION: *Back, straight. Seat frame construction,
as fig. 27. No bracing of seat frame. Knee brackets, small-headed
nails. No bracket responds. Horizontal shaping. No through tenons.
Seating of splat in shoe.*
NOTES: *The back post, below seat, is straight for a considerable
distance before chamfering begins, as if to accommodate a bracket
respond.*

179

Low side chair, Rhode Island, 1755–95. Mr. Norman Herreshoff.

PRIMARY WOOD: *walnut.* SECONDARY WOOD: *pine corner blocks.*
DIMENSIONS: *height, 35½ inches; width, 20½; height of seat
rail, 13¼.*
DESIGN AND CONSTRUCTION: *Back, straight. Seat frame construction,
as fig. 27. Bracing of seat frame, as fig. 28, large, secured with
large-headed nails. No bracket responds. Horizontal shaping. No
through tenons. Seating of splat in shoe.*
NOTES: *See note on preceding chair, which also applies here.*

180

Side chair, Rhode Island, 1755–95. Courtesy of The Rhode Island
Historical Society (Acc. no. 1953.1.24).

PRIMARY WOOD: *mahogany*. SECONDARY WOOD: *maple slip seat frame*.
DIMENSIONS: *height, 37¾ inches; width, 22⅛; height of seat rail, 16⅞*.
DESIGN AND CONSTRUCTION: *Back, straight. Seat frame construction,
as fig. 27. No traces of corner blocks. Knee brackets, small-headed
nails. No bracket responds. Horizontal shaping. No through tenons.
Seating of splat in shoe.*
NOTES: *"Massachusetts" retracted claw; inner curves of back posts
above seat pieced out.*

181

Side chair, English, 1750–80. High Wycombe Art Gallery and
Museum, England (Acc. no. 49–827).

PRIMARY WOOD: *walnut*.
NOTES: *This chair investigated, but measurements not recorded.*

182

Side chair, Rhode Island, 1760–95. Courtesy of Henry Francis du Pont Winterthur Museum (Acc. no. 58.18.2).

PRIMARY WOOD: *mahogany*. SECONDARY WOOD: *maple slip seat frame*. DIMENSIONS: *height, 37⅝ inches; width, 20; height of seat rail, 16⅞*. DESIGN AND CONSTRUCTION: *Back, straight. Seat frame construction, as fig. 19. Bracing of seat frame, corner blocks, new. No bracket responds. No horizontal shaping. No through tenons. Seating of splat in shoe.*

183

Side chair, Rhode Island, 1760–95. Courtesy of Israel Sack, Inc., New York City, New York.

PRIMARY WOOD: *mahogany*. SECONDARY WOOD: *maple slip seat frame*. DIMENSIONS: *height, 38½ inches; width, 22; height of seat rail, 16¾*. DESIGN AND CONSTRUCTION: *Back, bowed. Seat frame construction, as fig. 19. No trace of corner blocks. No bracket responds. No horizontal shaping. No through tenons. Seating of splat in shoe.* NOTES: *The tenons of slip seat frame are pinned through.*

Connecticut Valley

FIGURES 184–201

184

Side chair, Connecticut, 1730–60. The Metropolitan Museum of Art; Gift of Mrs. J. Insley Blair, 1946 (Acc. no. 46.194.4).

PRIMARY WOOD: *maple, painted red.*
DIMENSIONS: *height, 43¼ inches; width, 21½; height of seat rail, 17.*
DESIGN AND CONSTRUCTION: *Back, spooned. Seat frame construction, as fig. 19. No bracing of seat frame. Knee brackets, glued to face of seat rail. No bracket responds. Horizontal shaping, but rear of side rails shaped to curve related to knee blocks. No through tenons. Seating of splat in shoe.*
NOTES: *This is one of a related group of chairs owned by the museum; the information was recorded from Acc. no. 46.194.4 and the photograph is Acc. no. 46.194.3a, b. Original seat cover. Tradition says that this chair was made by the Southmayd family of Middletown, Connecticut. Recent research by Houghton Bulkeley has failed to discover any Southmayd of Middletown who was a cabinetmaker in the first half of the eighteenth century, and no Southmayd inventory of related dates shows cabinetmaker's tools.*

185

186

Side chair, Connecticut, 1730–80. The Connecticut Historical
Society.

PRIMARY WOOD: *maple*. SECONDARY WOOD: *maple slip seat frame*.
DIMENSIONS: *height, 41½ inches; width, 20¼; height of seat rail,
17⅜.*
DESIGN AND CONSTRUCTION: *Back, spooned. Seat frame construction,
as fig. 19. No trace of corner blocks. No knee brackets. No bracket
responds. Horizontal shaping. Through tenons. Seating of splat in
shoe, which projects behind splat.*
NOTES: *Applied seat molding to contain slip seat; normally it is cut
from the solid except on horseshoe-shaped seats constructed as in
Philadelphia (fig. 17). Absence of knee brackets.*

Side chair, Connecticut, Wethersfield area, 1730–80. Mabel Brady
Garvan Collection, Yale University Art Gallery (Acc. no. 1963.10).

PRIMARY WOOD: *cherry*. SECONDARY WOODS: *soft maple and pine
slip seat frame.*
DIMENSIONS: *height, 41¼ inches; width, 20⅛; height of seat rail,
17¼.*
DESIGN AND CONSTRUCTION: *Back, spooned. Seat frame construction,
as fig. 17. Bracing of seat frame, the depth of the seat frame. Knee
brackets, nailed. Bracket responds, horizontal grain, nailed. No
horizontal shaping. Through tenons. Seating of splat in shoe.*
NOTES: *This chair is recorded as having belonged to Ezekiel Porter
(1707–75) of Wethersfield, Connecticut (Lockwood, vol. II, p.
58, fig. 495). Original seat covering.*

187

Side chair, Connecticut, Norwich area?, 1730–80, possibly by Cheney (see Notes below). Courtesy of Henry Francis du Pont Winterthur Museum (Acc. no. 60.107).

PRIMARY WOOD: *cherry.* SECONDARY WOOD: *soft maple slip seat frame.*
DIMENSIONS: *height, 42 inches; width, 21¾; height of seat rail, 16⅞.*
DESIGN AND CONSTRUCTION: *Back, straight. Seat frame construction, as fig. 27. No trace of corner blocks. Knee brackets, nailed. No bracket responds. Horizontal shaping. No through tenons. Seating of splat in shoe.*
NOTES: *"Cheney" is written in chalk on the slip seat frame, and is probably original; it may be an owner's or the maker's name. Benjamin Cheney worked in East Hartford, Connecticut from about 1721 to 1760; Silas E. Cheney (1776–1821) worked in Litchfield, Connecticut.*

188

Arm chair, Connecticut, Norwich area?, 1730–80. Mr. William Welles Lyman.

PRIMARY WOOD: *cherry.* SECONDARY WOOD: *pine.*
DIMENSIONS: *height, 41 inches; width, 27⅝; height of seat rail, 17.*
DESIGN AND CONSTRUCTION: *Back, straight. Seat frame construction, as fig. 27. No evidence of corner blocks. Horizontal shaping. No through tenons. Seating of splat in shoe.*

189

Side chair, Connecticut, 1730–80. Collection of Frederick K. and Margaret R. Barbour, The Connecticut Historical Society.

PRIMARY WOOD: *cherry.* SECONDARY WOOD: *pine corner blocks and plank slip seat.*

DIMENSIONS: *height, 43 inches; width, 21; height of seat rail, 17⅜.*

DESIGN AND CONSTRUCTION: *Back, straight. Seat frame construction, as fig. 27. Bracing of seat frame, at front, small vertical grain squared pieces fill corners between leg and seat frame. Knee brackets, small-headed nails; shallow in depth. No bracket responds. Through tenons. Seating of splat in shoe, which projects behind splat and beyond front of back posts.*

NOTES: *Slip seat is not a frame but a solid plank of wood.*

190

Side chair, Connecticut, 1730–80. Mabel Brady Garvan Collection, Yale University Art Gallery (Acc. no. 1930.2416).

PRIMARY WOOD: *cherry.* SECONDARY WOODS: *cherry plank slip seat, maple shoe.*

DIMENSIONS: *height, 40¾ inches; width, 21½; height of seat rail, 16¾.*

DESIGN AND CONSTRUCTION: *Back, straight. Seat frame construction, as fig. 19. Bracing of seat frame, corner blocks, new. Knee brackets, glued to face of seat rail. No bracket responds. Horizontal shaping. No through tenons. Seating of splat in shoe.*

NOTES: *Slip seat is not a frame but a plank of wood.*

191

Side chair, Connecticut, Norwich area?, 1755–90. Courtesy of
Wadsworth Atheneum (Acc. no. 1928.1).

PRIMARY WOOD: *cherry*. SECONDARY WOODS: *maple corner blocks
and slip seat frame; birch stretchers.*
DIMENSIONS: *height, 42⅜ inches; width, 21¾; height of seat rail, 17¼.*
DESIGN AND CONSTRUCTION: *Back, straight. Seat frame construction,
as fig. 27. Bracing of seat frame, corner blocks, as fig. 28, with
large-headed nails. Knee brackets, small-headed nails. No bracket
responds. Horizontal shaping. No through tenons. Seating of splat
in shoe.*
NOTES: *Birch stretchers. Traces of original leather webbing on slip
seat frame. According to tradition, this chair belonged to William
Pitkin, governor of Connecticut from 1766 to 1769 and great-
grandfather of the donor (Wadsworth Atheneum files).*

192

Arm chair, English, Norwich, 1740–61, branded by Samuel Sharp,
made freeman of Norwich (Norfolk) in 1737; will filed 1761.
Victoria and Albert Museum, London (Acc. no. W.60-1936).

PRIMARY WOODS: *walnut, walnut veneer.* SECONDARY WOODS: *oak, beech.*
DIMENSIONS: *height, 36⅞ inches; width, 28½; height of seat rail, 16¼.*
DESIGN AND CONSTRUCTION: *Seat frame construction, as fig. 19.
Bracing of seat frame, corner blocks, as fig. 19; right front block
original. Knee brackets, thin in depth and attached to seat rail which
drops behind them. Bracket responds, cut from solid and veneered
along with seat rail. No horizontal shaping. No through tenons.
Seating of splat in shoe.*
NOTES: *Slip seat frame and back feet restored according to local
practice. Splat, back posts above seat, and seat rail veneered.*

193

194

Side chair, Connecticut, East Windsor, 1781, by Eliphalet Chapin (1741–1807), active about 1771–95, East Windsor. Mabel Brady Garvan Collection, Yale University Art Gallery (Acc. no. 1930.2516a).

PRIMARY WOOD: *cherry.* SECONDARY WOOD: *white pine corner blocks, slip seat frame, and board inside rear seat rail.*
DIMENSIONS: *height, 38⅝ inches; width, 22½; height of seat rail, 16¼.*
DESIGN AND CONSTRUCTION: *Back, bowed. Seat frame construction, as fig. 19. Bracing of seat frame, corner blocks, as fig. 19. Knee brackets, small-headed nails. No bracket responds. Horizontal shaping. Through tenons. Seating of splat in shoe.*
NOTES: *Pine board applied to inside of rear seat rail. Irving W. Lyon saw the bill of sale for this chair and its mates. "They were made for Alexander King in 1781 when he was married . . ." (recorded on slip seat of chair by Lyon when he owned the chair). King lived in Windsor Hill, Connecticut, and Eliphalet Chapin in East Windsor.*

Side chair, Connecticut, East Windsor, 1771–95, probably by Eliphalet Chapin (1741–1807), active about 1771–95, East Windsor. Mabel Brady Garvan Collection, Yale University Art Gallery (Acc. no. 1930.2561).

PRIMARY WOOD: *cherry.* SECONDARY WOODS: *white pine corner blocks; white oak slip seat frame.*
DIMENSIONS: *height, 38½ inches; width, 22½; height of seat rail, 16⅜.*
DESIGN AND CONSTRUCTION: *Back, bowed. Seat frame construction, as fig. 19. Bracing of seat frame, corner blocks, as fig. 19, large and bold. Knee brackets, small-headed nails. No bracket responds. Horizontal shaping. Through tenons. Seating of splat in shoe.*
NOTES: *Attribution based on similarity to fig. 193.*

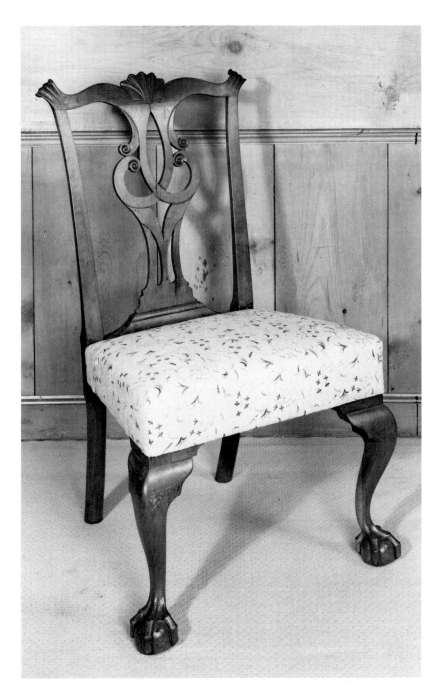

195

Arm chair, Connecticut, East Windsor, 1771–95, probably by
Eliphalet Chapin (1741–1807), active about 1771–95, East Windsor.
Mabel Brady Garvan Collection, Yale University Art Gallery (Acc.
no. 1965.21).

PRIMARY WOOD: *cherry.* SECONDARY WOOD: *white pine corner blocks
and slip seat frame.*
DIMENSIONS: *height, 40½ inches; width, 27¾; height of seat rail,
16½.*
DESIGN AND CONSTRUCTION: *Back, bowed. Seat frame construction,
as fig. 19. Bracing of seat frame, corner blocks, as fig. 19. Knee
brackets, small-headed nails. No bracket responds. Horizontal shaping.
Through tenons. Seating of splat in shoe.*
NOTES: *Attribution based on similarity to fig. 193.*

196

Side chair, Connecticut, East Windsor, 1771–95, probably by
Eliphalet Chapin (1741–1807), active about 1771–95, East Windsor.
Collection of Frederick K. and Margaret R. Barbour, The Connecticut
Historical Society.

PRIMARY WOOD: *cherry.* SECONDARY WOOD: *pine corner blocks.*
DIMENSIONS: *height, 38½ inches; width, 23⅝; height of seat rail, 16¾.*
DESIGN AND CONSTRUCTION: *Back, bowed. Seat frame construction,
as fig. 19. Bracing of seat frame, corner blocks, as fig. 19. Knee
brackets, small-headed nails, probably original. No bracket responds.
Horizontal shaping. Through tenons. Seating of splat in seat rail,
passing behind shoe.*
NOTES: *Rear seat rail of same depth as back posts. Attribution based
on similarity to fig. 193. Partial over-upholstery. Some Connecticut
chairs are reported (by Frederick Barbour) to have removable slip seats
and original over-upholstery, implying that chairs were sometimes
made up in advance of order.*

201

Side chair, Connecticut, Norwich area, 1760–95 (see Notes below for possible attribution). Courtesy of Israel Sack, Inc., New York City, New York.

PRIMARY WOOD: *mahogany*. SECONDARY WOOD: *maple slip seat frame*.
DIMENSIONS: *height, 37¼ inches; width, 20¼; height of seat rail, 17¼.*
DESIGN AND CONSTRUCTION: *Back, straight. Seat frame construction, as fig. 19. Bracing of seat frame, corner blocks, new. Knee brackets, curved pierced brackets in front. No bracket responds. No horizontal shaping. No through tenons. Seating of splat in shoe.*
NOTES: *Front edge of medial stretcher, outside edge of side stretcher, and back edge of rear stretcher all molded. Medial stretcher dovetailed into side stretchers. Seat frame stamped* J. A. BELL, *possibly the maker or original owner. The chair carries the label: "This chair was in the / Jabez Huntington House, / 16 Huntington Lane, Norwich / Town, Conn. Bought by / Edith (Huntington) Wilson in 1922. This chair left / by her to her cousin / Sydney (Stevens) Williston in 1939."*

The South

FIGURES 202–224

202

Speaker's arm chair, Virginia, probably about 1753 (see Notes below). Courtesy of Colonial Williamsburg (Acc. no. L 1933-504).

PRIMARY WOOD: *walnut.* SECONDARY WOODS: *tulip poplar and yellow pine braces.*
DIMENSIONS: *height, 97½ inches; width, 36¾ (arms); height of seat rail, 18.*
DESIGN AND CONSTRUCTION: *Back, straight. Seat frame construction, as fig. 19. Bracing of seat frame, new crossed braces. Knee brackets, applied to face of seat rail which drops behind them. Bracket responds, rear corner blocks. Horizontal shaping, ends covered with corner blocks. No through tenons. Seating of splat in rail (there is no shoe).*
NOTES: *The second Capitol was built in 1753 and there is no evidence to suggest that this chair was saved from the fire which destroyed the first Capitol.*

203

Side chair, English, 1740–80. Mr. and Mrs. Graham Hood.

PRIMARY WOOD: *walnut.*
DIMENSIONS: *height, 37½ inches; width, 18⅝; height of seat rail, 16⅞.*
DESIGN AND CONSTRUCTION: *Back, straight. Seat frame construction, as fig. 19. No traces of corner blocks. No knee brackets. No bracket responds. No horizontal shaping. No through tenons. Seating of splat in back rail, passing behind shoe.*

208

209

Side chair, Southern, Virginia?, 1755–95. Museum of Early
Southern Decorative Arts (Acc. no. 2151).

PRIMARY WOOD: *mahogany*. SECONDARY WOODS: *tulip poplar rear
corner blocks; yellow pine rear seat rail and slip seat frame.*
DIMENSIONS: *height, 38½ inches; width, 22¾; height of seat rail, 17⅜.*
DESIGN AND CONSTRUCTION: *Back, straight. Seat frame construction,
as fig. 19. Bracing of seat frame, new front corner blocks; rear, as
fig. 19, with later wire nails. Knee brackets, later wire nails. Bracket
responds, horizontal grain, right one replaced. Horizontal shaping
at rear only; lower points are level with base of side bracket responds,
so that they resemble bracket responds cut from the solid. Through
tenons. Seating of splat in shoe.*
NOTES: *Front corners of seat frame chamfered and fluted. Rear
surface of rear seat rail faced with ⅜ inch mahogany "veneer." Left
and center dots of splats restored.*

Side chair, Southern, Virginia?, 1760–1810. Courtesy of Colonial
Williamsburg (Acc. no. 1933.11).

PRIMARY WOOD: *walnut.* SECONDARY WOOD: *yellow pine corner
blocks and slip seat frame.*
DIMENSIONS: *height, 37½ inches; width, 21; height of seat rail, 16⅝.*
DESIGN AND CONSTRUCTION: *Back, bowed. Seat frame construction,
as fig. 19. Bracing of seat frame, corner blocks in front, as fig. 18,
except each part is one quarter round. No knee brackets. No bracket
responds. No horizontal shaping. No through tenons. Seating of
splat in shoe.*
NOTES: *Strip of walnut on inner face of thin rear seat rail to support
shoe further. Splat made of two pieces seamed down the center.
Slip seat frame made of unusually wide members. Later strips inside
rear and right seat rails. Base of right rear leg restored.*

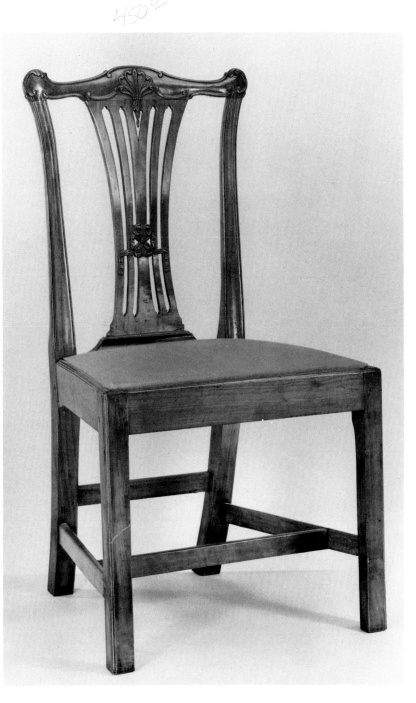

210

Side chair, Southern, Virginia?, 1760–1810. Courtesy of Colonial Williamsburg (Acc. no. 1933.40.1).

PRIMARY WOOD: *walnut.* SECONDARY WOOD: *yellow pine slip seat frame.*

DIMENSIONS: *height, 37⅜ inches; width, 19¾; height of seat rail, 16½.*

DESIGN AND CONSTRUCTION: *Back, straight. Seat frame construction, as fig. 19. No traces of corner blocks. No knee brackets. No bracket responds. No horizontal shaping. No through tenons. Seating of splat in shoe.*

NOTES: *Later small strip inside rear seat rail.*

211

Side chair, Virginia, Williamsburg?, 1760–95. Courtesy of Colonial Williamsburg (Acc. no. G1965.184).

PRIMARY WOOD: *cherry.* SECONDARY WOOD: *ash (Williamsburg reports oak) slip seat frame.*

DIMENSIONS: *height, 39 inches; width, 21¼; height of seat rail, 17⅞.*

DESIGN AND CONSTRUCTION: *Back, straight. Seat frame construction, as fig. 19. Bracing of seat frame, rear corner blocks, and half of right front corner block, original, as fig. 19; other half of right and left front replaced. No knee brackets. No bracket responds. Horizontal shaping in rear only. No through tenons. Seating of splat in shoe, which is one piece with rear seat rail.*

NOTES: *"Credible tradition of ownership by Benjamin Waller (1716–1786), a resident of Williamsburg" (files of Colonial Williamsburg).*

216

Side chair, Southern, Virginia?, 1760–1810. Courtesy of Colonial Williamsburg (Acc. no. 1930.60.1).

PRIMARY WOOD: *walnut.* SECONDARY WOOD: *yellow pine slip seat frame.*

DIMENSIONS: *height, 37¾ inches; width, 21⅛; height of seat rail, 17⅝.*

DESIGN AND CONSTRUCTION: *Back, slight bow to splat, probably not original. Seat frame construction, as fig. 19. No traces of corner blocks. No knee brackets. No bracket responds. No horizontal shaping. No through tenons. Seating of splat in shoe, which is one piece with rear seat rail.*

NOTES: *Back rail same depth as rear legs.*

217

Side chair, Southern, Virginia?, 1760–1810. Courtesy of Colonial Williamsburg (Acc. no. 1930.411).

PRIMARY WOOD: *walnut.* SECONDARY WOOD: *yellow pine slip seat frame.*

DIMENSIONS: *height, 37½ inches; width, 20; height of seat rail, 16½.*

DESIGN AND CONSTRUCTION: *Back, straight. Seat frame construction, as fig. 19. Bracing of seat frame, new corner blocks. No knee brackets. No bracket responds. No horizontal shaping. No through tenons. Seating of splat in shoe.*

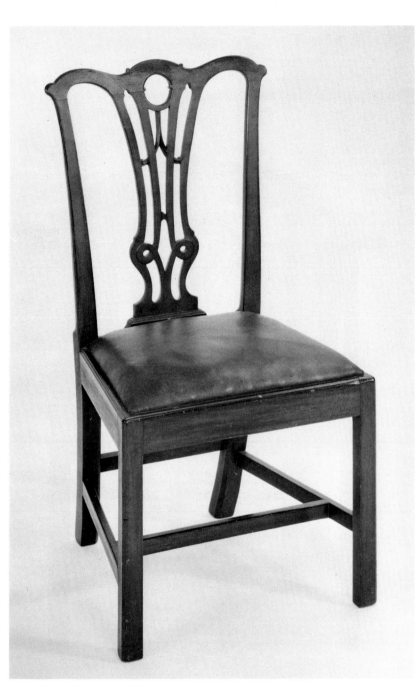

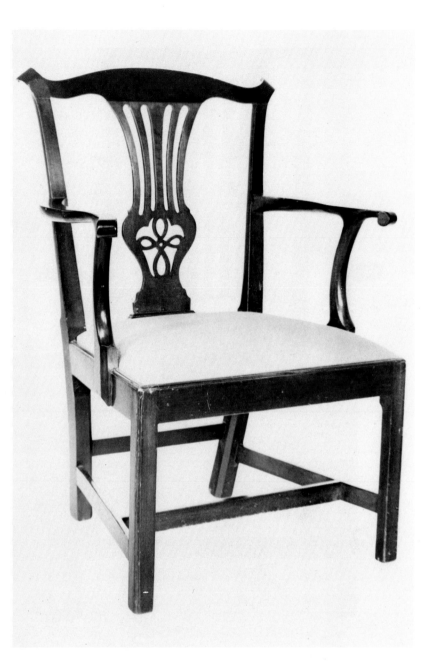

218

Side chair, Southern, South Carolina?, 1760–1800. Courtesy of Colonial Williamsburg (Acc. no. 1967.60).

PRIMARY WOOD: *mahogany*. SECONDARY WOOD: *yellow pine slip seat frame and inner face of rear seat rail (7/16 inch thick, to support shoe).*

DIMENSIONS: *height, 38 inches; width, 21⅛; height of seat rail, 16⅞.*

DESIGN AND CONSTRUCTION: *Back, bowed. Seat frame construction, as fig. 19. Bracing of seat frame, traces of corner blocks in front, new corner blocks in rear. No knee brackets. No bracket responds. No horizontal shaping. No through tenons. Seating of splat in shoe.*

NOTES: *"History of ownership by Mordecai Gist . . . resident of Baltimore before the Revolution and South Carolina after the Revolution" (files of Colonial Williamsburg).*

219

Arm chair, North Carolina, Edenton area?, 1760–1800. Museum of Early Southern Decorative Arts (Acc. no. 2024.72).

PRIMARY WOOD: *mahogany*. SECONDARY WOODS: *white pine corner blocks, yellow pine slip seat frame.*

DIMENSIONS: *height, 37⅞ inches; width, 26¾; height of seat rail, 16⅜.*

DESIGN AND CONSTRCTION: *Back, straight. Seat frame construction, as fig. 19. Bracing of seat frame, corner blocks as fig. 19. No knee brackets. No bracket responds. No horizontal shaping. No through tenons. Seating of splat in shoe.*

NOTES: *Rear seat rail set in from rear face of back posts ¼ inch. " . . . History of having been handed down through Edenton families. . . . " (files of MESDA).*

224

Side chair, South Carolina, Charleston, 1755–95. The Charleston Museum.

PRIMARY WOOD: *mahogany.* SECONDARY WOOD: *yellow pine slip seat frame.*

DIMENSIONS: *height, 38⅛ inches; width, 21⅞; height of seat rail, 17½.*

DESIGN AND CONSTRUCTION: *Back splat straight, posts bowed. Seat frame construction, as fig. 19. No trace of corner blocks. Knee brackets, missing. Bracket responds, missing. No horizontal shaping. No through tenons. Seating of splat in shoe.*

NOTES: *The leafage of the center of the crest rail and splat is gilded, which appears original.*

III

REGIONAL

AESTHETICS

1. Philadelphia

HAVING STUDIED the Queen Anne and Chippendale chairs of six American areas, what can we say about their original context, their European source of design, and their makers' understanding of aesthetics? From observing the quantity of American furniture still extant we know that, except in part of the South, English furniture did not fill the rooms of American eighteenth-century homes. It was extremely expensive to import bulky objects from England, and Philadelphia furniture was cheaper than the imported English counterpart. Also the Americans, always practical, soon realized that American wood did not succumb as readily to worms as the English, and that the American climate was far drier than the constant damp of England, even before central heating. This meant that English furniture imported into America would dry and twist when brought into the American climate, a fact that eighteenth-century colonists actually recorded. Today it is often the custom for importers of English furniture to place newly acquired objects in a warehouse where they can twist away while becoming accustomed to the American climate; later, after they have adjusted themselves, they are repaired and put in order for resale. The nonimportation agreement signed by many Philadelphia cabinetmakers in 1765 cut British imports by half between the years 1768 and 1769. Captain Samuel Morris, much of whose furniture is still known, wrote in 1765 to his nephew Samuel Powell, Jr., then in London, "Household goods may be had here as cheap and as well made from English patterns. In the humor people are in here, a man is in danger of becoming Invidiously distinguished, who buys anything in England which our Tradesmen can furnish. I have heard the joiners here object this against Dr. Morgan & others who brought their furnishing with them."[1] There is no question that English furniture was indeed brought to these shores, but the ownership of locally made products was practically, as well as politically, more acceptable. Many of the

goods reported in the inventories of eighteenth-century Americans as English are the type of thing, such as fine textiles, not made here. Governor John Penn, grandson of William Penn, possibly brought a cabinetmaker to Philadelphia when he arrived in 1763. At Penn's death, his house contained American furniture valued at £581.9s. and imported goods at £277.2s.3d., most of the latter probably the kind of products easily transported and unattainable in the New World.[2]

The majority of the people who came with William Penn in 1682 were of the middle class; as soon as they could, they built homes that reflected their former way of life and by 1740 Philadelphia was a thriving metropolis. At the time of the Revolution, Philadelphia was second only to London, within the British Empire, for size, importance, and lavish living. The town had grown from a population of 13,000 in 1742 to 40,000 in 1775.[3] Some designers in Philadelphia advertised that they had formerly worked for kings and nobility. The customers of the best eighteenth-century cabinetmakers were sophisticated people who knew some of the finest things available in England to the non-nobility. On these shores they became the most important people and it is interesting that, now transformed into the upper class, they did not surround themselves with objects suitable to the English nobility. The grandest American homes were small in comparison to the great homes of England, and the furniture that became the model for American products was not the finest court product of England. The lavishly carved and inlaid work of the late seventeenth century did not become popular here, nor did the elaborate, almost ritualistic, furniture of the eighteenth century. In fact Philadelphia, like the rest of America, took what was England's simpler,

[1] Hornor, p. 81.

[2] Hornor, p. 239. He also lists from whom Penn purchased goods.

[3] Carl Bridenbaugh, *Cities in the Wilderness* (New York: The Ronald Press Co., 1938), p. 303; and Carl Bridenbaugh, *Cities in Revolt, Urban Life in America, 1743–1776* (New York: Alfred A. Knopf, 1955), p. 216.

and in a sense, second-rate, work as models and transformed it into first-rate products.

What then is the difference between the second-rate furniture the American designer-makers copied and the first-rate they produced? It is possible to say that in America the bones of the object were emphasized. In England, some of the finest carving is done upon a background which American taste would consider awkward in form. For example, the cabriole legs of some English chairs are only a background for the rich embellishments; it is impossible to imagine the leg without the carving, for what would be left would be undefined backing. On the finest English product, this dissolving of the form is the result of a true baroque or rococo understanding; but on the lesser pieces, related to ours, it produces a strangely shaped leg which seems to hide beneath the carving. In Philadelphia, where complete surface enrichment is rare, the basic line itself, the form of the basic unit, is drawn to an incredible degree of simple excellence.

The eighteenth-century American's consciousness of the difference between his way of life and that of the upper class in England caused the cabinetmakers who came to Philadelphia to produce, not the more exotic work of which they were often capable, but work in what we now know as the Philadelphia taste. Thomas Affleck, who made the now famous Penn-Affleck furniture for Governor John Penn in the prevailing London taste,[4] later also made the "Mifflin-Morris-Hacker" chair with a solid splat and a crest rail decorated with Queen Anne scrolls, both long out of fashion in London.[5] This use of earlier forms transformed into a distinct Philadelphia taste did not represent a degeneration in Affleck's taste; rather, it was either a recognition of a different but good style, or a reflection of the demand by his public for something they preferred.

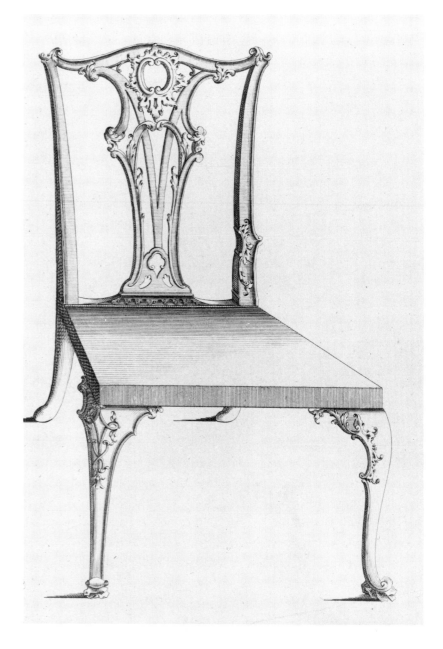

225

Drawing from Chippendale's The Gentleman and Cabinet-Maker's Director, *1754 and 1755 editions; plate XII, dated 1753; 1762 edition, plate XIII (other drawings on same page, design credit and date changed, but this drawing unaltered).*

[4] I am indebted to Charles F. Hummel for telling me that his research has not located sources to document Hornor's statements (Hornor, pp. 73–4, 176, and 184) that Affleck was born in Scotland, trained in London, came to America with Governor John Penn in 1763, and that he paid the highest tax and was therefore the most important cabinetmaker. Hummell points out that a tax list in the Historical Society of Pennsylvania for 1772 rated Benjamin Randolph twelve times higher than Affleck, and William Savery (who deducted from payments because of a fire) six times higher. Hummel further relates that Hornor based his statement on a tax list of the 1780's after Randolph was out of business. Hummel supports Hornor's statement that Affleck presented his Certificate to the Philadelphia Monthly Meeting of the Religious Society of Friends in 1763. It must be remembered that Randolph engaged in other business than furniture-making and much of his income may have been from his nonfurniture activities.

[5] Hornor, plates 259 and 132, p. 180, and elsewhere.

Another factor which contributed to Philadelphia's creation of a peculiar taste is that it was a center which drew many immigrating groups. From the beginning, the colony was open to everyone and people swarmed in from all Europe. For some years we have known the role that Ireland played in the eighteenth century in influencing the design and construction of Philadelphia furniture. This was the result of the great influx of Irish workers at the end of the first quarter of the eighteenth century. It has been estimated that between 1,500 and 2,000 Irish Quakers came to that region during its first sixty-eight years. Governor James Logan wrote in 1729, "It looks as if Ireland is to send all her inhabitants hither: for last week not less than six ships arrived and every day, two or three also arrive. The common fear is THAT IF THEY CONTINUE TO COME, they will make themselves proprietors of the Province."[6]

We must recognize, however, that Chippendale's pattern book, the *Director,* also played a part in Philadelphia, and that some of the most famous cabinetmakers were not of Irish descent. Perhaps even more noticeable than the Irish influence is the affinity of many English and Philadelphia pieces. Several English examples are included here to help define the transformation of the simpler English product into a refined Philadelphia piece. Figure 86 is an English chair made of mahogany. This Gothic splat became standard in Philadelphia and straight legs and stretchers common. However, in Philadelphia the central strapwork of the splat almost never violates the unity of a crest rail by breaking into it in this manner; rather, on carved chairs a husk is used for central emphasis, eliminating this finality of a rising point which divides left from right. In the English chair, figure 74, it is possible to see the heaviness of parts typical of pieces that served as models for Philadelphia work. It was made just before the emergence of the Chippendale period or during it; note the relationship in design to figure 75. On the English example the carving is of primary importance, rather than secondary to the basic form and movement, as it is in the Philadelphia chair; its decoration seems applied or laid on, rather than intrinsic, whereas in the Philadelphia example the basic form and the decoration work together as one.

It is instructive to take plates from Chippendale's pattern books and to see how they were used differently by cabinetmakers working for English, Irish, and American clients, though the purchasers were possibly living at a comparable socio-economic level. Figure 225 is a drawing that appeared in all three editions of Chippendale's *Director*[7] and it shows a refined sense of drawing,

226

English side chair, 1754–80. Victoria and Albert Museum (Acc. no. W62–1940). Mahogany. Height 37¼ inches; width 23. The shoe is inscribed in pencil, " '6 pedestals for Mr. Chippendale's backs.' This implies either that the 'backs' were obtained ready-made from Chippendale, or that they were copied from his designs." (Ralph Edwards, English Chairs: Victoria and Albert Museum [London, His Majesty's Stationery Office 1951], p. 26.) The latter seems more likely the case considering their lack of grace, though the carving is good. See also note 8, p. 168. (This chair was not investigated personally.)

---

[6] Quoted in David Stockwell, "Irish Influence in Pennsylvania Queen Anne Furniture," *Antiques,* 79 (March 1961), pp. 269–71, from the Logan Papers.

[7] This drawing is on the right of no. XII in Chippendale's *Director* of 1754 and of 1755, and no. XIII in that of 1762 (the latter has been republished with a biographical sketch by N. I. Bienenstock [New York: Dover Publications, Inc., 1966]).

227

Irish side chair, 1754–80. National Museum of Ireland (Acc. no. 6492, C1). Mahogany. (This chair was not investigated personally.)

among the heavy members; the carving is sporadic or scattered across the crest rail, which is altered from its original sweeping line to a scallop-like form; and the piercing at the bottom of the splat seems small.[8] Part of the heaviness is produced by the fact that the English worker made all the parts thicker or broader than the drawing suggests. It is indeed not the finest interpretation of the Chippendale drawing made in England, but it typifies the better than standard objects made there during this period. Had the people who owned the American furniture included here remained in England, this is the type of chair they might have possessed. Figure 227 is an Irish interpretation of the same pattern, showing the earthy, complex heaviness of one extreme of their work, a degree of heaviness even greater than that of the English interpretation. This is not the side of their work that has made people cite them as a source for Philadelphia but it, too, had some impact on Philadelphia work. Figure 228 is another drawing by Chippendale published in the 1762 edition. As in the first Chippendale drawing, its splat has a light, fanciful movement of complex interlacing scrolls and strapwork; the C scrolls lap onto the crest rail, joining to the lambrequin C shape to end in fanciful scroll-leafage ears. The base of the shoe is also carved to C scrolls flanking central leafage. Figure 229 was probably executed by Thomas Affleck in Philadelphia[9] and is obviously derived from this drawing; Affleck may have owned a copy of the *Director*. Whereas the English interpretation of the Chippendale drawing made all the members heavier than the drawing suggested, in the American interpretation they were made at least as light as suggested, being open and delicate, without losing the suggested thrust and counterpoint.

It is informative to observe what was left out when the design was used in Philadelphia. While in the English version the simplification produced boredom, in the American product there has been a clarification and unification of the parts. Now the crest rail moves down into the splat, uniting the two visually. The C scrolls move sideways, then down and in, providing a more encompassing movement. Perhaps the bottom of the splat appears overly simplified without the complex shoe suggested by the drawing. There it seems to balance the splat in mid-air. But the American solution is more in accord with the Philadelphia desire for stability and

with delicate leafage carving introduced onto the ears, splat, front legs, and one of the suggested back posts above the seat. The English chair, figure 226, uses this back design on a chair with straight legs. The chair appears broad and heavy to an American eye, with little flow movement; the piercing at the top seems insignificant

[8] This back is known on an English example with simple cabriole legs and club feet, showing that England too continued to use this less expensive foot with updated backs; Ralph Edwards, *The Shorter Dictionary of English Furniture* (London: Country Life Ltd., 1964), p. 146, fig. 114.

[9] Hornor, plates 113–15, p. 204, and elsewhere.

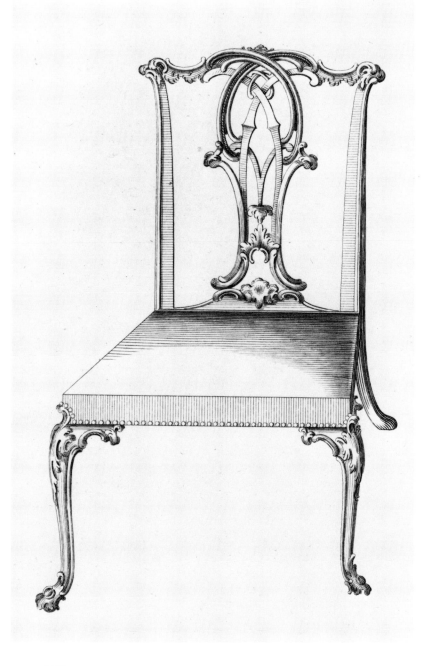

228

Drawing from Chippendale's The Gentleman and Cabinet-Maker's Director, *included in the 1762 edition only, plate IX.*

229

Seen also as fig. 94. Possibly made by Thomas Affleck in Philadelphia, this chair is based on Chippendale's drawing, fig. 228.

mass, rather than for the instability of things just touching, not interlocking, as though poised without involvement.

Another noticeable feature in the handling of the pattern book drawing is that the American chair emphasizes the vertical. The chair is narrow at the back of the seat, and thrusts up and out

to the top rail, while the English chair broadens a vertically oriented drawing. The Philadelphia exceptions are the vase-baluster chairs (fig. 80), which usually retain English breadth, and such chairs as the labeled Randolph chair, figure 92. This verticality exists in Philadelphia for both styles (and to some degree in the Queen Anne chairs of Connecticut and Massachusetts); compare figure 68 with a Massachusetts chair, figure 106, or with a New York chair, figure 139, or an English chair, figure 74. Typical of this desire for a lean, upward thrust is the fact that rolled arms (fig. 57), which accent breadth and the horizontal, though popular in England, are seldom found in Philadelphia. Instead, Philadelphia develops the scooped arm support, figure 58, which gives an additional upward motion.

We have said that in a Philadelphia chair all parts are related in scale, line, and decoration. Let us look in detail at one of the finest Philadelphia examples, figure 230. The feet, magnificently carved to strong but visually proper size, swing into a strongly curving leg that moves in, out, and in again to the seat rail. The knee, with simple, crisply delineated carving that spills down the leg without disturbing its line, is accented by a central daisy. The whole thrust of the leg springs one's eye into the seat rail, which is lightened by horizontal shaping, and the central accent is made by the time-honored shell, repeated in a larger form on the crest rail, bringing the eye up to the back and center. The ears, large, which flow down and into the crest rail (just as the front feet flow into the leg and up toward the seat rail) are visually a part both of the fluted posts and of the top rail, thus uniting the two. The top rail flows down into the splat, which is formed of marvelously fluid strapwork. The only straight line is the top of the seat rail, framing the elaborate textile whose pattern relates to the movement of the back, and the latter is likewise framed on either side by the back posts. The linear accents established by the gadrooning of the shells are repeated in the fluting of the back posts. No part is conceived alone, no area expressed except in relation to another. This chair has the movement and grace of spring plants. It is American eighteenth-century sculpture. Being original, not overly dominated by London, the furniture designers expressed themselves freely, carving or leaving alone a line, attenuating or thickening, retaining forms of feet and other details long out of fashion in Europe, doing what suited their purpose. This chair and others are great original designs. Where English chairs often show a tight, not powerfully tight, but tense, nervous line, or again a rather placid line, the great Philadelphia chairs are like a taut, powerful bow, all grace and strength, rhythm and flow, always conscious of simple harmonic relationships. This consciousness is constantly reflected in such small details as the fact that back posts rounded above the seat (fig. 53) were almost wholly discarded, perhaps because such a surface was unrelated to the flat planes of the upper part of the chair. Other American chairs never

230

Seen also as fig. 69. The integration of motif, form, and movement seen in this chair epitomizes the best Philadelphia taste during the Chippendale period.

achieve this level of consciousness, nor the sinuous, lithe quality of Philadelphia. New York and Massachusetts will show their unique character; only Connecticut has a related aesthetic, but the manner of expression is different.

Having looked both at Philadelphia's construction characteristics and the attitude to design, it is possible to see that a chair which may at first sight appear to be a Philadelphia piece comes in fact from elsewhere. Figure 232 is similar in shape and carving to the Philadelphia chair, figure 231, but there are, upon close study, noticeable differences: its members are heavier; the front legs are thicker, the ankles extremely so. The carving is much coarser: the shell on the front rail appears as seven separate lobes placed in conjunction, not as a united shell form; the same is true of the shell of the top rail; and the flanking acanthus is stiff and seemingly artificial. The carving on the knee is also stilted, the daisy noticeably so: in figure 231, it flows into its allotted space, being a plastic form nearly triangular; in figure 232, it has become a stiff, three-pronged cutout. It does not spring from the wood, is not organically part of the chair; it is simply a decoration that looks

231

Seen also as fig. 72. A comparison between this Philadelphia chair and the perhaps Newtown, Pennsylvania, chair, fig. 232, demonstrates the difference between a high-style product and a rural one.

232

Seen also as fig. 73. This possibly Newtown, Pennsylvania, chair is a rural interpretation of such chairs as fig. 231.

applied. The movement of the basic parts of figure 232 is clumsy in comparison to figure 231, the subtle curves are gone, a lightness and quickness is lacking. The ears project upward and outward from a cruder back post. The strapwork of the splat moves ponderously along its course without the quick springing motion of the other example. So like the Philadelphia chair and yet so different. Where was this piece made? Except for the use of cherry, it is purely Philadelphia in detail and construction, and cherry was used to a limited extent for Philadelphia high-style pieces. We are not surprised to find it has a Newtown, Pennsylvania, history, placing it north of Philadelphia, where the Philadelphia style might dominate but become less suave. This chair is typical of much country Pennsylvania cabinetwork, carried out by more rural designers for a different milieu. Though it does not have subtle grace, it has a simple power typical of some of the very fine country furniture. Here, regionalizing is a question of the visual experience of the chair as a whole and not of a description of its details, for a simple description of detail alone would have assigned it to Philadelphia.

Figure 46 shows a chair that has been classified by many as a Philadelphia example; to a great extent, the presence of through tenons was the deciding factor, though the general design was considered to be like Philadelphia work. Admittedly, rounded back posts (fig. 53), C-scroll knees (fig. 58), and a single rear stretcher (fig. 48) are all known in Philadelphia, but they are rare, and rounded back posts usually show a reverse curve on the front plane. This type of shoed club foot has not been found there; the seating of the splat—on a slip seat chair—directly into the back seat rail, passing behind the shoe, has also not been found there. The heavy straight base of the back feet we have not seen in American work; the shape of the splat, with its slow-moving reverse curve, is not a Philadelphia line; and the front legs lack the action that we have come to expect of that area. In short, it does not fit into the Philadelphia group. And it is in fact an English chair. English authorities have accepted it as such, it has an English history, and is classified at Williamsburg as English, probably from the North Country, where we have seen through tenons. The slow movement and blandness so like certain other English chairs makes it hard for us to understand how this chair could ever have been attributed to Philadelphia. Its incorrect assignment was caused, in this instance, by a misunderstanding both of Philadelphia's method of construction and detail, and of the approach to design. The reassigning of these two chairs is not difficult. But more knotty problems do exist.

233

Seen also as fig. 83. A chair of questionable age, bearing the label of Benjamin Randolph.

To those who know Philadelphia chairs, it will perhaps be surprising that figures 80–82 are not assigned to Benjamin Randolph and that the well-known labeled Randolph chairs of the Boston Museum are not given eighteenth-century dates. The chairs in the Boston Museum are a pair of Philadelphia Chippendale side chairs, one of which bears the label of Benjamin Randolph (fig. 233). Upon investigation, these chairs show some variations from what we have come to expect of Philadelphia examples, and they need to be examined carefully.

In the Mabel Brady Garvan Collection at the Yale University Art Gallery, there are five chairs (three included here, figs. 80–82) which offer a useful "control group" by which to gauge the variation from the norm found in the Boston chairs. For several reasons, the Garvan chairs serve as an excellent control group: first, they were purchased from several different sources; second, though they are basically similar in construction and design, the very differences in the handling of the details show the freedom and variety within an individual style that characterizes the work of an authentic "period" cabinetmaker or group of cabinetmakers. Thus the back height, width, and seat height of these chairs differ as much as ⅞ of an inch. In two of the chairs the side seat rails tenon through the back posts, while the third has blind tenons. The manner of executing the carving on figure 80 differs from the other two, showing the hand of at least two carvers or one carver working at different times. There are marked differences in the way of decorating the front seat rail. All three chairs have their original pine seat frames. Two of the chairs retain all or part of their original pine corner blocks. The details, such as the carving of the decoration and feet, though varied, are essentially handled with the same spirit of crispness and life and correspond in every way to the Philadelphia chairs we have seen. These chairs were presumably made at about the same time, but for different customers. Briefly outlined below are sixteen points concerning the two Boston chairs, which indicate precisely where they differ from the Garvan chairs and from other Philadelphia chairs studied earlier:

1. On both chairs all corner blocks are of new stained pine.

2. Both seat frames are of oak, not nearly as common as pine.

3. The four knee brackets of each chair are not applied with large-headed, hand-made nails as was standard in Philadelphia but show wooden pegs, which are perhaps plugs covering screws (these may be original, not a later addition).

4. The C-scroll carving on the front seat rails is applied, rather than carved from the solid as is standard in Philadelphia.

5. The outside ends of the C scroll, where they fall below the seat rail, are backed by applied pieces rather than by the extension of the rail itself, not a Philadelphia practice.

6. There is a groove carved above the carved scroll edging to make it appear deeper, an unusual practice for the eighteenth century.

7. The rear part of the horizontal shaping of the side seat rails is applied like a bracket respond and is an uninspired curve. Two of the Garvan chairs have true side shaping, that is, not formed of a separate piece but cut from the solid as is standard in eighteenth-century Philadelphia chairs, and the back part of the shaping of the Garvan chairs shows a subtle curve; the Boston chairs have a simple straight lower edge where it meets the leg. The third Garvan chair has no horizontal shaping.

8. Points 5–7 show an attempt to save wood not customary in Philadelphia or indeed in American work of the eighteenth century.

9. The height of the through tenons is ¾ of an inch less than the side seat rail, whereas usually they are nearly the same depth.

10. The rear of the horizontal shaping, which is a separate piece like a bracket respond, is applied with a through tenon, not normal on Philadelphia eighteenth-century Chippendale chairs.

11. The carving is not alive; that is, it is correct in detail but spiritless in execution, like the work of a copyist.

12. The front seat rail is shaped to a loose, serpentine line, with its higher corners rather flat, and depends for effect upon the applied carving. The line itself lacks character.

13. Contrary to the opinion expressed by Hipkiss,[10] the shape and carving of the legs do not correspond to those of the highboy to which he related them in supplements 33 and 89 of his book. In comparison, the chair legs lack spring and strength of line and the carving is far less inspired; for example, all the leafage springs from one point.

14. It is not unusual for a label to lose part of its edge through cleaning and general wear. When this happens, the wood under the removed part is lighter than the surrounding area because less air has reached it. Often, various areas of missing labels show various colors, since they were removed at

[10] Hipkiss, plate 89 and supplements 33 and 89.

different times. On the Boston chair, this variation does not appear (see detail of label). A stain has been applied around the label, leaving a lighter area at the upper right hand corner which does not actually correspond to the area the complete label would originally have covered. The stain does not cover the whole back rail; there are light patches near the corner blocks as well. These light areas are of the same color as the inside of the back rail of the unlabeled chair; that is, they are the natural age color and differ from the color of the stained part. Thus, the color where the label is missing appears lighter only because of the stain around it. This suggests that an old label was attached to the chair and stain applied to leave a "light" area which *nearly* corresponds to the missing part of the label.

15. In approach to design, the chairs do not resemble the other known labeled Randolph chair; figure 92 is a Gothic splat chair in the Garvan Collection which meets all the requirements of authenticity as to its label and construction. Two other chairs recorded with Randolph labels have the same simple, stripped-down quality of this Gothic back chair. None show the super-refinement of decoration present on figures 80–82.[11]

---

[11] See labeled Randolph chairs: Samuel W. Woodhouse, Jr., "More About Benjamin Randolph," *Antiques,* 17 (January 1930), p. 23, fig. 4; advertisement, *Antiques* 59 (April 1951), p. 248 [illustrated]. What contact Randolph ever had with much of the elaborate Chippendale furniture assigned to him is much in question. The six famous "sample" chairs are often used to demonstrate his skill as a carver and they lack any proof of origin. Hornor says in a footnote on p. 94: ". . . the six Sample Chairs were not preserved by the descendents of Benjamin Randolph, but have come down through those of his second wife, Mary Wilkinson, who previously had been married twice. Randolph died in 1790, leaving but £20 to his wife; yet considerable property, including all of his household goods not bequeathed to a ward, was left to his daughter who continued to reside in Randolph's Burlington County home, Speedwell. By the will of Mary Randolph dated 1816, the six superlative chairs are *thought* [sic] to have been included in 'the remainder of my household goods I give unto my son Nathaniel Fenimore,' in whose family these same chairs descended. This pedigree lacks the first two and most important links in the whole chain, which at best is only circumstantial . . . all six Sample Chairs have been located in the families of Mary Randolph's great grandchildren."

Thus the household goods went to a ward and a daughter, not to the thrice-married wife who probably had her own goods, and the chairs are only "thought" to have been amongst what she left to her son.

Four of the chairs (at the Metropolitan, the Philadelphia Museum, Colonial Williamsburg, and Winterthur) have been investigated and accepted as made in Philadelphia. They were, however, not included here as they were not considered typical of Philadelphia work, shedding little light on the basic attitude or desire of the region. If they were samples, and Philadelphia customers liked them, why are there not many like products in existence?

16. The back design of the Garvan and Boston chairs is English in its breadth and general treatment and corresponds to the Affleck-Penn chair shown in plate 260 of Hornor's *Blue Book, Philadelphia Furniture.* As we have seen, Affleck came to America in 1763 and made furniture for the Governor's Mansion in the English style. In 1775, Affleck was still using this crest rail (see Hornor, plate 265). This would make it natural to attribute the Garvan chairs tentatively to Affleck. If the Boston chairs had appeared on the market without one being labeled, they would never have been attributed to Randolph.

In construction and design, the Boston chairs differ significantly from other Philadelphia chairs we have seen. Though none of these sixteen points provides conclusive proof, in itself, of a later date than the eighteenth century, taken together they certainly suggest it. The chairs do show patina resulting from use; this would be explained if they were found to be nineteenth-century chairs made to fill out a set of authentic chairs of like design—a rather common practice—which would mean that the labels had been attached recently to enhance their value.

2. *Massachusetts*

SINCE THE BEGINNING of a broad interest in American antiques in the early years of this century, Boston chairs have been second in popularity only to those of Philadelphia, but they have never commanded the same price because they have not the rich, free movement of Philadelphia. This difference in desirability in no way reflects the quality of construction—in fact, the retention of stretchers, so common in Massachusetts, creates a sturdier chair; nor does it imply lesser designers, for the shaping of parts and the stance of the chairs is often of the highest development. What then is the difference? Viewing a Massachusetts Queen Anne chair squarely from the front (fig. 235), the curves and the straights form a fine composition. Quiet in line, restrained in movement, composed of slowly moving curves which are repeated and recalled throughout the total object, it appears at first beautiful and restful. But from an angle, as chairs are usually seen (fig. 234), and to one accustomed to Philadelphia, the squares and the straights begin to clash with, rather than to harmonize with, the curves. In figure 101, where the seat is shaped further to carry out the Queen Anne use of the reverse curve, bringing more harmony throughout the chair, the straight columnar-turned side stretchers and the equally unrelated medial and rear stretchers introduce a discordant note, and throughout our entire period the use of these

235

Seen also as fig. 100. Seen from the front, the incongruity of Massachusetts makers using straight stretchers and seat rails with a reverse-curve back and front legs is not immediately evident.

234

Seen also as fig. 97. Seen from an angle, the straight parts of a typical Massachusetts Queen Anne–style chair do not relate to the curves of the back and front legs.

straight unharmonious stretchers is continued. Behind this inconsistency of line movement is the lack of a sense of design harmony toward the total object.

Massachusetts's concept of design differs from that of other areas of America. During the Chippendale period, the curves that had never fully flowed earlier became tight and brittle. The moving lines of the central upper scrolls of the standard splat (figs. 103–109) are styled to solidified reverse curves. The top rail where it flows into the splat is nearly frozen in its movement and the top of the splat is suspended above the base without having any visual relationship to it. Figure 237 is symptomatic of the problem. It is handsome, and one of the finest and most typical of the Massachusetts chairs. At first glance it is both an emotional and an intellectual experience, but in time the intellectual appreciation

237

Seen also as fig. 106. One of the finest interpretations of the standard Massachusetts Chippendale chair, which borrows almost all of its features from England (see fig. 105).

236

Seen also as fig. 104. The shaping of the strap work of the splat and the straightness of the back is typical of Massachusetts Chippendale; unusual is the use of a horseshoe-shaped seat rail and the absence of stretchers.

alone holds one's interest. The stretchers, legs, seat, back post, crest rail, and splat, though each beautifully drawn, seem to have been conceived of separately; they never really achieve any unified movement. One feels it would be possible to exchange the legs or splats or seats with any other related chair and still have a good typical Massachusetts product. Figure 237 is a more successful chair than is figure 107 only because its proportions and execution are finer, not because there is more response or harmony between parts. Let us look at a chair, figure 236, which is one of the most graceful of those made in Massachusetts. Its base is freed of straight stretchers; its front legs and seat, with their reverse curves, are harmonious; even the back posts below the seat, with their bracket responds and quietly flaring feet, pick up the movement of the rest. But, in this respect, it is not typical of Massachusetts and even this great chair can be criticized. The base alone, if looked at with the upper half covered, would lead one to expect a more flowing, pulsating, richly developed back; instead, the rigidity of the straight back is not relieved to flow by the simple use of spooning or bowing as it would have been in Philadelphia.

It has been said that when creating a piece of furniture, the Massachusetts designer used one area or part of the object as a foil for another; that one part was left plain to provide a contrast to a carved area;[1] this is seen in figure 113, where carved legs are placed with an uncarved back. Though a simpler explanation for this particular inconsistency is perhaps the factor of economics, the use of a plain back and carved legs does tell us something about the taste of the region. In Philadelphia, the reverse of this division would be found: the back, the most readily noticeable part of the chair, would have been the most fully developed area. It seems that in Massachusetts, rather than a plain surface being thought of as a foil for another area, the conception of a "totality" or "whole" differed radically from elsewhere. In Massachusetts, the parts of the chair seem to have been created separately and to be seen as a whole only when assembled. There is no consistency in idea or movement between parts: for example, the motifs that appear below are not recalled above. What unites the chair is that the parts are of a consistent weight or mass; that is, the width of the parts and details is visually balanced, whereas in New York we shall see that the parts often did not relate even in scale or weight.[2]

[1] Richard Randall, Jr., "A Question of Taste," *The Ellis Memorial Antique Show* (1961; no publishing data), pp. 51, 53, 55, 57, and 59.

[2] The inconsistency between one part and another can be easily seen by studying the typical Massachusetts "blocked" chest-on-chest. The bottom chest is blocked, which provides three vertical parts; the upper chest is flanked by two wide, fluted pilasters; and the whole is crowned by a broken arch pediment without rosettes, accented by three flame finials. In such a piece, the motifs of one part are not repeated on the other, the blocking below is not recalled above, the wide pilasters above are not seen below, and the fan that decorates the top center drawer is not echoed on the base. What unites the piece is the relationship of the weight masses of the individual parts; the pilasters are wide enough to provide a bulk that is in harmony with the weight of the blocking below, and the pediment is bold enough to terminate the strong vertical accent created by the blocking. (For example, see Nutting, fig. 302.)

Another unifying factor in Massachusetts furniture is that though the drawing shows rigidity, there is a unified clarity and clearness of parts. The drawing, the outline, is sharp and clear, with no soft edges. Though this lack of roundness can lead to stiffness it can also, as in figure 237, lead to a marvelously clear delineation of the object. The finest Massachusetts case piece has clear linear drawing, a precise distinction of parts, and there is a refinement, a fineness of definition. The same is true of the best Massachusetts chairs; let us again consider figure 237. This chair looks as if it were drawn with a finely sharpened pencil. There is no fuzziness or softness of line, there is, rather, a crisp, precise outlining of parts. This unifying clarity, however, does not carry with it a sense of interaction. The acanthus carving of the knee in no way disturbs the underlying leg. It appears almost as hair, combed lightly though stiffly across the knee. It does not spring from the knee bracket, in fact, the word "spring" seems the opposite of its action; it merely covers the area. It would not be possible, as it is in Philadelphia, to apply such verbs as "spring," "pulsate," or "flow" to these members or this carving. Nothing is allowed to disturb the brittleness, the almost austere aloofness of the piece. A lack of flowing carving produces some of this Massachusetts tightness; no shells appear on Queen Anne chairs and only semi-shells later on. What leafage there is is tight, linear, and confined; it seems laid on begrudgingly. In Philadelphia this amount of leafage would appear rich and lush.

It is revealing of Massachusetts's taste that it should choose from many existing English attitudes this particular one, with its lean, tautly drawn lines. The sameness of so many of the chairs implies that a standard pattern was chosen, perhaps partly by chance, and repeated again and again, the difference between particular chairs lying in the cabinetmaker's skill in developing each member in itself. A skillful man produced clearly defined and well-executed parts, and thus a fine example; another man, not such good parts, and thus a less refined chair.

This approach to design is to some extent the creation of Massachusetts itself, but it has its source in England. For example, figure 105 is a mahogany chair made in England in the eighteenth century for Løvenborg Manor House in Denmark; it was probably purchased through the family's London agent, John Collett, who died in 1759. This English chair has what we would call pure Massachusetts features: the splat, crest rail, central conventionalized shell, ears, knee carving, back post, with the slight flare forming a foot in this manner, and the lightness of the seat rail, all could have appeared in this manner in Massachusetts. The lack of stretchers, though not typical in Massachusetts, is known. The front feet are less defined than those on the finer Massachusetts products but resemble those of figure 109, and the back posts above the seat show a double molding that is uncommon, though not unknown here.[3] Again, the arrangement of the strapwork of the splat of another English chair, figure 110, is also characteristic of Massachusetts, as are the ears, crest rail, shell, and character of the back. The rear corner blocks of this mahogany chair are made in the Massachusetts form, though in front there are the narrow cross-ties we have seen in this country, prior to 1780, only in New York. Also unusual for America is the fact that the shoe holding the splat is tenoned into the back posts instead of being simply nailed to the seat rail. Again, we note the double molding of the back posts, as well as the gadrooning that is not typical of Massachusetts. Although cartouche-carved knees would be surprising in Massachusetts, we find related carving on figure 123.

The direct dependence of Massachusetts chairs on English is shown once more by the comparison of the back of figure 122 and that of the English chair back, figure 121. The same Gothic effect and carving is present on both.

Attempts are continually made to find pattern book sources for American designs, with the emphasis given to Chippendale. It is far more logical, and accurate, to discover a parallel European object. European-trained men would repeat similar designs here as long as the public tolerated them, as they did in Massachusetts and New York (and in the South), and what European objects were imported proved stronger influences than drawings. True, we have examples of Americans using pattern sources, as we saw under Philadelphia; but this is *extremely* rare before the classical patterns of Hepplewhite and Sheraton. Again and again, we can find English objects that are much more similar to existing American ones than any design book drawing. (An example of object rather than design book source [figs. 241–243], is discussed in Part III under New York.

A distinctive feature of Massachusetts Chippendale chairs is their form of the claw and ball foot, with its two flanking talons. Although this retracted claw appears to some extent on English chairs (figs. 105 and 110), it seems, at least at present, that it can be considered an American development when carried to the extreme of figure 122. It should be remembered that we noted retracted claws in Philadelphia (fig. 90) and Rhode Island (fig.

180) and a comparison with the feet of figures 106–109 provides a study in quality of carving.

Massachusetts in its direct borrowing of English designs shows less reinterpretation of, or renewal of, its source material than we found in Philadelphia. Few if any of the Philadelphia Chippendale chairs are *exact* copies from any English example or pattern book source, and where the Philadelphia products do come close to the patterns, the variants are perhaps more interesting than the direct following of details. In Massachusetts we have seen that some of the standard chairs are, detail for detail, like English sources. This makes it more difficult to perceive an absolutely standard Massachusetts attitude toward design. It eliminates the consistency developed by an area which, taking former sources, alters them to a great degree to its own taste. Direct borrowing means that the inconsistencies found in England are directly copied here, and perhaps it means that they are intensified. This led to the necessity of considering two basic groups in Massachusetts chairs; and in New York, where this copying is perhaps more absolute, or at least of a different nature, we needed to form many separate groups. Philadelphia, in reorienting the European forms, imposed upon them its own peculiar standards of taste, bringing them more into conformity.

Of the two basic Massachusetts groups, the first (i.e., fig. 106) has its parallel in such chairs as figure 105; the backs are alike but the front legs and feet of the American chair show the intensely crisp delineation of line so typical of Massachusetts. The variant of this group, figure 111, is just as closely related to its sources as the rest of the group. The second Massachusetts group (figs. 113–125) is perhaps equally close to English sources while showing the same tendency to leanness, thinness of parts, spareness of movement, and flatness of carving. As many of the motifs, details, and basic forms are found in both groups, their joint presence in Massachusetts is in no way inconsistent. Many of the latter group are documented to the area (fig. 123). This at first caused raised eyebrows. Now it is possible to see them as a key to what was the prevailing taste, for the recognition of their presence and role in the area forced us to re-examine previous inadequate and oversimplified conclusions based on the desire to assume that America invented much, if not the majority, of its designs.

It would be unfair to assume because of the parallelism of these English and American chairs that Massachusetts created nothing on its own. The very act of choosing this particular attitude to form when so many lavish, rich, full-blown designs were

---

[3] Nutting, fig. 2226, although this, too, may be an English example.

238

*Seen also as fig. 98. This English Queen Anne style
chair shows the type of design that inspired such Massachusetts
chairs as fig. 239.*

239

*Seen also as fig. 99. Closely related to the English chair
(fig. 238), but with a greater sense of curving motion.*

prevalent shows the cabinetmakers' personal choice; moreover, having borrowed this particular type of English product, with its spareness and linear quality, they often intensified and clarified the design even further.

Perhaps Massachusetts did alter its European sources more during the Queen Anne period than the Chippendale. A comparison of the English chair, figure 238, and the similar American chair, figure 239, both of walnut, shows Massachusetts's liking for stripped-down, delineated designs. In the American chair, we see a graceful design that accents the vertical without the heaviness, breadth, or horizontality of the English example. Our understanding of Massachusetts's appreciation of simplicity and spareness is intensified when we notice that even the simple shells appearing on the English example are not present on the American product. In comparison with the English example, the American seems graceful. One might say that the drawing of the basic chair is more consciously curvilinear. The stretchers on the Massachusetts chair, though detrimental to the design as a whole, reflect more consciousness of movement than do those on the English chair, where a simple straight bar, bearing no relationship to the curves of the chair, forms the medial and rear stretcher. However, though the straight stretcher has not yet appeared in Massachusetts, the characteristically American stretcher does have an English prototype. This again shows Massachusetts's selectivity, choosing the stretcher that will relate, to some degree, to the curves around it.

This peculiar taste was probably created in great part by cabinetmakers who came from an area of England where it prevailed. Even earlier than Queen Anne we see in Massachusetts a clarification of line in, for example, the fine early eighteenth-century bannister-back chairs. Disregarding the more emotional Flemish-curve caned chairs of the time, Massachusetts showed a liking for the related but sparer designs we now know so well,[4] and this again indicates Massachusetts's early selection of a particular taste.

3. New York

PRIOR TO THE REVOLUTION, New York was not at all the important center of furniture design it was to become after 1784 when it was chosen as the federal capital. Then, designer-craftsmen such as Duncan Phyfe flocked to meet the new demands for classical elegance. Before this only a few cabinetmakers are remembered and relatively few pieces of New York furniture are known; the furniture of Albany is always included, as it is here, to pad out the examples.

New York chairs are related to the London chairs of about 1730, being George II in style, and show little later influence.

[4] For example, John T. Kirk, *Early American Furniture* (New York: Alfred A. Knopf, Inc., 1970), fig. 37.

English George II furniture has a heavy, ponderous, baroque quality, with wide, slow-moving, often complex curves, and generally a lack of consistency in the motifs (in England this gives way, by 1750, to the nervous quickness of the rococo period).

New York chairs, reflecting this English prototype, are lower, broader, and more slowly ponderous than the Philadelphia or Massachusetts examples. All show a full, broad, generous mass. The splats are wider and heavier. There is no airy rococo; the languid English reverse curve of 1730 predominates. The forms are all slow-moving and seem somber. There is little order in, or relationship between, parts. The chair is not an integral whole. The carving is stiff and hard; seemingly stiff in conception, it is equally stiff in execution. A stiff straight leg is put with a curvilinear back splat (fig. 131) and a stiff back is put with a full reverse-curve leg (fig. 133). The ornamentation is often unrelated to its surface, as we have seen on English examples, or to other ornamentation on the same chair. New York, it seems, liked this style to the exclusion of the later, lighter Chippendale forms, and continued to use it at least until 1795; whereas Philadelphia, Boston, and other areas seem to have gone directly from what the English would call Queen Anne and George I to the mid-century or Chippendale style, with only a minor use of George II.

Looking at standard examples from New York, we find this continuation of the first variation of the baroque-rococo style to be typical of a general lack of elegant refinement. An example of these ponderous, rather confused designs is figure 147. Here clumsy feet support heavy legs with knee brackets carved to squared leafage. This decorative form is not repeated elsewhere, and a quatrefoil daisy appears on the top rail, which is unrelated to any other area of carving. The ears are grooved into two parts, visually dividing the back post from the top rail and making three seemingly unrelated units. Compare this and two other New York splats, figures 146 and 148, with other interpretations of related splats, figures 77–78 and 181–182. Figure 240, with rather crisply carved knees, has heavy legs and a light back carved to static boredom. The back posts with two stopped flutes, always a static number, support a light crest rail over a splat which is purely European in form and illogical in design; it provides neither flow nor rhythm. The leafage on the ears, related to the knee carving, seems an afterthought. The central husk is suspended over a skirting of leafage and none of this carving is related to the complex gadrooning of the splat; the introduction of the Gothic arch with members crossing at dots is completely extraneous to any other detail of the chair. Even the greatly prized tassel and ruffle chairs shaped rear stretcher. The seat rails of figures 129–133 are not horizontally shaped and have loose curves that move slowly across to be supported on wide, unrelated knees. Each part of the chair seems to be treated as a separate unit, with no overall concept. The parts are not even related in scale or mass. Here, then, is not even the consistency of scale or clarity of drawing that we saw in Massachusetts. The great William Johnson chair (fig. 143) shows more continuity. Long thought to be a Philadelphia piece, it has much of that quality. The beautiful feet and legs are Philadelphia in character and the near harmony of parts is also related; but the knee carving, spilling from under the seat rail, breaks the flow, and the top rail, though it moves gracefully into the splat, has ears suddenly carved with shells that are unrelated in form to its central shell. It is, alas, only nearly harmonic.

We have seen how Philadelphia reinterpreted its sources and how Massachusetts, though in many cases adhering closely to its source material, did at times simplify to a refined aesthetic the simpler objects it chose to copy. New York also slavishly adhered to its prototypes and chose to confine itself to the heavier Georgian forms. The backs of many New York chairs, like those of Massachusetts, are identical to the English models from which they were drawn. Figures 151 and 242 are English chairs which show patterns used in New York with little or no rethinking. Compare the splat and crest rail of figure 151 to those of the New York chair, figure 152; though, as we have seen, the English form of gadrooning is not the most common form in New York, it is not unknown there. Figure 242 shows an English back; note that the molded back posts, the carving and piercing of the splat, and the shaping of the crest rail are also standard in New York (fig. 243). These two chairs permit us to compare the Chippendale drawing, figure 241, with its English and American applications. This demonstrates the American cabinetmaker's dependence on actual objects from England rather than upon pattern book sources. The American chair is closer to the European example than to the drawing. It would of course be unfair to think there was no originality or alteration from English patterns, but the main point is that these alterations remained within a basic English taste, without bringing forth anything that can be titled, in the obvious sense, American. To see New York in relationship to Philadelphia is to see a lesser style center (during this period) with little organization compared to a highly developed and integrated style center. Philadelphia shows originality in creating a new concept of design which differs from the British; when New York does vary from its source, it shows only a simplification of English and Irish designs, and the changes

240

Seen also as fig. 150. Typical of many New York Chippendale chairs, the splat and crest rail has juxtaposed motifs or parts with little flow or harmony between them.

(fig. 136) are squared off, never to flow or unite the separate parts into an integrated whole. The carving, too, is scattered about: ears, central ornament, flanking scrolls, tassel, again flanking scrolls, "ruffle," handholds, knee carving, and gadrooning, all appear separate units, simply placed side by side. How low and unrelated are the stretchers on figure 130, and what a statically complex a system of classification in handling the variety of New York types, in contrast to the comparatively simple system that could be used in other areas. There was not sufficient new energy generated by a sophisticated buying market, no controlling active taste to focus and unify the various borrowings from England, let alone call forth great new aesthetic expressions different from the European models.

This seemingly negative evaluation does not reflect a blanket condemnation of New York craftsmen. Before the Revolution New York produced some of the finest American silver and after the Revolution it gave America some of its finest original furniture. But its pre-Revolutionary chairs are inferior when viewed as pieces of design, though they possess the sturdy richness of their

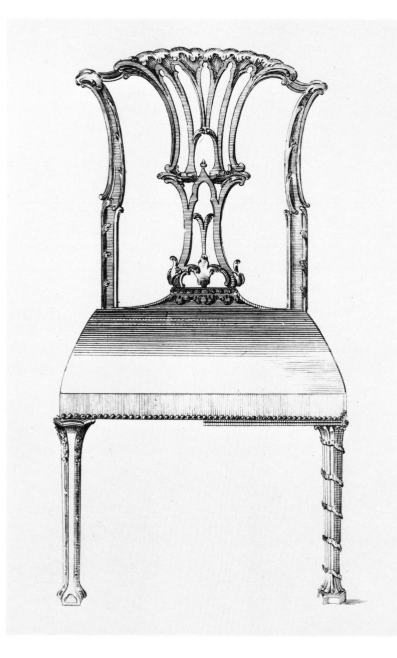

241

Drawing from Chippendale's The Gentleman and Cabinet-Maker's Director, *included in the 1762 edition only, plate 12.*

242

Back of English side chair, 1762–80. Present location unknown. Mahogany. (This chair was not investigated personally.) Based on the Chippendale drawing, fig. 241, this type of chair was the source for New York chairs such as fig. 243.

seem to express a rural quality rather than the creation of a new mode of aesthetics. Philadelphia purified itself to three basic chair backs; New York seems to have groupings perhaps only because a man or a group of men made a single standard pattern (figs. 129–131). This direct borrowing without the clarity that comes from focus probably accounts for the fact that we had to resort to so

made elsewhere; here let us look at a chair (fig. 244) once thought to have been made in Philadelphia, whereas actually it was made in New York. It became one of the most famous New York chairs, for it was believed that it was signed by a New York cabinetmaker, as discussed earlier. It was classified in the Sack sale of 1932 at the

243

Seen also as fig. 149. The back of this chair is closer to the English chair back, fig. 242, than it is to the drawing, fig. 241, suggesting that its design source was not a drawing but similar English objects.

244

Seen also as fig. 139. Once catalogued as Philadelphia, probably because of its through-tenoned seat rails and rounded back legs, this chair has a typical New York design attitude.

English counterparts. New York did achieve a masterpiece during our period in the great New York card tables, and it is interesting that an English precedent for these has been found as well.

At the end of the section on Philadelphia we looked at two chairs thought to be from that area which turned out to have been

American Art Association, Anderson Galleries, as "Philadelphia 1760–70," although it had been in the Van Rensselaer family of Rensselaer, New York. (Later, what was probably its mate appeared in a loan exhibition of New York furniture in 1934). The obvious reason for this attribution is the presence of through tenons and rounded back legs. The concentration on transferable details that have a European source comprises one of the main stumbling blocks in this field because they are such a handy, simple way to regionalize an object. The change to a New York attribution was based on the discovery of writing in pencil on the inside of the back seat rail.[1] The chair is stiff and decorated with "here-and-there" leafage, with little flow or rhythm, and it has the boxiness we now expect from New York. The splat has a two-part feeling, with the upper section compounded of C scrolls; neither the division nor these C scrolls are known in Philadelphia. The width of the chair as a whole, and the splat in particular, is typical of the New York spirit. The former incorrect designation appears surprising today, as the chair so obviously fits into the New York fold. Here again, then, is the curse of our problem, the dependence on small details which results in sacrificing real understanding for simple answers.

Another chair difficult to place was figure 134. Looking at it, we find that a careful investigation of details and construction does not solve the place of its origin but rather only makes us wish to assign it to two homes. It has been assigned to New York because "The front feet are like those of the Beekman dining table . . . shod and pointed. . . ."[2] This type of foot is indeed found in New York, but it also appeared in Connecticut, perhaps in several areas. In the Mary Allis Collection in Fairfield, there is a tea table with these wide, pointed-pad feet, which was found locally and which seems to have been made there.[3] There is also a highboy that was built into the wall in the Old Inn, South Woodstock, Connecticut,[4] which has similar feet. In addition, there is a Connecticut Valley chest of drawers with a Deerfield history which had related feet,[5] and two pieces with such feet were found in the Woodbury area. It must then be accepted that Connecticut as well as New York used this style of foot. The wood is cherry, and though it was used in New York, it was far more popular in Con-

[1] See page 42 and note 1.

[2] Downs, figs. 108 and 318.

[3] [Kirk], *Connecticut Furniture*, fig. 160.

[4] Nutting, fig. 352.

[5] *Antiques*, 70 (September 1956), p. 225 [illustrated].

necticut. The corner blocks are composed of two large vertical pieces of square section, similar in placement to the Philadelphia-New York-Connecticut practice, but they do not overlap to form a quarter-round section. The use of bracket responds cut from the solid is very unusual, and rounded back posts are not common in either place. Nothing so far provides grounds upon which we can ascribe the piece. The most helpful feature is perhaps the back. Spooned backs appear to some degree in both areas. The back posts above the seat are straight from the front; this is found on Connecticut Queen Anne chairs, and not on any known New York ones. The back posts below the seat kick strongly backwards, which is a Connecticut practice. On the basis of the kind of study discussed in Part II it would be hard to favor either area, but on the basis of the total design the assignment to New York becomes reasonable. The movement is broad and slow without the open feeling for space we associate with Connecticut. Its lack of decoration is not typical of New York, but the heaviness of parts is. Seen from the front the splat is broad and the seat and back wide and square. It is therefore tentatively assigned to New York.

4. Rhode Island

THE 1965 LOAN SHOW held by The Rhode Island Historical Society in the John Brown House provided an opportunity to see together some of the finest examples of Rhode Island furniture. A study of the assembled objects made it possible to see that there were in Rhode Island two basic approaches to design. Although this is more easily demonstrated by studying the facade of case pieces, it is possible to perceive in chairs the same division. The first approach was the flat, rectilinear, basically two-plane style. The pieces that form this group bring to mind the suggestion of some scholars that the drawings in Chippendale's pattern book were produced in two stages. First, the basic units which provided the portions and general functions were drawn by Chippendale and then the rococo ornamentation that formed the surface decorations was added by others. This flat, two-plane Rhode Island furniture is like Chippendale furniture before the ornamental overlay. The powerful design of figure 245 best represents the style. The back, including posts and splats, seems cut from a flat board; the piercing, instead of providing any sense of roundness,

245

*Seen also as fig. 172. Using a straight back, seat rail,
and straight-sided cabriole legs, this chair shows one extreme
of Rhode Island design attitude.*

lieve the squared-off quality, and even the back legs remain square, without the chamfered corners usually found in other areas between the seat rail and stretchers. The shell does not seem an organic part but simply placed on the face of the crest rail, intensifying the sense of the chair's flatness.

Though the back of figure 155 is spooned, it too shows this two-plane quality. The back, the broad flat splat, the squared seat, and the typical squared cabriole of Rhode Island recall the squarish English Queen Anne chairs of about 1700 (fig. 153), which were to some degree copied from Chinese examples.[1] In many of these English source chairs all the members, including the cabriole legs, are square in section, providing a marvelous brittleness of movement within a contained form, and this English example has cabriole rear legs as on figures 165 and 166. The standard Newport highboy shows this same attitude toward design. It is basically composed of a facade of two superimposed rectangles, the lower on squared cabriole legs. Here again, there is little feeling of surface plasticity. It seems conceived of in two-dimensional terms. The front of the base is normally flat, with the shell flush within the skirt, rather than appearing to grow out of it as is normal in other regions. The cabriole legs themselves are normally flat on four sides rather than rounded in cross-section. The upper case is again flat across the front, usually without even the relief of engaged fluted quarter columns. Often the bonnet is closed behind the only finial, rather than open as in other regions, and since the eye cannot penetrate behind the finial the pediment too has a flush, flat quality.[2]

The second basic style is most easily recalled by the great Goddard and Townsend shell-carved block front secretaries, where the whole surface pulsates as it moves from the positive to the negative, bringing to America one of its fullest developments of the baroque idea.[3] Figure 246 perhaps best typifies this attitude in chairs, though figure 158 presents the same generosity of movement. Full-flown curves are the keynote of this style, but they lack the ponderous quality of the related New York pieces; here there is not the breadth and awkwardness usually seen there. Figures 175 and 176 seem to combine these two attitudes; the backs are

only intensifies the flatness. The front rail again emphasizes the straight, and the knees move out in a straight flat line to the squared cabriole legs with four flat sides. A sense of roundness appears only as we see the ball of the foot, which the long talons seem to divide into four parts. The columnar-turned stretchers do not re-

[1] The straight splat, the spooning of a splat, and the eared crest rail have definite Chinese origins, while a Chinese origin for the rolled shoulder is only surmised: George N. Kates, *Chinese Household Furniture* (1948; reprinted, New York: Dover Publications, Inc., 1962), fig. 86.

[2] For example, Sack, *Fine Points*, p. 183.

[3] For example, Sack, *Fine Points*, p. 158, bottom of page; Downs, fig. 232; Nutting, fig. 701; Kirk, *Early American Furniture*, figs. 19 and 20.

flat, with little openness of movement, but the bottom halves show the generous boldness experienced in the great block front pieces. It seems at first curious that these two attitudes should appear on the same chair, but it becomes less strange when we realize that the same workshops made many of the flat, rectilinear highboys and probably most of the full-blown shell block front pieces.

246

Seen also as fig. 156. Using echoing and re-echoing curves, this chair demonstrates Rhode Island's baroque extreme.

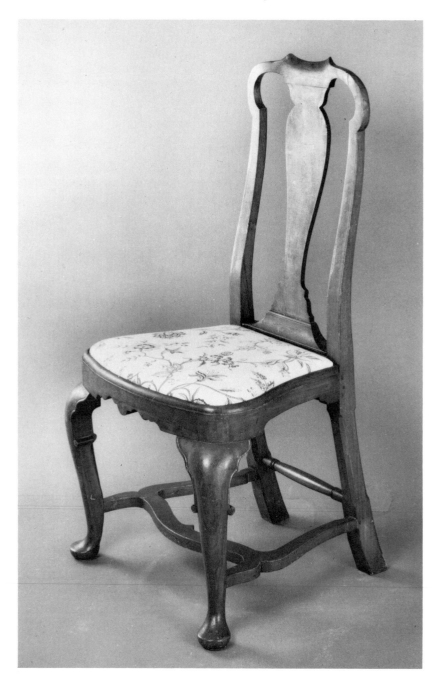

Here as in Massachusetts the turned stretchers seem unrelated to the reverse curves of the period, figure 170 appearing less cluttered than figure 169 even though on the former the seat rail looks slightly heavy since it lacks horizontal shaping. Though the flat stretchers with the reverse-curve movement seem more in accord with the prevailing style, they may appear low, almost as if they had slipped from a higher position, and the accompanying unfortunately turned rear stretcher seems completely extraneous. The straight-turned rear stretcher of figure 158 is a form that happily appeared rarely in America.

A chair such as figure 174, without any distinguishing form of surface decoration, makes a statement of impressive clarity. Nicely flowing strapwork and simple cabriole legs present quietly the best of its region. It lacks the suave grace of Philadelphia and the excitement of Connecticut; it seems to be consciously and clearly designed without fussiness or brittleness. Figure 182, so typical of many Rhode Island chairs, shows this sense of delineated clarity carried to an extreme. It recalls the surface movement of the Chapin chair, figure 194, having the polished smoothness of line that makes one think of forms found today only in plastic.

In Rhode Island there is not the suaveness or airy rococo of Philadelphia, no leafage decoration flows across the crest rails or knees, there is no sense of young plant growth. On the other hand, there is not the brittleness of Massachusetts nor the ponderous quality of New York. Rhode Island seems between the extremes. However, though many Rhode Island features appear to the north and south (for example, the knee blocks of figure 170 were found in New York and Massachusetts), to say that Rhode Island taste is a logical development in a place between two strong regions, a mere compromise between them, would be naïve in the extreme. Although Rhode Island was clearly influenced by both places, as Connecticut was influenced by several American regions, its basic source was Europe; and, although this is not as yet clear, perhaps some of its attitudes were borrowed from German or Low Country sources.

5. Connecticut Valley

THE PREVIOUS four style centers received their sources of design almost completely from Europe. Connecticut, New Hampshire, and other rural areas without the same traffic with England drew their inspiration from two places: from Europe, and, to a great degree, from furniture made in the dominating America style centers. Connecticut drew on the four Northern style centers we have studied, and the result shows the difference in design that developed when rural craftsmen received their ideas from several "second-hand" sources, and then reinterpreted them to conform to their own peculiar taste and situation.

The influence of Europe on Connecticut came directly through the English cabinetmakers who settled in the Connecticut Valley. The influence of American centers, on the other hand, came about in several ways. Many young Connecticut Valley men were apprenticed in the larger centers, to return home with new ideas. Also, Connecticut men with business in the large American coastal cities returned home with some longing for the latest fashion they had just seen, and their concept of this fashion would usually be an American expression. The Connecticut Valley's being at a second remove from England, along with its open social structure, allowed its designers a freedom not found in the major cities, which received their consciousness of style directly from Europe. Here, a combination and mingling of details and styles developed a richness of expression for which it is wholly insufficient to use the damning phrase "style lag." Rather, it seems to have been a deliberate choice to combine details according to personal likes, simply ignoring what did not appeal.

Since any sense of the true classical concepts was distant, a freedom arose that meant new combinations of motifs could be devised, creating and being created by a newly originated attitude to taste. For example, the square, tapered legs of the end of the eighteenth century were often combined with Chippendale backs, whereas in most of the other centers, the back would have been the most updated feature. Queen Anne splats appeared here in what are basically bannister-back chairs with high crests and ring-turned legs. In another rural area, New Hampshire, the originality that developed is typified by the products of the Dunlap family and it is not surprising to find that rural areas throughout the world show this same achievement of personalized statements.

It is not indeed sufficient to say, as so often happens, that "Anything odd and made of cherry is from Connecticut." Rather, the determining characteristic was a conscious demand for things that appealed personally to the people of the area, just as in other areas, as we saw with Affleck's adapting to a Philadelphia style. The most famous Connecticut cabinetmaker, Eliphalet Chapin, upon returning to Connecticut from Philadelphia[1] constructed

chairs as well as case pieces in a pure Philadelphia manner, but he borrowed motifs and details from many sources. In figure 247, the manner of handling the carving, the piercing of the splat, and the action of the chair are unlike any known Philadelphia example. New York and Rhode Island are recalled in the central grooving of the ear, and New York in the rolling backward of the front of the top rail (fig. 146) and the carving of the central shell (fig. 127); the strapwork of the splat is of the Massachusetts (fig. 111) and Rhode Island (fig. 174) form; and it is carved to an upper and lower division, in the Massachusetts and Rhode Island manner. The legs and feet are related to Philadelphia work but they are bolder in movement, more positive and delineated in their drawing, and the back posts below the seats are rounded, again in the Philadelphia manner; but the seat rail is simply shaped, without the shell accent we might expect on a Philadelphia chair of related development. This great chair reflects many areas of America, but its real greatness lies in its sense of movement and action, which differs from anything we have seen elsewhere. The whole action, the whole movement, the essence of the chair is in the back. The back posts strongly diverge upwards; the outward action is caught by prominent ears, brought back into the strongly bowed top rail, and moves with swift motion into the splat where it circles in upon itself. Its emphasis is on power and spirit and not on the suave grace we have seen in Philadelphia. Here Chapin is using Philadelphia's means of construction with through tenons, Philadelphia corner blocks, and back legs, where they are not visible to the beholder, and for the things that are visible he uses details borrowed from other areas. Then he combines them in a new and spirited way into a design with a sense of activity and sinewed strength. Though its sources can be discovered, it is a new expression, just as Philadelphia chairs are a new expression of English designs.

It seems that the Connecticut cabinetmaker felt free to make what he liked, or that his customers had a sense of individual choice. Something caused Chapin, as we have seen, to change from the purely Philadelphia style he must once have used there. Whether it was he or his public who caused this change we are

---

[1] I am indebted to Houghton Bulkeley, who did so much to advance our knowledge of Connecticut cabinetmakers, for the following information in a letter dated April 22, 1962. In 1767, Eliphalet Chapin left East Windsor, Connecticut, and lived for several years in Philadelphia. Mr. Bulkeley told me he used documents owned by Mrs. Hildreth Raymond of East Windsor, including a report of the clerk of the church society of East Windsor, which substantiate this.

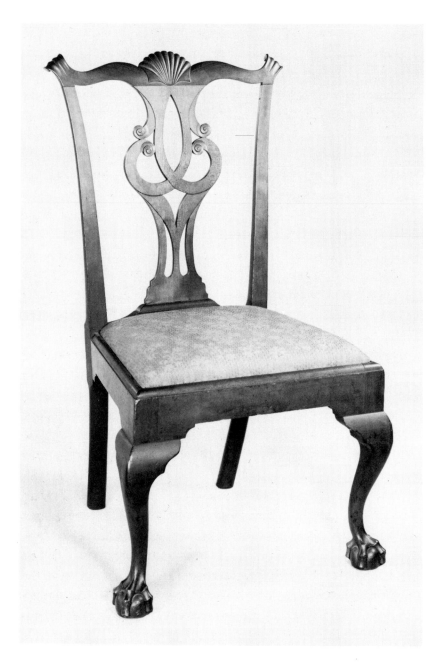

247

Seen also as fig. 194. One of the greatest of Connecticut's sculptural designs, this chair borrows ideas from Massachusetts, Rhode Island, New York, and Philadelphia.

Connecticut objects are much later in date than their form suggests. The key Chapin chair (fig. 193) was made in 1781, and Chippendale furniture was being made in quantity in this area at least as late as 1810 and quite probably well into the nineteenth century.

While the Chapin chair represents one of the two basic Connecticut attitudes toward furniture, the Queen Anne chair, figure 248, shows the other. It is also Philadelphia in construction but even less like Philadelphia in feeling than the Chapin chair. No Philadelphia chair ever resembled this. Its leg grows from a club foot with no visual break, seeming almost as though it were pulled from taffy; both are of a continuous line differing only in width. This splat would never have been made in Philadelphia; it is not rich enough, being of a simple baluster form, and the ring necking would have been thought naïve. The chair, *qua* design, is wholly a Connecticut product. Starting at one front foot, working up the delicately strong leg into the horseshoe-shaped seat, up the back posts and down the other side, it is pure line, completely independent of decoration. Powerful in line, it is individual in statement; it is simply itself, a thing strong, beautiful, and self-contained. These Connecticut chairs do, however, seem closely related to Philadelphia chairs in their sense of unity and overall organization toward the vertical. The difference is that in Philadelphia the chairs are tightly knit compositions, suaver, less bold, more richly developed, more elaborately conceived with many subtle interplays of line and movement, and less individual and simple in statement. The Philadelphia chairs seem to be cut from marble, as if the chair was present in the block needing only to have the waste removed. In Connecticut they seem to be created before you. Here the space between the splat and the back posts is as important as the wood area. All of these Connecticut chairs, though active and strong, allow space to move around and through them; like creatures, they seem to be aware of their movement through space; and the wood seems drawn out to create form patterns in the air, producing an open, flowing design.

These two basic attitudes toward design in Connecticut, typified by two chairs we have looked at in detail (figs. 248 and 247), can easily be seen in case pieces. The first is a sense of open, flowing curves uninterrupted by decoration. On case pieces this is perhaps best seen in the reverse serpentine Connecticut chest of drawers with its flat, slow-moving curves.[2] The second captures action and quickness, providing rich eye entertainment. On case

not sure, but probably the public had greater control. (Chippendale, late in his work, made furniture designed by Robert Adam.) Chapin's work certainly is related to the other furniture of Connecticut, as originality, cleverness, and an active line seem to be essential to some Connecticut work. Another factor is that often

[2] For example, Nutting, fig. 267, or [Kirk], *Connecticut Furniture*, fig. 66.

pieces, this takes the form of lavishly applied, active carving, enriching surfaces already active in line, setting up a counterpoint of interests.[3]

There are very few Connecticut high-style chairs but many simple chairs are known: ladder backs, bannister backs, various

[3] For example, Nutting, fig. 709, or [Kirk], *Connecticut Furniture,* fig. 126.

248

Seen also as fig. 186. Compared with fig. 247, this chair is at the opposite extreme of Connecticut's design attitude.

"stick chairs" and "country" Queen Anne, as well as straight-legged Chippendale chairs. Perhaps the rural population thought other forms too pretentious, but more probably they were simply too expensive. Also possibly some of what made a Philadelphia man conscious that he was not the aristocrat of England, though he was perhaps the most important citizen in Philadelphia, made the Connecticut purchaser conscious that his way of life was not less important but of a different nature to that of the wealthier, more polished urbanite.

We have noticed that the furniture of Connecticut and Philadelphia has many characteristics in common, and it has been assumed that Connecticut's style of furniture was heavily conditioned by Philadelphia. This, in fact, is only one of the many influences upon that region. As we have seen, other style areas of America played their role in the development of the Connecticut Valley taste. It is possible to say that Connecticut's taste and personal style are the ability to change and combine elements of various areas, turning them into personal statements. On the other hand, not only were some of these directly English but the overall designs, even the taste itself, derive to a degree from England. Like other areas, Connecticut had workers from England who had been trained there, and who brought to the valley the techniques and ideas of their previous home regions in England. The famous Connecticut Valley carved chests from Hadley, Massachusetts, southward, and their related brothers the "sunflower" chests from Wethersfield, Connecticut, as well as the painted chests traditionally from the Guilford-Saybrook area, all have related English patterns in Norfolk, Suffolk, Derbyshire, Lancashire, and the southern part of Yorkshire, with the Guilford painted pattern appearing in Pennsylvania in inlay, the medium in which it was executed in England. The eighteenth-century immigrants from England to the Connecticut Valley also brought designs. Compare the basic splats of figures 249 and 250, for instance. Figures 250 and 192 were made in a particular area of England and each reveals both Connecticut and Philadelphia characteristics.

Figure 192 shows the following Philadelphia features: the front feet are of the pad form known in Philadelphia rather than the simple club foot of New England; the flaring of the back feet resembles that on many Philadelphia Queen Anne chairs (they are restored but are considered by English scholars to be correct); the veneering of the seat frame and back posts above the seat, splat, and crest rail is another Philadelphia feature. Also the scrolling of the ears and the front ends of the arms. The movement of the scrolled strapwork of the splat is characteristic of New England

249

*Seen also as fig. 187. A Connecticut eared and fretted
solid baluster splat better known in Philadelphia (figs. 5 and 52)
with an English source (fig. 51, 59, and 250).*

work in general and of Connecticut chairs made by Eliphalet
Chapin in particular. The corner blocks, quarter-round in section,
of vertical grain, made in two pieces and fitting around the top
of the leg, are found in Philadelphia and Connecticut work. The
flowing movement of the front legs is also common to both areas,
as is most readily seen on figure 248. This chair is stamped
s: SHARP NORWICH and the will of Samuel Sharp, filed April 4,

250

*English arm chair, 1730–70. Southwell Cathedral, Southwell,
Nottinghamshire, England. Oak. Height without bishop's crest,
41½ inches; width, 28; height of seat rail, 17¾. Seat frame
construction, similar to fig. 19 (seat rail thickness, 1⅛ inches,
thicker than most American rails and demonstrating that thinness or
an attempt to save wood is not proof of an English origin). No
corner blocks. No bracket responds. No horizontal shaping. No
through tenons. Seating of splat in shoe. Board seat restored.*

1761, and now in the Norwich Public Library, records his work as a cabinetmaker in that region. (This Norwich chair has the same arms and arm supports as the American Norwich chair, fig. 188.) There is an English cherry ladder-back arm chair, perhaps from the Fen Country a little to the north and now in the collection of the Yale University Art Gallery, that shows the same Connecticut-Pennsylvania features.[4] In the Philadelphia Museum of Art is a Philadelphia Chippendale side table,[5] with its skirt cut to the multiple arches better known in Connecticut, and this skirt shaping was found in the same area of England. It is therefore possible to assume that some of what Connecticut and Philadelphia have in common is what designer-craftsmen from the same locality of England brought to these two regions of America. The differences, then, that arose between these American regions seem to be due at least in part to the fact that Philadelphia was a large style center with a sophisticated production that looked constantly to Europe for modes and manner of design, while Connecticut and the Connecticut Valley, being further removed, developed an originality of interpretation such as is seen in all countries in rural, country, or peasant work.

6. The South

THE VERY TERM "Southern Chairs" is such a broad generalization that it could prove harmful to any real understanding. Baltimore is over 500 miles from Charleston, whereas the just over 300 miles which separate Boston from Philadelphia include five distinct style centers, each of which has required detailed analysis. It is true that our main concentration—Winchester to Edenton, with brief stops in Roanoke, Williamsburg, and Suffolk—is only a distance of some 275 miles and there are no dominating centers that would control or focus any part of it; but a generalization will serve only to show how much there is to learn. And, as we said before, the real work that will turn guesses into certainties is properly being done by scholars working on a day-to-day basis in this area. Proceeding, then, to generalize, the Tidewater South (excluding Baltimore and Charleston) is heavily dependent on

England (but in fact no more so than either Massachusetts and New York) and the Piedmont areas on Pennsylvania. The elaborate chairs, figures 251 and 252, are heavy in design and seem more like many of the chairs on display in the National Museum of Ireland, which may be the result of Irish influence or of a similar ruralness. The two Southern chairs have broad parts that are slightly clumsy when compared with fine examples from other regions; for example, compare the splats, knee carving, and front seat rail shaping of figures 251 and 75. There is no lack of fundamental cabinetmaking skills; rather, the subtle eye and hand that could execute the Philadelphia chair were not present at the creation of the Southern one. The only regular chair with club feet (fig. 208) has, particularly in its back, a beautiful sense of spacing; it is quiet in balance and this makes it akin to many of the fine simpler Southern chairs. Figure 204 achieves great elegance as the straight line of the crest rail breaks back at its ends to the outer edge of the back posts, and under the crest rail the reverse-curve line that moves into and down the splat is strong and well drawn. The rest of the chair shows an interplay of horizontal and vertical rectangles of wood and space. Even the use of a front rather than a medial stretcher is harmonious in this play of parts. It has a direct English source in such chairs as figure 203, but the probably Virginia chair achieves a new lightness, a new opening up of the design. Although as provincial as figure 203, it is more direct and leaner. It alters its source design just as American high-style chairs altered their European sources.

Related to these two chairs, figure 220 has a similar crest rail, with angled ends and reverse curves. The splat is quietly rayed and increased in width by the addition of a fifth strap for the necessarily wider back. The restrained verticality of the back is continued by the general straightness of the arms, the straightness of the arm supports, and the straight legs. By comparison, the other simple chairs seem a bit naïve. Figure 206 appears spread out and low-backed and figure 217 a bit compact, but heaviness need not be a fault. Figure 209 has used it, even broadening its splat to five rather than the more general four ribs. Perhaps it is this added complexity and having kept the design more contained by not using outwardly scrolled ears that renders the heaviness here an asset rather than a fault.

A similar comparison is possible between the lighter figure 216 and the heavier figure 217. The ears of the first pull the design apart. Lightness however is one of the assets of figures 210, 218, and 219; here the wood draws somewhat delicate patterns which gently outline the spaces. That most of these chairs are

---

[4] [Kirk], *Connecticut Furniture,* fig. 275.

[5] Accession number 40–16–27.

based on English patterns is obvious, but that they looked directly to England for inspiration is not certain although comparison of 203 and 204 definitely suggests it. It may be that, like rural Connecticut, the rural South looked to Southern high-style centers. But here again we are confronted by a lack of centers to borrow from. It could therefore also be that, except for such pieces as the

252

Seen also as fig. 215. Like fig. 251, this Southern chair from Virginia has heavy, slow-moving parts.

251

Seen also as fig. 222. One of the most elaborately designed Southern chairs (possibly North Carolina, Edenton area). Revealing of this area's design taste is a comparison of this chair's splat with those of Philadelphia, fig. 75, and England, fig. 74.

probably Edenton chairs, figures 212 and 213 (which can only be seen as interesting rural uses of Pennsylvania designs, not as major sculptural forms), English makers and English chairs conditioned the designs; or it may have been some combination of both.

The two style centers that bracket Virginia and North Carolina did develop well-balanced, elaborate designs. On the North,

Annapolis, and later Baltimore, borrowed heavily from Philadelphia and many of their chairs and case pieces have a character that often develops in furniture that is dependent on a main design area. The pieces are a little bolder and the decoration is sometimes increased in size and amount. Part of this increase in decoration is probably an attempt at more elegance and therefore more Englishness; but a large pendant shell or an elaborate finickiness of carving is not always an advantage, although many of the Maryland highboys and dressing tables with huge pendant shells are dramatically interesting. They have not, however, the subtleness of the greatest pieces from Philadelphia.

The Maryland chair, figure 223, is a well-balanced design, but shows a provincial use of ideas borrowed from the neighboring major style center. Just as the possibly Newtown area chair, figure 73, used Philadelphia forms and details in its own way, so figure 223 transposed Philadelphia elements mostly by stylizing the details. The carving is more brittle and thinner in scale. On the knees, it looks laid on rather than brought out of the backing. On the crest rail, it is flat decoration rather than raised ornamentation. The arm supports, though like those particularly known in Philadelphia, are stiffer and more contained in movement. The splat's strapwork moves from shoe to crest rail and reflects Philadelphia Gothic splats, but it is frozen movement; the C scrolls particularly are fixed and help to make the whole chair appear less fluid than a related Philadelphia one.

The Charleston chair, figure 224, concentrates its elaborateness in the splat area. Milby Burton has said that after the Revolution some Philadelphia cabinetmakers moved to Charleston to benefit from increasing business and there is a set of chairs in Charleston that are pure Philadelphia in form and construction except that they have elaborate splats, more intricately designed than would have been favored in Philadelphia. It is reasonable to assume that these splats were elaborated for the Charleston taste, which always leaned toward England and the elegance that depends on intricately involved details.

After 1795, both Baltimore and Charleston became major design centers. While we have far to go in understanding what happened south of Philadelphia, it is clear that we are dealing with two major centers, one that depends upon both Philadelphia and England; the other, at least before the Revolution, upon England. But there was also a large expanse between, which showed similarities because of its ruralness—a quality which often makes things appear to have a similar source when that may not be the reason for likenesses. For example, Connecticut's Chapin is often discussed with New Hampshire's Dunlap when in fact their only similarity is their country attitude rather than a single source of design.

It may also prove true that similarities in the South exist because the makers had similar English sources, both in pieces brought to the South and in the men who migrated there. A few of the chairs included show that ruralness per se is not a drawback if the maker, who is usually also the designer, is good enough at both. Here the simpler chairs have often proved successful when attempts at elegance and complexity have failed.

Conclusion

For the furniture designer, the chair is perhaps the most demanding form since so many factors are necessarily present. Structurally, a chair involves all the major framing and strengthening problems. It puts the practical adequacy of a style to its most stringent test for it must withstand the hardest use of any furniture form—undergoing stress from a variety of angles. Other pieces seldom carry anything like the same weight for a given area. Also, a chair is portable and actively involved in day-to-day use.

Visually, the chair is always potentially awkward, for an inequity between the mass and three-dimensionality of the base and the lightness and the near two-dimensionality of the back is a given of the form. Moreover, the chair employs most of the individual features (both the basic units and the decorative motifs) that were the idiom of a period in its feet, legs, knees, splat, backposts, and crest rail. Yet the relative smallness of the chair means that all its elements come close together and therefore it demands the highest degree of unity; other equally small items, such as tables, present nothing like so complex a design problem. The designer of larger pieces, such as the chest-on-chest, can successfully plan its pediment and base as autonomous units that relate to each other only in scale and forcefulness and through the unity provided by the brasses. But for the chair designer, the whole piece must function as a tightly integrated design. The chair contrasts large areas against small, always seeking to produce an integrated sculptural whole when seen from any angle.

As is often the case, the almost too demanding problem of

combining all these factors pushes the best designers toward achieving the quintessence of the style in which they work, within the demands imposed on them by the local milieu. As a result, the chair is as much a sociological and economic object as a visual one.

When we add to all these considerations the fact that, at least after the seventeenth century, the chair provides us with the most numerous corpus of related design material, and permits us to compare variation after variation within a closely related format, we see why studying the chairs of a design period, like studying the sonnet in literature, is to study the nature of style itself. The very limitations involved in analyzing American Queen Anne and Chippendale chairs become a means of seeing more sharply than more heterogeneous material permits how the creations of one region differ from those of another, and, perhaps above all, how different the great achievements are from the small, how different two chairs can be whose verbal description would be identical.

If such a body of material can be thought of as providing an implicit definition of design standards, differentiating the aesthetically valuable from the historically illuminating, it also reveals the complexity of the methodology that the history of the decorative arts requires. As we have seen, method after method must be used. Yet each method must finally be tested not only against the results of the others but above all against a stringent visual and stylistic analysis of the completed design.

Paradoxically, it is only when we have thus, in a sense, subordinated the historical to the aesthetic that we can fully appreciate the major role the decorative arts can play for the historian of American society. These chairs throw into relief not only the assumptions about daily living that shaped and underlay American life in the eighteenth century, but demonstrate the strikingly different character of the many different cultures that were to come together at the end of our period to form the United States. Few "documents" exist that stand so uncompromisingly outside current mythologies about colonial history and that so directly witness to its actual character. The relation of American designers to their sources is a microcosm of the way in which this developing culture was related to that of Europe. Colonial furniture, based upon actual objects rather than upon pattern books, and in which artists worked less self-consciously and defensively than in painting and poetry, never thinking of visiting Europe for further training, demonstrates the nature of a region's self-appointed artistic and cultural demands. For the historian as well as the art historian, these chairs are among the primary documents for an understanding of America during the eighteenth century.

APPENDIX

There are a number of methods that could prove helpful in dividing the eastern seaboard into different regions that show genuine artistic cohesion. One of these is the division that results from dialect studies; although this field of study, like that of American furniture, is still immature it does show that dialect regions correspond to furniture regions. As further work is carried out on English sources for American dialects we shall be able to use this knowledge to further our understanding of American regional tastes in furniture. At present, the problem of discovering the European sources of our regional ideas of taste and construction is extremely complex. Locating the original sources in England of many American variations would be greatly simplified if the English were concerned with regionalizing their own pieces. It is still possible for an English furniture expert to say, in one breath, "All objects were made in London; all objects outside London are inferior; all objects made outside London cannot be regionalized as they are like the London products, since London completely conditioned the rural taste." Fortunately for us, some of those officially in charge of the greater collections of English furniture are broadening this view. It is also true that for some years a few individuals and local societies have given attention to this problem, and the recently formed Furniture History Society in England should be of great assistance.

But the information that exists so far has not yet been published, nor is it easily possible to find persons who can explain what little is known. It is also unfortunate that there are no detailed maps or studies of the immigration patterns from England to America to show the origin of the early settlers, for this would tell us where to look for prototypes. It is therefore, necessary to use other means to attempt to discover the answers. Much of the material on English sources included in this study was encountered during a necessarily random search across England for areas where furniture related to American designs seemed to congregate. Unsystematic as it was, this proved surprisingly productive, but it provides only a suggestion for further investigation.

This appendix is an attempt to use dialect areas to divide New England into areas of individual speech concentration and to see if these correspond to the stylistic divisions observed in the furniture. We will then try to see if we can suggest the sources of these American dialect groups in England. What we discover when we approach the question of regional dialects is that the Americans have given careful attention to dividing and sorting their dialect groups, and that the English, as with their furniture, have only now begun to apply the new techniques.[1] We can see divisions in New England and suggest English origins for a few of the dialect groups; but these must be taken only as a result of preliminary study.

Before modern research, it was though that "American English" was essentially the standard southern English of the seventeenth and eighteenth centuries as modified locally during the last century or two. New research has altered this view. "To my mind," says Hans Kurath, in an account of the studies which were to produce the monumental *Linguistic Atlas of New England* on which much of this discussion is based, "most of the dialectal differences . . . did not develop out of a uniform Southern English Standard, but have their bases partly in the regional variations of the Standard and partly in the strongly dialectal speech which the earlier settlers of these regions brought with them from England and Scotland."[2] That is, English was not a unified dialect with variations introduced after its arrival in America. The variations existed already in England, in its "Southern English Standard," and were complicated by the fact that other dialect groups outside the Standard added their own variations. In fact, the idea of there being only one correct version of the English language does not

---

[1] See Eugene Dieth, "A New Survey of English Dialects," *Essays and Studies by Members of the English Association*, XXXII (1947), pp. 74–104. A survey of dialects is in progress at the University of Leeds, under Eugene Dieth and Harold Orten, but only the introductory material has as yet been published.

[2] Hans Kurath, "The Origin of the Dialectal Differences in Spoken American English," *Modern Philology*, XXV (May 1928), p. 387.

arise until the mid-eighteenth century. Kurath distinguishes two kinds of local variations in England, the variations of what was supposed to be the London Standard, which we may relate to high-style furniture, and the genuine local dialect from the areas where we would expect to find provincial or folk furniture. Until pronouncing dictionaries, codifying the correct pronunciation of English, became popular in England at the end of the eighteenth century (they had been used abroad earlier by those wishing to learn English), England showed a lack of uniformity even among the educated. Kurath quotes such a dictionary of 1774:

... those at a considerable distance from the capitol do not only mispronounce many words taken separately, but they scarcely pronounce with purity a single word, syllable or letter. ... The best educated people in the provinces, if constantly resident there, are sure to be strongly tinctured with the dialect of the country in which they live.[3]

The most significant feature of Kurath's study of the distribution of word usage and pronunciation for the student of furniture is the fact that the *Atlas* divides New England not primarily by state areas but vertically into two basic dialect groups, an eastern and a western area, with a third or marginal area between. The eastern area was settled from the coast, the western area from the lower Connecticut Valley and Long Island Sound. One of the differentiating features most readily recognized by the average listener is the absence of the "post-vocalic 'r'" in the east and its presence in the west; where the western New Englander says "barn," the easterner generally says "bahn." The basic dividing line goes straight north from the mouth of the Connecticut River, through Connecticut and Massachusetts, to the southern boundary of Franklin County in Massachusetts. From there it goes directly west along the boundary to the Berkshires, then heads due north along the crest of the Green Mountains to the northern boundary of Vermont. Between these two areas, that of the coast and that of the Connecticut River settlements, there was little contact until about 1735.[4]

The eastern area is composed of the original settlements along the coast, except for New London which will be dealt with later. The coast was settled by large groups that had been formed by common philosophy or theology in England; they came together and settled together in the New World.

Many churches in eastern Massachusetts had been founded on the other side of the Atlantic; the members sailed together to the New World, and ultimately settled as neighbors in the center of a township, of which the uncleared lands were gradually occupied by their descendents for two or three generations.[5]

This of course fits with the previously suggested idea of large groups of people coming with cabinetmakers to America from a given area in England to settle together and continue their taste in furniture as well as their way of speaking. Kurath stresses the fact that such cultural patterns were not obliterated by later immigration: "In the Boston area, the stock provided by the original 'planting' determined social customs and intellectual standards, which were accepted by later additions to the population."[6] During the 150 years after 1640, which was the end of the "great migration," new settlers were continually coming to New England, but they came as individuals or rather small groups and those that did come in large bodies such as the Scots-Irish tended to settle on the frontiers.[7]

Since different parts of the coast were settled by different incoming groups, there is variation within the large eastern dialect unit, and it is possible to see subdivisions in that area:

I. The Narragansett Bay of Rhode Island is quite distinct from the other areas and in the use of some words unique. Rhode Island shows little effect from any later influx into its population, the colony remaining closely knit together in clans and groups descended from the original settlers.[8] There were, however, a few exceptions. A colony of French Huguenots arrived late in the seventeenth century although they moved on to East Greenwich and from thence dispersed. There was an influx of Jews from Curaçao and Brazil in 1658 and a century later from Portugal; and later still there was some immigration from Ireland.[9] From Rhode Island groups went to settle Long Island early in the eighteenth century, to New Jersey, and in the 1760's to Nova Scotia, though they were to return later from Nova Scotia to Maine. Some settlers continued to go from Rhode Island to the Berkshires until 1790 and then to Vermont and New Hampshire, as well as to the valleys of central New York.[10]

II. The Plymouth area, including the Old Colony, Martha's Vineyard, and Nantucket, shows few distinctive features, perhaps

[3] Kurath, "Origin," p. 395*n*.

[4] Hans Kurath, *et al.*, *Handbook of the Linguistic Geography of New England* (Providence, Rhode Island: Brown University, 1939), p. 8.

[5] Kurath, *Handbook*, p. 63.

[6] Kurath, *Handbook*, p. 62.

[7] Kurath, *Handbook*, p. 62.

[8] Kurath, *Handbook*, p. 74.

[9] Kurath, *Handbook*, pp. 74-5.

[10] Kurath, *Handbook*, p. 75.

the result of never having achieved the unity that would have been provided had it been an important economic unit.

III. The Boston area, the Massachusetts Bay Colony minus Essex County, affected the educated speech even into the lower Connecticut Valley, and thus has "intruded" into some of the larger coastal areas, a fact which has sometimes caused confusion in the study of dialects. These areas, if considered in terms only of educated speech, would seem to set themselves aside from their surrounding areas. It is, however, only a question of this intrusion of speech brought from Boston.

Kurath's IV, V, and VI are closely related; IV is Essex County whose furniture is termed that of the North Shore area, which we mentioned under Massachusetts chairs as showing a difference from Boston. V, the Merrimack Valley of New Hampshire, though largely settled from Essex County to the south, shows distinct dialect differences. VI is eastern New Hampshire, called "old New Hampshire," being the towns along the coast settled above the Merrimack River. Strangely enough, this area has a relationship with an area inland, around Lake Winnepesaukee. It would have seemed logical that the lake area should have more in common with group V, since it is at the headwaters of the Merrimack River. However, this does not prove to be the case, and there were perhaps settlements that went across land to that area rather than up the river valley. This area shows certain English West Country features, suggesting that there were strong immigration relationships between the two areas.[11]

Group VII is York County, Maine, which has some relationship to IV, V, and VI but, like them, also sufficient differences to set it apart.

Group VIII consists of the majority of Maine: Casco Bay, Penobscot Bay, eastern Maine, and northern Maine (which is distinct and has some features in common with the whole western group beyond the Connecticut Valley); this area was largely settled from the Massachusetts Bay and Plymouth Bay colonies, and therefore shows some relationship to groups II and III.

There is a clear "seam" between the basic eastern and western areas, making it possible to divide them. The eastern area also shows a vertical band running up its western or inland side, called the "eastern marginal area," between the coast towns and the boundary of the western dialect area. It consists of New London, an original settlement, and a series of secondary settlements made

[11] Kurath, *Handbook*, p. 16.

by groups from the eastern coast towns as their population began to spread inland. The eastern marginal area is divided into three groups:

I. The New London area, which is not strongly distinctive and includes some westernism from the Connecticut Valley and some Narragansett Bay features, especially around the area of Stonington, Connecticut. Pieces of furniture have been found in Stonington which show a strong Rhode Island flavor, so much so that some have been assigned to Newport because of their similarity to the cabinetwork from there. This New London area provided the settlers of the upper Connecticut Valley and the Berkshires. We have noted that the line dividing east from west which goes directly north from the mouth of the Connecticut River breaks to the west two-thirds of the way up Massachusetts, and goes across under this settlement from New London.

II. The second marginal area is the Worcester area, including northern Windham County, in Connecticut.

III. Closely linked to that area is the third, the upper Connecticut Valley from Franklin County, Massachusetts, northward to Canada, above the break in the straight line north. This upper Connecticut Valley, as we have seen, was partly populated by settlers from New London. By 1750 the western movement from the coast had reached the Connecticut River, which was already settled. The new movement from the coast was then deflected northward into this area, so that it was settled as well by people from the Massachusetts Bay Colony, the Plymouth Bay Colony, and by some Irish settlers direct from Europe. Though this is an area distinct from the whole western dialect group, its location being at the upper part of the valley and movement by water being easy, it did acquire some of the lower Connecticut Valley features. The trade up the Connecticut River caused a superimposition of lower valley dialects upon the original dialect.

The second major area of New England, the western area, runs from the "seam" with the eastern area as far west as the Hudson River and the Lakes. Most of the Connecticut Valley is included, and thus forms a distinct subculture cut off from the coast and showing affinities with the Hudson Valley of New York. The western area is also divided into subareas, since it was settled by two different thrusts or movements:

I. The lower Connecticut Valley unit consists of Hartford County, Tolland County, most of Litchfield County, northern

Middlesex County, Hampton County, and Hampshire County, the last two in Massachusetts. This coincides with our observations of the valley furniture styles being unified beyond state boundaries. Windsor was settled in 1633, Wethersfield in 1634, and Hartford in 1635. Springfield, on the other hand, settled in 1636, had direct contacts across land to the Massachusetts Bay Colony, and was further linked by reason of religious differences, river taxes, and the fact that the Enfield Falls divided it from the lower towns; it failed to join in the Pequot war in 1637, it broke its earlier contact with the other valley towns, and, in 1649, it had a deputy admitted to the general court of Massachusetts. Also, a crossland route connected it with the eastern Massachusetts area. It is thus not unexpected that some of the elaborately inlaid furniture known to be from the Springfield area shows a distinct mixture of valley and eastern Massachusetts tastes.

Towns further to the north of Springfield show strong relationships with lower towns in Connecticut. Northampton to the north was settled in 1653 by families from Hartford. It is therefore not surprising to find distinct relationships between the Hadley-type carved chests and the carved chests from the Wethersfield area, traditionally called "sunflower" chests, both of the late seventeenth century.[12] Deerfield further to the north was settled directly from the Massachusetts Bay Colony and shows, as did Springfield, influences from the east.[13] The eastern boundary of the lower Connecticut Valley is clear, being New London, Windham, and Worcester counties, and it is even sharper in Connecticut than in Massachusetts. To the north, it fades off into the upper Connecticut Valley and Deerfield, though it is still distinct; to the west, it fades off into the Berkshires toward the Hudson Valley which we shall mention later.

II. The settlers of New Haven, Milford, Guilford, Branford, Stratford, Fairfield, and Norwalk seem to have come, to a great degree, directly from England and are a different settlement thrust than that which went up the valley from Old Lyme.[14]

As the eastern area had a marginal area to its left, there is a group to the left of the western area called the "Western Fringe"; this includes the western part of Connecticut, Massachusetts, and Vermont.[15]

The distribution of the postvocalic "r" shows a strong connection between the Connecticut Valley and the Hudson Valley, from New York through Albany as far as Lake Champlain. It is not surprising to see the Connecticut Valley's relationship to New York's taste, found in country furniture and in the work of Eliphalet Chapin, etc. It is generally believed that eastern New England was settled from "the south eastern counties of England, Essex, Norfolk, Suffolk, Kent, etc.," but western New England "received a considerable admixture of Scotch-Irish in the half century preceding the Revolution. It is the speech of the west of New England that became established in New York State and in the Western Reserve of Ohio."[16]

In addition to marking off these basic dialect areas, the *Atlas* shows a number of additional patterns superimposed upon them, and these, too, confirm significant trends we have seen in furniture. The first is the fact that some areas show a conservatism which is not reflected by the surrounding areas. That is, within a large area there are often smaller areas or towns that continue a conservative approach reflected in the retention of an earlier form of speech.[17] This of course would suggest that these areas also were conservative in their attitude toward design. The relationship between such areas is not that they once or originally had things in common; it is only that later, when the majority of New England had progressed, they remained to a great degree static. Their relationship then lies in their conservatism, not in originally having had contacts.

The southern seaboard area shows a retention of features once common to all of New England, particularly Long Island Sound and the eastern coast of Cape Cod, except for the Boston area. These features can be distinguished, or isolated, because they are invariably found in the even more conservative coastal communities north of Boston. There is a conservative retention also in northern New England, that is, Vermont to eastern Maine, and in an area apparently without any geographical connection to the rest, Litchfield County, Connecticut. The northern Vermont and eastern Maine areas also show in their architecture and simple furniture the continuation of forms long outdated elsewhere; this is typified by the fact that ladder-back chairs long out of date in the more progressive areas continue, to this day, to be made.

A second variation superimposed upon the basic groupings of

---

[12] [Kirk], *Connecticut Furniture,* p. xii.

[13] Kurath, *Handbook,* pp. 94 and 97.

[14] Kurath, *Handbook,* p. 95.

[15] Kurath, *Handbook,* pp. 19–22.

[16] Kurath, "Origin," p. 391.

[17] Kurath, *Handbook,* p. 22.

dialect is that which is called the spreading of innovations. That is, certain areas of New England have in common the originating of new sounds which cut across other divisions. The first is from Long Island Sound east to Narragansett Bay or perhaps even on to Cape Cod, Martha's Vineyard, and Nantucket. The rough shape of this group is a triangle, with its base in western Connecticut tapering off to the east, the tip extending past Narragansett Bay to Buzzard's Bay, or perhaps to Cape Cod and the islands near it. This would reinforce again the idea of a relationship between Connecticut and Rhode Island furniture. Another area of innovation extends from Narragansett Bay, east to Buzzard's Bay, and west to New London again, reinforcing the idea of there being contact between Rhode Island and Stonington and the area north of New London.[18]

Kurath and McDavid in their more general study recognize the following main dialect areas:

1. Eastern New England
2. The lower Connecticut Valley
3. Metropolitan New York
4. Upstate New York and western New England
5. Pennsylvania east, and Pennsylvania west: related but showing variations
6. The south midland, New Jersey, Maryland, etc.
7. The upper South
8. The lower South.

This study gives no evidence for the divisions, but it is interesting that they again show the Connecticut Valley as an independent area with eastern New England to the right and the New York area to the left.[19]

At the time of the Revolution, Pennsylvania was composed of three basic groups; one-third Quaker, with affiliations with the north and northern Midlands of England; one-third Scots-Irish; and one-third German. This created the principal dialect that moved straight west. The Scots-Irish had taken their dialect down behind the mountains into the Piedmont of Virginia and the Carolinas during the half century preceding the Revolution. Tidewater Virginia was settled from southeastern England, as was the coastal area of New England. Kentucky, Tennessee, the southern portions

of Ohio, Indiana, and Illinois, and much of Missouri received most of their early population from the valley of Virginia and from the Piedmont, where the Scots-Irish predominated; whereas the cotton belt of western Georgia, Alabama, Louisiana, Mississippi, and eastern Tennessee was settled very largely by the cotton growers of the Tidewater of Virginia and the Carolinas.[20]

In a more detailed study of vocabulary distribution, Kurath confirms the impression of diversity between Southern regions suggested by the furniture we have seen. He observes that "Speech boundaries within the Southern area are rather more clearly marked than elsewhere in the Eastern States," and notes more specifically:

The South is more diversified in speech, both regionally and socially, than the North or the Midland. Localisms abound, especially in the coastal areas. The Virginia Piedmont has attained a degree of regional unity; perhaps also the piedmont of South Carolina below the Peedee. Another fairly unified area appears to be developing in the upper piedmont of North Carolina.[21]

The boundary Kurath defines between the Midland and the South is interesting, not least for what it implies about the affiliations of such style centers as Baltimore. The boundary forms

an arc from the Atlantic coast in central Delaware through Baltimore to the Blue Ridge, then along the Blue Ridge to the James River, where it swings out into the piedmont and runs in a southerly direction through North Carolina, reverting to the Blue Ridge in South Carolina.[22]

The chief subregions of the South he notes as: "(1) the highly diversified Chesapeake Bay area, (2) the relatively unified Virginia Piedmont, and (3) the Carolinas east of the Midland boundary, with several distinct sub-divisions."[23]

One specialized study that should be mentioned here is Cleanth Brooks's analysis of a small dialect area which includes part of Alabama and part of Georgia, the dialect preserved in the Uncle Remus stories. Though this is not directly related to our study it shows, first, that areas of unity disregard state boundaries; and secondly, that it is possible to identify a specific complex of

[18] Kurath, *Handbook*, pp. 22–3.

[19] Hans Kurath and Raven I. McDavid, Jr., *The Pronunciation of English in the Atlantic States* (Ann Arbor, Mich.: The University of Michigan Press, 1961), pp. 121–3.

[20] Kurath, "Origin," pp. 391–2.

[21] Hans Kurath, *A Word Geography of the Eastern United States,* (Ann Arbor, Mich.: The University of Michigan Press, 1949), p. 37.

[22] Kurath, *Geography*, p. 37. Elsewhere he notes that the boundary meets the Atlantic coast below Dover, Delaware (p. 27).

[23] Kurath, *Geography*, p. 37.

English background; for the American dialect in this case derives from that of Devonshire and Dorset during the seventeenth and early eighteenth centuries.[24] This scholar demonstrates a longed-for correlation between American and English dialects, making us eagerly await such a correlation for other areas.

We can already accept the statement that "it is abundantly clear that many local dialectal differences are traceable directly to local dialectal differences in England which were transferred from England to America."[25] It also seems possible to see that there is a relationship between New England, especially eastern Massachusetts, and the county of Essex in England. This is established by the relationship in the drawl, rhythm, and phrases as well as by the town names.[26] Grouped together on the east coast of England are counties and a town with the following names: Norfolk, Suffolk, Cambridge, Essex, and Middlesex; and down the eastern coast of Massachusetts there are the following townships and towns: Essex, Middlesex, Cambridge, Suffolk, and Norfolk.

Along with others, then, we who are interested in the origins of furniture must eagerly await further developments in an understanding of the English dialectal areas.

[24] Cleanth Brooks, Jr., *The Relation of the Alabama-Georgia Dialect to the Provincial Dialects of Great Britain* (Baton Rouge, La.: Louisiana State University Press, 1935).

[25] George, Philip Knapp, *The English Language in America* (New York: Frederick Ungar Publishing Company, 1960; originally published 1925), vol. I., p. 53.

[26] Krapp, vol. II, pp. 24–5.

The index indicates page references by roman type and figure numbers and their captions by underlining. Captions to the figures are not indexed except for cabinetmakers, provenance, original owners, and a few significantly recurrent constructional peculiarities.

Footnotes are not indexed except where they contain a significant point different from that made in the corresponding passage in the main text.

Books cited are indexed by author, not title.

Only the principal areas referred to in the Appendix are indexed.

Since "Queen Anne" and "Chippendale" recur constantly, only substantive discussions of them are indexed.

An indexed item often occurs more than once on a cited page.

In general, the primary discussion of any constructional or design feature, which provides the necessary background for subsequent discussion, is to be found under the subentry Philadelphia.

INDEX

CORRESPONDENCE OF PLATES AND TEXT

A chair is often mentioned more than once on the page cited. Material in the caption is not indexed except that cross references indicate when a chair appears in more than one illustration. Footnotes are cited only when the chair in question is not mentioned in the corresponding text.

FIGURE	PAGES
1.	7, 34; *see also* fig. 45
2.	7
3.	7, 34; *see also* fig. 54
4.	7, 34; *see also* fig. 70
5.	7
6.	7, 34
7.	7; *see also* fig. 111
8.	8; *see also* fig. 151
9.	22; *see also* fig. 52
10.	24; *see also* fig. 69
11.	24; *see also* fig. 80
12.	24; *see also* fig. 91
13.	25; *see also* fig. 52
14.	25
15.	27
16.	21, 27–8; *see also* fig. 54
17.	28, 56; *see also* fig. 54
18.	29; *see also* fig. 70
19.	29, 30, 56; *see also* fig. 70
20.	30–1; *see also* fig. 52
21.	31–2; *see also* fig. 52
22.	32; *see also* fig. 70
23.	32–3; *see also* fig. 69
24.	37; *see also* fig. 68
25.	37; *see also* fig. 103
26.	38
27.	28, 38, 56
28.	28, 36
29.	40; *see also* fig. 117
30.	40, 42; *see also* fig. 123
31.	45, 64; *see also* fig. 143
32.	45, 64; *see also* fig. 146
33.	45, 64; *see also* fig. 130
34.	45; *see also* fig. 136
35.	48; *see also* fig. 143
36.	50; *see also* fig. 174
37.	53; *see also* fig. 171
38.	53; *see also* fig. 172
39.	55; *see also* fig. 194
40.	56

FIGURE	PAGES
41.	59; *see also* fig. 205
42.	60; *see also* fig. 211
43.	63; *see also* fig. 222
44.	23, 36
45.	21, 23, 28, 32, 35, 36, 49; *see also* fig. 1
46.	35, 172
47.	21, 22, 23, 26, 29
48.	21, 22, 23, 32, 34, 35, 172
49.	22, 23, 26, 34
50.	23, 29, 34, 35, 50, 64
51.	46
52.	23, 24, 31, 32, 50; *see also* figs. 9, 13, 20
53.	22, 23, 28, 32, 63, 64, 170, 172
54.	*see* figs. 3, 16, 17
55.	32, 35, 54, 64
56.	28
57.	26, 28, 29, 170
58.	32, 170, 172; *see also* frontispiece
59.	23, 48, 59
60.	7, 22
61.	11, 23, 34
62.	23, 32, 34
63.	22
64.	11
65.	caption only
66.	23, 26, 28, 32, 34, 64
67.	22, 29, 64
68.	22, 25, 29, 32, 33, 34, 170; *see also* fig. 24
69.	22, 23, 24, 31, 34; *see also* figs. 10, 23, 230
70.	22, 32; *see also* figs. 4, 18, 19, 22
71.	23, 24
72.	23, 34, 51; *see also* fig. 231
73.	193; *see also* fig. 232

FIGURE	PAGES
74.	24, 63, 167, 170
75.	24, 33, 63, 64, 167, 191
76.	caption only
77.	24, 47, 51, 180
78.	24, 47, 51, 180
79.	24, 62
80.	22, 31, 62, 169, 172, 174; *see also* fig. 11
81.	172, 174
82.	23, 24, 26, 34, 54, 172, 173, 174
83.	*see* fig. 233
83 a.	173–4
84.	173–4
85.	23, 24, 29, 34
86.	27, 52, 167
87.	23, 25
88.	caption only
89.	24, 29, 33, 34
90.	24, 34, 55, 64, 178
91.	24, 29, 30, 34, 39; *see also* fig. 12
92.	31, 64, 169, 174
93.	27, 29, 34, 47
94.	*see* fig. 228
95.	23, 24; *see also* frontispiece
96.	51, 63
97.	23, 36, 38, 39, 49, 64; *see also* fig. 234
98.	36; *see also* fig. 238
99.	54; *see also* fig. 239
100.	38; *see also* fig. 235 and frontispiece
101.	40, 175
102.	36, 49, 50
103.	35, 38, 51, 55, 64, 175–6; *see also* fig. 25
104.	37, 38, 40, 52, 64, 175–6; *see also* fig. 236
105.	175–6, 177–8

A NOTE ON THE TYPE

The text of this book is set on the Linotype in Fairfield, the first type face from the hand of the distinguished American artist and engraver Rudolph Ruzicka. In its structure Fairfield displays the sober and sane qualities of a master craftsman whose talent has long been dedicated to clarity. It is this trait that accounts for the trim grace and virility, the spirited design and sensitive balance of this original type face.

Rudolph Ruzicka was born in Bohemia in 1883 and came to America in 1894. He set up his own shop devoted to wood engraving and printing in New York in 1913, after a varied career as a wood-engraver, in photoengraving and bank-note printing plants, and as art director and free-lance artist. He has designed and illustrated many books and has created a considerable list of individual prints—wood engravings, line engravings on copper, aquatints. W. A. Dwiggins once wrote : "Until you see the things themselves you have no sense of the artist behind them. His outstanding quality, as artist and person, is *sanity*. Complete esthetic equipment, all managed by good sound judgment about ways and means, aims and purposes, utilities and 'functions'—and all this level-headed balance-mechanism added to the lively mental state that makes an artist an artist. Fortunate equipment in a disordered world. . . ."

Composed by H. Wolff Book Manufacturing Company, Inc., New York;
printed by Halliday Lithograph Corp., West Hanover, Mass.;
and bound by A. Horowitz and Son, Clifton, N.J.

Typography and binding design by Philip Grushkin.